APPLIED PSYCHOLINGUISTICS AND MENTAL HEALTH

APPLIED PSYCHOLINGUISTICS
AND COMMUNICATION DISORDERS

APPLIED PSYCHOLINGUISTICS AND MENTAL HEALTH
Edited by R. W. Rieber

PSYCHOLOGY OF LANGUAGE AND THOUGHT
Essays on the Theory and History of Psycholinguistics
Edited by R. W. Rieber

A Continuation Order Plan is available for this series. A continuation order will bring delivery of each new volume immediately upon publication. Volumes are billed only upon actual shipment. For further information please contact the publisher.

APPLIED PSYCHOLINGUISTICS AND MENTAL HEALTH

EDITED BY

R.W. RIEBER

John Jay College, CUNY, and
Columbia University College of Physicians and Surgeons
New York, New York

PLENUM PRESS · NEW YORK AND LONDON

Library of Congress Cataloging in Publication Data

Main entry under title:

Applied psycholinguistics and mental health.

(Studies in applied psycholinguistics)
Includes index.
1. Psycholinguistics. 2. Psychology, Pathological. 3. Schizophrenics — Lan-
guage. I. Rieber, Robert W. II. Series.
RC455.4.P78A66   616.8'9   79-24915
ISBN 0-306-40392-7

© 1980 Plenum Press, New York
A Division of Plenum Publishing Corporation
227 West 17th Street, New York, N.Y. 10011

Printed in the United States of America

To my mother,
Rose Rieber,
with all my love and respect,
and to the memory of my father,
John Rieber

CONTRIBUTORS

Murray Alpert · Department of Psychology, New York University School of Medicine, New York, New York

Marshall Edelson · Department of Psychiatry, Yale University School of Medicine, New Haven, Connecticut

Richard S. Feldman · New York State Psychiatric Institute, New York, New York

Sheldon M. Frank · Departments of Psychiatry and Pediatrics, University of Miami, School of Medicine, Miami, Florida

Joseph Jaffe · New York State Psychiatric Institute, and Department of Psychology, Columbia University, New York, New York

Luis R. Marcos · Department of Psychiatry, New York University School of Medicine, New York, New York, and Department of Psychiatry, Gouverneur Hospital, New York, New York

Peter Ostwald · Langley Porter Institute, University of California, San Francisco, California

Jeanne Patenaude-Lane · New York State Psychiatric Institute, New York, New York

Stephanie Portnoy · New York State Psychiatric Institute, New York, New York

Mario I. Rendon · 333 East 30 Street, New York, New York

R. W. Rieber · Department of Psychology, John Jay College of Criminal

Justice, City University of the City of New York, and Columbia University College of Physicians and Surgeons, New York, New York

Sherry Rochester · Clarke Institute of Psychiatry, University of Toronto, Toronto, Ontario, Canada

Kurt Salzinger · National Science Foundation, Washington, D. C.

Gregory Siomopoulous · Army Medical Department, Athens, Greece

Theodore Shapiro · Cornell University Medical College, New York, New York

Donald P. Spence · CMDNJ, Rutgers Medical School, New Brunswick, New Jersey

Valentina Zavarin · Langley Porter Institute, University of California, San Francisco, California

CONTENTS

PART I

INTRODUCTION

R. W. Rieber and Joseph Jaffe

PSYCHOLINGUISTICS AND MENTAL HEALTH
THE STATE OF THE ART

This is the first book to attempt to integrate psychiatry and the burgeoning field of applied psycholinguistics. The ideal application involves the *scientific* study of the psychology of language and thought as it relates to the gamut of psychological disorders. In general, psychiatrists are not primarily concerned with aphasia, stuttering, mental deficiency, and other related neurolinguistic communication disorders. Accordingly, we have narrowed the scope of the book to exclude these conditions. Another application, namely, to affective disorders, is also omitted, even though some of our authors have worked in this area (Jaffe, Anderson, & Rieber, 1973). Finally, areas of linguistic interest such as autism and childhood schizophrenia are absent, as this work is reviewed in Frank and Rieber (in press).

The assumption that underlies the conception of this book is that there is heuristic value in the scientific study of the psychology of language and thought, the eventual outcome of which will be improved diagnosis, prognosis, and treatment of mental illness.

Verbal interaction is an essential tool in medicine generally, but is

R. W. Rieber ● Department of Psychology, John Jay College of Criminal Justice, City University of the City of New York, and Columbia University College of Physicians and Surgeons, New York, New York 10019. *Joseph Jaffe* ● New York State Psychiatric Institute, and Department of Psychology, Columbia University, New York, New York 10019.

indispensable in psychiatry, in which laboratory procedures cannot supplant history taking. There are no laboratory tests for belief systems. Furthermore, since existing therapies for mental illness are often verbal, it is our hope that this book may contribute to the clarification of communication in psychotherapy.

At present, psychiatry is in the midst of a neurobiological revolution, with relatively less emphasis on psychodynamics than in the past. This comes at a time when both linguists and psycholinguists are themselves very much concerned with the biological foundations of language. Thus, there is a convergence of interests, as expressed in the title of this book.

Given the state of the art, the chapters in this volume represent a variety of approaches to their chosen topics. This nonpartisan eclecticism seems wise at present. It is premature to foster any extreme theoretical or methodological bias. The emergent discipline is in its preadolescence at best, and any coherent, unified approach is fanciful. Nevertheless, one should be aware of the long history of the discipline from infancy to preadolescence in the convergence.

It was in 1903 that psychiatry took serious interest in the relationships of language, thought, and mental illness (Liebmann & Edel, 1903). Although psychiatrists had acknowledged the importance of such phenomena, they were primarily understood as a means of communicating in everyday life. Liebmann's book was the first attempt in the field to set the stage for future contributions in this area. The literature before the publication of the Liebmann monograph was mostly anecdotal in nature, and a few examples should serve to illustrate this point.

Wyllie (1895) gave a fine review of the literature during the period of the nineteenth century. He pointed out that in mental illness the function of thought appears to be more damaged than the function of speech and language. According to Wyllie, the functions of both thinking and speaking must be directly related to the operations of the mind, both normal and abnormal. He then recommended that we look at language and thought as it relates to mental illness from several different vantage points. His first task was to demonstrate the manner in which the various disorders of the mind are mirrored in the language of the mental patient. Second, he pointed out that auditory-verbal hallucinations in mental illness must be dealt with in such a way as to relate them to the disturbances in the cortical speech centers. His third suggestion was that the scientist should look at language and thought disturbance in mental illness as an important area of study in itself; he also emphasized that speech and language deteriorate less, both qualitatively and quantitatively, during the course of mental illness than the processes of thought.

Wyllie used as his authorities Esquerol's classic work on *Malades mentalles* and Seglas's book on *Les troubles du langue chez les aliénés*. Esquerol had stressed the importance of the study of language to understand a mental disorder, whereas Seglas had stressed the importance of the study of verbal hallucinations for the same purpose. Both of these approaches are being explored at the present time, and this fact is reflected in several of the chapters in this book (see especially Chapters 5 and 7).

It was not until the mid-1920s that scientists began to investigate this area with a greater emphasis. In May 1929, William Alanson White read a paper entitled "The Language of the Psychoses" at the American Psychiatric Association meetings in Atlanta, Georgia (White, 1930). In this paper, White discussed many aspects of language and psychosis, including intonation pattern, modulations of voice, gestures, and other factors to better reflect the state of the mind of the patient. He dealt with both the microscopic and macroscopic levels of language and was also very much aware of the importance of the intrinsic relationship of mental development and language development for a better understanding of the nature of mental illness—especially psychosis.

White's paper attempted to elaborate further some of his ideas that were previously published in 1926. In that paper, he had dealt with language and schizophrenia. Scientific research in the field of psycholinguistics and mental health was undertaken in a serious manner only sporadically. For an excellent review of the literature from the 1930s to the 1960s, see Vetter (1969).

Let us now examine briefly the remaining chapters in this volume. In Part II, Chapters 2 through 5 focus on the perennial problem of the role of thought disorder in schizophrenia. Rochester has attempted to operationalize the phenomenon of thought disorder, utilizing a psycholinguistic frame of reference that is based on an average listener's comprehension task (Rochester & Martin, 1980). Her chapter suggests how this approach may facilitate our studies of etiology and treatment in light of a review of six decades of observation and research.

In Chapter 3, Ostwald and Zavarin summarize the Soviet literature, which appears less monolithic than often depicted and displays the tension that exists between primarily mentalistic, internal-cognitive, and external behavioristic approaches. The nature of thought disorder as illogicality versus improbability is also addressed. The contemporary Soviet trend toward emphasis on the pragmatic dimension of communicative behavior parallels, to a large extent, what is currently happening in the United States.

In Chapter 4, Salzinger, Portnoy, and Feldman present a radical behaviorist position which carefully avoids cognitive and psychodynamic questions regarding the relations between language and thought. Dealing with thinking as a private phenomenon, they avoid speculation about it and concentrate on measurements of language behavior. A long-term prognostic study of schizophrenia by this method is of particular significance.

In contrast, Frank, Rendon, and Siomopoulous approach hallucinated speech psychodynamically. In Chapter 5, they discuss, among other things, the intriguing pragmatic notion of an imaginary conversational partner as a model for verbal hallucinations.

Thus, we leave the problem of thought disorder in schizophrenia with many new, stimulating ideas but, as one would anticipate, no definitive solutions.

Part III deals with semantics in psychopathology. Semantics, along with pragmatics, seem today to constitute the leading edge of psycholinguistic research. In Chapter 6, Marcos and Alpert discuss the complex phenomenon of bilingualism in the evaluation of psychopathology. They indicate how bilingualism may be an asset or a liability from both the patient's and the clinician's viewpoints.

In Chapter 7, Spence shows how contemporary scientific psycholinguistics can deepen the insights so classically documented in Freud's *Psychopathology of Everyday Life*. This contribution should be of particular interest to psychotherapists and to the research investigators of the therapy process.

The final two chapters center around the indispensable feature which especially characterizes psychiatry, namely, the patient–therapist dialogue. The enticing analogy between mental operations in psychodynamics and deep structures of transformational models in linguistics is explored by the authors represented here. Since both mental operations and deep structures may be out of awareness, yet subject to introspection, the analogy suggests interdisciplinary convergence and is certain to be controversial.

In Chapter 8, which is especially addressed to physicians and medical students, Edelson argues that language is the key to the study of man, that it provides a model for thinking about human relations, and that a knowledge of linguistics will deepen the understanding of the patient and his illness.

Shapiro in Chapter 9 uses psycholinguistics as a tool to understand and improve our conversations with youth, particularly adolescents.

In summary, it is clear that, regardless of etiology, all mental illness ultimately involves a disorder of communication; that is, interpersonal communication is the final common path by means of which psychiatric disorders are detected, diagnosed, and often treated. It is also the arena in which therapy is evaluated. At the present time, the scientific study of language and communication has had little impact upon psychiatry. However, we trust that this volume will illustrate and promote such cross-disciplinary fertilization.

1.1. References

Frank, S. M., & Rieber, R. W., Language development and language disorders in children and adolescents. In R. W. Rieber (Ed.), *Communication disorders.* New York: Plenum, in press.

Jaffe, J., Anderson, S. W., & Rieber, R. W. Research and clinical approaches to disorders of speech rate. *Journal of Communicative Disorders*, 1973, 6 225–246.

Liebmann, A., & Edel, M. Die Spreche der Geisteskranken nach stenographischen Aufzeichnungen. Halle a.S.: Verlag von Carl Marhold, 1903.

Vetter, H. J. *Language behavior and psychopathology.* Chicago, Ill.: Rand-McNally, 1969.

White, W. A. The language of the psychoses. *The American Journal of Psychiatry.* 1930, 9(4), 221–229.

Wyllie, S. *Disorders of speech.* London: Oliver and Boyd. 1895.

Rochester, S., & Martin, J. R. *Crazy talk: A study of the discourse of schizophrenic speakers.* New York: Plenum, 1980.

PART II

THOUGHT DISORDER, LANGUAGE, AND SCHIZOPHRENIA

Sherry Rochester

THOUGHT DISORDER AND LANGUAGE USE IN SCHIZOPHRENIA

> It is frequently observed that though schizophrenics use proper words and produce reasonably well-formed sentences, one is unable after having heard a series of such sentences, to comprehend what has been said. (Pavy, 1968, p. 175)

Schizophrenic speakers sometimes fail to speak coherently. Operationally, this means that listeners sometimes cannot follow schizophrenic speakers even though the speakers are using familiar words in well-formed sentences. It also means that the listeners are agreed on this matter, saying, in effect, "These speakers cannot be understood through any reasonable effort." It is not always true that schizophrenic speakers fail to produce coherent discourse. However, when they do fail, their failures are regarded as significant, as, in Norman Cameron's words, "one of the most outstanding characteristics of schizophrenic thinking" (1938b, p. 2).

In this chapter, the notion of discourse failures forms the central theme. The schizophrenic speaker is viewed as someone whose talk can sometimes not be understood by ordinary listeners. In Section 2.1., I consider the role of discourse failures in the original definition of schiz-

---

Sherry Rochester ● Clarke Institute of Psychiatry, University of Toronto, Toronto, Ontario, Canada M5T 1R8. With a few modifications, this chapter appears as Chapter 1 in Rochester and Martin (1979).

ophrenia and explore how these failures have come to be termed "thought disorders." I found that the notion of "thought disorder" has been and still is an elusive and difficult concept to study. In Section 2.2., I examine the premises underlying studies of language use in schizophrenia. Although there have been many reviews of the experimental work in recent years, there have been no overviews of the assumptions underlying these studies and no summaries of the recent, exciting descriptions by linguists and asphasiologists. The premises of experiments and naturalistic studies in the field are outlined, and some of the problems associated with these premises are discussed.

Finally, in Section 2.3., I consider the study of discourse failures or "thought disorders" in light of the premises that have been adopted by students of schizophrenic language. The central issue is whether one should pay attention to schizophrenia or to language. As will be evident, the approach in this chapter is to argue for the detailed study of language use—of language in action. The alternative to ignoring language *per se* and seeing it only as one more "behavior" has not been successful. Language studies in schizophrenia have not produced useful insights into the origins of or cures for any aspects of the schizophrenic syndromes. A systematic approach through the study of language use at least offers a promise of models of the schizophrenic speaker which can be mapped onto models of the normal speakers. This means we shall be able to describe what the schizophrenic speaker *can* do, as well as what he or she cannot do. This option may be significant in helping us understand the processes underlying the discourse failures that have come to be known as "thought disorders."

2.1. Discourse Failures and the Schizophrenic Speaker

2.1.1. "Schizophrenia" and Discourse Failures

The term "schizophrenia" was coined, in part, to describe discourse failures. In 1911, Eugen Bleuler reported his experience of being a confused listener in the presence of incoherent speakers. He described listening to patients whose speech was difficult to comprehend, where "fragments of ideas are connected in an illogical way to constitute a new idea," and where "new ideas crop up which neither the patient nor the observer can bring into any connection with the previous stream of thought" (1950, p.9). These disruptions in the patient's discourse Bleuler took to be indications of a "splitting" of psychic functions, the "schizo" of schizophrenia.

Although Bleuler regarded thought and speech as distinct contructs,[1] those who followed him often treated speech as a direct reflection of cognition. From about the middle 1930s until the present day, schizophrenic patients who have failed to speak coherently have been said to show "thought process disorder" or "formal thought disorder." They have rarely been described in terms of their "discourse failures" or "language disorders" or "communication disorders."

This tendency to infer disordered thought from disordered speech has caused many problems and obscured some interesting issues, as we shall see presently. In recent years, several workers have commented on the confusion which results from assuming that speech is isomorphic to thought (e.g., Andreasen, 1979a,b; Chaika, 1974a,b; Lecours & Vanier-Clément, 1976; Seeman, 1970; and Singer & Wynne, 1963). But there is a second step that makes the matter even more complicated.

To say that a speaker is incoherent is only to say that one cannot understand that speaker. So to make a statement about incoherent discourse is really to make a statement about one's own confusion as a listener. It is therefore just as appropriate to study what it is about the listener that makes him or her "confusable" as it is to study what it is about the speaker that makes him or her "confusing." The focus of study depends simply on the direction of attribution.

Historically, the direction of attribution has been from clinician to patient. So when a clinician experiences confusion in the presence of a patient, as Bleuler and so many after him did, it is natural to look to the patient's behavior for an explanation of that confusion. Sensitive clinicians treat themselves as measuring instruments which detect difficulties and then signal that something is amiss in the environment.

---

[1] If one reads carefully, it is clear that Bleuler did not regard speech as a mirror image of thought. He notes, for example, that a speaker may appear confused when only the "manner of expression" is obscure. In such a case, "logical transitions may be assumed to exist" (1950, p. 21). And elsewhere he observes that a "gap in associations" in the speaker's thoughts may be bridged in speech by grammatical forms. In this case, speech that appears to be reflecting coherent thoughts is, in fact, only simulating them. Thus, the patient's speech may be confusing while the thoughts are logical; or the thoughts may be unconnected while the speech is linked through grammatical forms. Speech is one thing, Bleuler seems to be saying, and thought another; and though the two often meet, they are not inseparable.

For example, a clinician might experience a headache or at least a sense of bewilderment in the presence of certain speakers and infer that some aspects of the speaker's behavior are responsible for this experience.

This inferential tradition is valuable because it relies on the profound sensitivity of native members of a culture—a sensitivity linguists and psycholinguists are very far from capturing at the present time. But it is also a troublesome tradition, for it obscures the inferential status of many of the clinician's observations. In particular, it obscures two inferences: (a) the assessment of "thought disorder" is based on an inference from talk not thought; and (b) "talk failures" are inferences based on the *listener's* experience of confusion. In the first inferential step, one is moving from the speaker's utterance to his or her thoughts, and the issue is: To what extent is speech a reflection of thought? In the second inferential step, one is proceeding from the listener's experience of confusion to attribute confusing behavior to the speaker. The issue here is: To what extent is the speaker's utterance responsible for the listener's confusion?

There is one more complication in this process. It occurs because the second inference (from listener to speaker) was originally made by Bleuler in 1911 and has been reified in the ensuing years. Bleuler attempted to account for his experience of confusion in several ways, suggesting that his patients' discourse was "vague and wooly" and full of "loose associations" and "long silences" and "rhyming words"; that it was "haphazard" and "bizarre" and "lacking in goals." Most of these are behaviors that Bleuler presumed were disruptive to his own comprehension. One does not know whether all were actually disruptive; whether some were more disruptive than others; whether there were other behaviors that might have confused Bleuler but were not mentioned; or whether those behaviors would be confusing to other listeners. In short, we do not *know* that Bleuler's list describes behaviors which actually are disruptive and confusing to listeners. We only know that Bleuler suspected these behaviors as the sources of his confusion.

It is the largely uncritical acceptance of Bleuler's list as truth rather than speculation that makes it a problem. As a result of this enduring acceptance and the supportive (but equally speculative) observations of later writers, there are actually two ways in which today's clinicians make inferences of thought disorder. Thought disorder is said to exist if (a) the listener (a clinician) feels confused and cannot follow what the speaker (a patient) is saying; and/or (b) the listener observes that the speaker is producing discourse which contains events described by Bleuler and later observers in their efforts to explain their own confusion. The inferential status of thought disorder is not different in (a) and (b). Rather, in (a) clinicians rely on their own experience, and in (b) they rely on the experience and inferences of others. In both cases, a double inference is being made: from the listener's experience to the speaker's utterance, and from the speaker's utterance to the speaker's own cognition.

Figure 2.1. Imaginary conversation between student and textbook writer.

2.1.2. Defining "Thought Disorder"

The double inference behind the designation of "thought disorder" makes a stubborn tangle for young clinicians hoping to learn its meaning. In one popular modern textbook, for example, thought process disorder is said to be "manifested by irrelevance and incoherence of the patient's verbal productions." The manifestations can range from "simple blocking and mild circumstantiality to total loosening of associations as in word salad" (Freedman, Kaplan, & Sadock, 1976, p. 1333).

The definition is evidently vague, but what is even more frustrating is that it is circular. As it stands—and the above definition is typical, not exceptional—the definition suggests that thought disorder can be inferred from speech events. But if one pursues the definitions of these speech events, one is led back to a description of thought disorder. For example, "loosening of associations" is defined not in terms of discourse events but in terms of cognition. "In the loosening of associations," the reader is told, "the flow of thought may seem haphazard, purposeless, illogical, confused, abrupt, and bizarre." The same circularity is true with "circumstantiality" which "is a disorder of association in which too many associated ideas come into consciousness because of too little selective suppression" (Freedman et al., 1976, p. 385). As the perplexed student observes in Figure 2.1., thought disorder is when talk is incoherent. And talk is incoherent when the thought is disordered.

2.1.3. "Thought Disorder" and Schizophrenia

> The potential payoff of success in understanding schizophrenic thought disorder is great. Schizophrenia is the most massive unsolved puzzle in the whole field of psychopathology, and thought disorder is schizophrenia's most prominent symptom. A true understanding of the nature of the thought disorder might illuminate the nature of schizophrenia itself. (Chapman & Chapman, 1973, p.ix)

"Thought disorder," as we have seen, is a central concept in the diagnosis of schizophrenia. For most clinicians, the assessment of "thought disorder" is based on inferences from the discourse of patients. Because the inferential status is not explicit, many young (and old) clinicians find the diagnosis of thought disorder mystifying and attempt to dispose of it by resorting to lists of phenomena given by Bleuler or presented in textbooks. As I have argued, using these lists does not change the inferential status of the construct. Nor, as we have just seen, is it much help in picking out just what it is that makes a discourse incoherent.

Students and young clinicians are not the only ones inconvenienced by the problematic status of "thought disorder." Investigators from several different areas find the construct's shifting definition an impediment. It complicates the efforts of clinical investigators who wish to describe the onset and remission of schizophrenic symptoms. It limits the work of those who propose that schizophrenia involves some dysfunction of the left hemisphere, especially the left temporal lobes (e.g., Flor-Henry, 1976; Gruzelier, 1978). And for a long time the elusive construct has both attracted and hindered those who hypothesize that schizophrenia may involve an episodic aphasia (cf. Benson, 1973; Chaika, 1974a).

Why, if "thought disorder" is potentially so valuable to a variety of workers, have we had no systematic descriptions of the discourse failures on which this designation is based? Or, to put this another way, why has "thought disorder" been described in terms of thought-based rather than language-based variables?

The short answer to this question is that clinicians seeking to describe language use in schizophrenia have not noticed the inferential status of their own descriptions and have relied on metaphors to convey their experiences. Experimenters, on the other hand, have tended to produce studies which were methodologically rigorous but which in no way captured the complexity of the phenomenon they were trying to study. The longer answer is that research into language use in schizophrenia has been a microcosm of psycholinguistics. When the psychology of language flourished, as it did in the period from about 1870 to 1920, Bleuler presented his epoch-making descriptions of language use in schizophrenia. And when these studies declined and virtually disappeared in North America from about 1920 until the 1960s, the study of language use in schizophrenia languished as well. In the following section, I discuss some of these trends.

2.2. Studies of Language Use in Schizophrenia and Their Premises

"What are you working on these days?"
"Language and schizophrenia."
"It's a graveyard." (Overheard conversation, Toronto, 1973)

The study of language use in schizophrenia has not been a happy enterprise. Every major reviewer in the last decade has observed that there is no adequate theory of why schizophrenic speakers produce aberrant discourse. And, though most reviewers argue otherwise, there is also a lack of satisfactory data. In this section, I suggest why, after some fifty years of effort, promising models and adequate data are still lacking in this field.

2.2.1. The Reviewers

There is no promising model of language use in schizophrenia, and every reviewer in the last decade has commented on this fact. Harold Vetter, for example, after publishing several books and articles reviewing psychopathological language, observed that "even by the most pragmatic criteria, the results of forty years of research on schizophrenic language . . . have proven to be quite disappointing." What we know after all this effort, he continues, is mainly "the rather obvious fact that schizophrenics often differ strikingly from normal persons in what they talk about and how they talk about it" (Vetter, 1968, p.25).

David Pavy, in an important and comprehensive review of the field published in the same year, noted cautiously that "modern investigators of speech in schizophrenia are to be commended for their experimental rigor." Nevertheless, "one must conclude that we are far from specifying the nature of verbal disorder in schizophrenia" (Pavy, 1968, p.171).

Perhaps the most elegantly phrased observation was made by Brendan Maher in a careful and patient review of the host of experimental studies from the 1930s into the early 1960s. He writes that, in the attempts to specify the nature of verbal disorder in schizophrenia, "hypothesis struggles with hypothesis in a conflict in which new contenders enter the field but the defeated never retire" (Maher, 1966, p.433).

The gloomy consensus is that there has been little progress, if any, in experimental studies of schizophrenic language use and no generally accepted formulations of why schizophrenic speakers produce aberrant discourse. Experiments have been unsuccessful, it is suggested, because they have not led to theories which are both testable and relevant to the confusing productions of the schizophrenic speaker.

It is also implied by some observers that, though there is a lack of theory, there are more than enough data. I disagree. Rather, there seems to be (a) a very broad base of data from clinical observations that is speculative and essentially metaphorical, and (b) a very narrow base of experimental observations (e.g., statistical summaries of word class occurrences, listener's responses to individual sentences) that are not representative of language use in schizophrenic patients. In the next section, I suggest that the lack of promising theoretical models is related to the lack of broadly based, systematic observations. In the absence of a theory of language use, it seems, observations are constrained. And in the absence of adequate data, fruitful theories are not developed.

2.2.2. Studies of Language Use in Schizophrenia: The Early Premises

Although experimental studies of language use in schizophrenia have been reviewed extensively, the reviews have been either summaries of the literature or methodological critiques. In addition to those cited above, there is a comprehensive methodological critique by Chapman and Chapman (1973), a valuable review of the European literature by Bär (1976), and a review of some clinical observations and theories by Reed (1970). Very little has been attempted in the way of an examination of the premises in the field. In the following discussion, I pursue this examination.

2.2.2.1. A Microcosm of Psycholinguistics. The study of language use in schizophrenia is a poor stepchild of the development of psycholinguistics. It is, to use Titchener's (1905) term, a "microcosm, perfect to the last detail," exemplifying the course of development of psycholinguistic concepts and methods.

From about 1920 until the 1950s, psycholinguistics in North America was almost nonexistent. Those who studied language said that they studied "verbal behavior." They took their methods and concepts from those who studied white rats and other domestic animals in laboratories and modified them slightly to fit the behavior of college undergraduates in laboratories. As I indicate below, the concern at this time was to treat language use as a behavior "just like any other behavior."

Although it can hardly be said that those who studied "verbal behavior" were concerned with language use, they were concerned with the specification of normal processes. To the extent that language use was a normal process, therefore, it was interesting. These workers were not concerned with the use of language by schizophrenic patients, or with other groups that seemed aberrant in their functioning. Thus, the study of schizophrenic speakers was neglected by those who had a particular interest in language.

Clinicians, on the other hand, were intrigued by their patients' perplexing discourse and, by the 1920s, were attempting to study these productions with some care. But these observers were often primarily concerned with the personality of their schizophrenic patients and with the cause of the schizophrenia. For them, language was an epiphenomenon to be used to understand other, presumably more basic, issues. Again, the language use of schizophrenic speakers was neglected.

It was ultimately the clinicians who attempted to study the productions of schizophrenic patients by borrowing methods and concepts from their experimental colleagues. The exuberant discourse of schizophrenic speakers was thus squeezed into a behavioristic framework— and the fit was not a good one.

In retrospect, there seems to have been little alternative to the practice of using behavioristic techniques to study the remarkable productions of schizophrenic speakers. As we have seen, experimentalists were not interested in aberrant language functioning, and clinicians were not particularly interested in language use. In fact, the last point is not quite correct. Several clinicians were fascinated by their patients' use of language, but the reports they produced were almost impossible to use in the experimental frameworks of the time. The clinical accounts relied on evocative descriptions of thinking "which tends to stick to everything it touches" (Cameron, 1938b, p. 29), or which is like a "train which becomes derailed" (Kraepelin, 1919), or like an onion coming unpeeled (Storch, 1924). The descriptions were so elusive and so unsystematic that most of those who attempted experiments were unable or unwilling to grapple with them (a notable exception is Cameron, 1938a,b, 1944).

So perhaps it was inevitable that a full appreciation of the schizophrenic's discourse was neglected. But what is surprising or at least disconcerting to recognize in this retrospective view, is the fact that clinicians were no less enthusiastic than experimentalists in adopting the behavioristic approach. With awesome certainty, experienced clinicians assured their readers that, though the methods being used might appear to be "a naive or sterile approach to the complexity of language," in fact the tabulations of grammatical categories and cumulations of word frequencies were revealing significant information about the schizophrenic speaker's use of language (Lorenz & Cobb, 1954, p. 665). Although the techniques "may appear somewhat stilted and oblique," another respected clinician and his colleague assured their audience, counts of the number of different words used by schizophrenic speakers offer "a significant and fascinating approach to the study of mentation in psychotic conditions" (Whitehorn & Zipf, 1943, pp. 831–832).

If the clinical investigators had insisted on the primacy of natural language data—which they did not, and if the experimentalists had been willing to listen—which they almost certainly were not, then things might have been different. The productions of the schizophrenic speaker might have revealed the stunning inadequacy of behavioristic principles to deal with natural language. It would have been evident, as it finally was to Lashley in 1948, to Chomsky in 1957, and to most psycholinguists by the middle 1960s, that reducing language use to a matter of conditioning "treats only the simplest 1% of the psycholinguistic problem" (Miller, 1962), and that our crucially important human skill in conversing with each other is largely ignored by the reduction of language use to conditioned habits.

2.2.2.2. *The Early Premises.* In large part, the reticence of the clinical investigators and the indifference of the experimentalists seem to have been due to the assumptions of the behavior theory paradigm that prevailed from about 1920 until the 1960s in North America. These assumptions were so powerful, Robert Lockard (1971) has observed, that they functioned "mainly as beliefs beyond confirmation." They were so widely accepted and formed so coherent a view of the world that "individual investigators and even whole disciplines were unable to break out of the framework provided" (p. 170).

The study of the psychology of language was no exception. From a profound interest in natural language processes in the late 19th century, psychologists turned to conditioning studies with animals by about 1920. And linguists, following Leonard Bloomfield (1933), developed an antimentalistic, taxonomic approach to language. Throughout North America and Europe, in both psychology and linguistics, there was an orientation away from studies of the production and comprehension of natural language and toward prescriptions for segmenting, classifying, and counting behaviors and speech elements (cf. the valuable account of this period by Blumenthal, 1970).

By about 1950, the study of "verbal behavior," like the enterprise of psychology itself, had worked itself into a very narrow scientific position. Lockard's (1971, p. 169) comment about comparative psychology in this period is appropriate to the study of "verbal behavior" as well: the discipline had ignored all but a tiny fraction of the behavior it purported to study and had incorporated an elaborate set of premises about behavior into a dogmatic tradition.

The premises underlying the study of "verbal behavior" in 1950 are important to us here. They were influential into the early 1960s in the study of normal language processes and, in the study of schizophrenic language processes, are widely accepted even today.

Some of the premises about language which would generally have been accepted in 1950 are as follows:

1. Language use is learned behavior. Its full complexity is developed through the combining of stimulus–response connections.
2. Biology is of little interest in the study of language.
3. There is nothing unique about the use of language. An underlying equivalence exists between natural language behavior and other behaviors (e.g., motor behavior, rote learning).
4. The best way to study language is to study how words are used.

These premises were influential into the 1960s in many psycholinguistic endeavors (cf. the discussion of these issues by Reber, 1973). But by 1965, after an acrimonious series of debates, it was clear that the behavioristic approach to language processing had been rejected in North America. Fodor's (1965) logical critique of neo-behaviorist explanations of language marks the culmination of attacks on what had been "a most strongly established approach to language in the English-speaking world" (Blumenthal, 1970, p. 181).

The study of language use in schizophrenia, however, has lagged behind. At the time of this writing, in the end of the 1970s, many investigators are still adhering to the premises outlined above, and critics are still using these premises as the basis from which to evaluate experiments. For example, in Chapman and Chapman's (1973) review of studies on schizophrenic thought disorder (perhaps the most comprehensive and careful critique of experimental studies in schizophrenia published to date) there is a firm adherence to these premises. There is no concern for the fact that of the 200 or so studies reviewed that require verbal responses from the patients, perhaps three succeed in capturing the central issue of thought disorder. The issue which has been central historically and which is critical at present is this: How or why does the schizophrenic speaker produce language which is so confusing to listeners? This, as suggested in the introduction, became confounded into: Why is the language of the schizophrenic speaker so confusing? And from that into: Why is the thought of the schizophrenic patient so confused? It is this last question which Chapman and Chapman consider, neglecting the more elementary ones.

Every reviewer cited thus far, with the exception of Pavy, falls prey to the attraction of the behavioristic principles that were once so powerful in the study of "verbal behavior." These principles are inappropriate and often misleading in several ways. In order to discuss some of their difficulties, we can focus on studies conducted after 1960 and divide the studies into planned experiments and naturalistic research.

2.2.3. Experimental Studies and Their Premises

Experimental studies that require "verbal responses" from schizophrenic patients can be further divided into (1) investigations of information processing capacities, and (2) investigations of psycholinguistic abilities.

2.2.3.1. Investigations of Information Processing Capacities. Originating perhaps with the work of Weckowicz and Blewett in 1959 (cf. Chapman & Chapman, 1973, Ch. 13), there have been over 100 studies through the last two decades in which "verbal responses" were used as measures of the schizophrenic patient's ability to attend to "stimuli." The stimuli were sometimes words presented in isolation or in lists, and sometimes target words presented in sentences. Occasionally, patients were presented with strings of words in which attempts were made to vary the amount of "information" or redundancy. In addition, there have been perhaps another 20 experiments devoted particularly to memory for lists of words (cf. review by Koh, 1978; and Traupmann, 1975).

These studies have been extensively reviewed by several writers and need not be reviewed again. However, let us consider one that can serve as an example for discussion. Chapman, Chapman, and Daut (1976) report a study in which chronic schizophrenic patients are given two multiple-choice subtests. The patients are asked to read a series of statements of the following form:

> Mark the statement or statements which tell what a *book* is often like.
> (a) You read it. ("strong meaning response")
> (b) It has a back. ("weak meaning response")
> (c) It's edible. ("irrelevant alternative")
> (d) None of the above.

The study was designed to follow up a number of earlier studies in which it appeared that chronic patients would choose the "strong meaning response" whether it was appropriate or not, whereas normal subjects would choose that response only when it fit the sentence frame. In the present experiment, the investigators offered a second series of statements which resembled the first but which, instead of having a strong and a weak meaning response, had two weak meaning responses. They were attempting to test the hypothesis proposed by Cromwell and Dokecki (1968) that schizophrenics neglect weak meaning aspects of words only in situations in which a strong aspect of meaning is present. In a carefully controlled experiment, the investigators found no difference in the patients' responses to the two types of statements. They conclude that their findings lend no support to the hypotheses, and the most likely explanation is "a schizophrenic defect in the screening of their potential responses for appropriateness" (Chapman *et al.*, 1976, p. 39).

This study and many others like it are tempting sources of inference about language use because they suggest that schizophrenic patients have some difficulty using context in their interpretation of discourse. However, there are two difficulties with studies of "verbal responses" like this one: they do not inform us about actual language use, and they may mislead us about information processes. Let us consider these problems in turn.

2.2.3.1.1. Language Use. Studies that require patients to respond in terms of a single word may be tapping specific skills and not a general ability to use semantic information. In this task, as in word association experiments, the subject's response is likely to involve stages in which (1) the subject must "understand" the stimulus; (2) and "operate" on the meaning of the stimulus; and (3) produce a response. Clark (1970) argues that it is the unique second stage that sets tasks of this sort apart from situations in which natural language is used. In having to choose between several printed sentences in the multiple-choice task, or in having to associate to or discriminate between target words in word association experiments, the subject is asked to engage in a selection process which may be unrepresentative of ordinary language operations.

There is some support for this assertion. In three experiments, tests that required responses to single words or target words seemed to tap specific information rather than processing abilities. Boland and Chapman (1971) and Rattan and Chapman (1973) demonstrated that normal adults give "schizophrenic-like" responses when they do not know the correct answer in multiple-choice tests. That is, they choose words that are similar to the test word, or sound like it, or occur with it in some contexts. In a related study, Stolz and Tiffany (1972), report that adults make word choices just as children (and schizophrenics) do when the frequency of occurrence of the word is low. In general, studies which restrict themselves to the meanings of words that are isolated or are presented in multiple-choice or discrimination tasks are studying "verbal behavior" in unusual situations. In extrapolating from such tasks, one must be carful to limit generalizations to these unrepresentative kinds of language use.

2.2.3.1.2. *Information Processing.* To say that a set of experiments is unrepresentative of natural language use means that one cannot characterize the listener's behavior in ordinary situations. However, it need not mean that such studies are uninformative. Very many studies have been predicated on the assumption that verbal responses are just as appropriate as any other responses to test hypotheses about selective attention, discrimination, and recognition processes in schizophrenia.

There are several reasons for arguing, however, that "verbal behavior" studies provide the wrong sort of evidence from which to infer information processing operations. First, and most seriously, observations of "verbal behavior" are only very tangentially connected to the information processing constructs used for their explanation. This was not always so. In the early 1950s, psycholinguists often tried to formulate the operations of speakers and hearers in terms of the redundancy in language. The development of information measures in communications theory offered a formal way of discussing language performance, and grammatical structures were seen as the basis for establishing sequential constraints in language. Grammar was what made words more predictable. So knowledge of the rules of English was seen as allowing one to reduce the range of possible completions for sentences, such as "The bright _____ shone for _____ first time _____ three days."

Sequential constraints were studied with procedures developed by Miller and Selfridge (1950) and by Taylor (1953). By the 1960s, these procedures were adopted and used widely in studies of schizophrenic "verbal behavior." However, although the techniques themselves might be useful as an approximate measure of structure when nothing about the underlying processes is postulated (cf. Olson & Clark, 1976, p. 38), the models underlying these techniques are not appropriate models of language users. Chomsky's formal demonstrations of the inadequacy of statistical conceptions of language structure (1957, 1965) and the joint discussions of such demonstrations by Chomsky and Miller (1963; Miller & Chomsky, 1963) have shown the limitations of such models. As a result of these demonstrations, the analysis of linguistic strings based on information theory is no longer an acceptable means of representing the language user.

But without such a model, there is no set of intermediate steps between the behavior of the language user and information processing models of the sort proposed in studies of schizophrenic patients. Thus, although investigators argue vigorously about which information processing construct is the correct one in any given study of "verbal behavior," all such arguments are, in fact, highly speculative and probably unproductive.

A second problem in these studies is the difficulty in specifying which "information process" is being measured. For example, if one presents patients with pairs of words to be discriminated, one may be studying discrimination processes, or linguistic abilities associated with semantic knowledge, or some complex combination of discrimination and language processes. If one assumes that verbal responses are not different from responses in other systems, then this will not be a problem. However, if one questions this assumption, then it is difficult to know how to interpret a host of studies that rely on verbal responses. In particular, 90% of the 20 studies of memory published since 1960 use words or sentences as the items to be remembered; an additional 5% present spatial patterns but rely on exceedingly complex verbal instructions. Consequently, although it may appear that quite a bit is known about schizophrenic memory processes, in fact we know only about verbal memory for words. We are ignorant of how schizophrenic subjects remember faces and locations, and rhythms and intonation patterns and music. By not distinguishing "verbal" from non-verbal responses, there is a danger of interpreting the available data too broadly and overlooking observations which are essential to understand the system under study.

A third difficulty is presented by the use of a task in which one may be demanding a special skill from the subject, instead of a general process. As we mentioned, one probably cannot extrapolate from the experimental results to patients' language comprehension in everyday situations. The problem with regard to information processes is related, but a little different. Because the tasks are unrepresentative of normal processing, they may demand a skill from the subjects which is irrelevant to such processes. Though one can devise tasks on which schizophrenic patients are different from control patients, there is no guarantee that such tasks reveal factors which *make a difference* to any significant behavior or experience of the patients. Though the question of relevance is always an issue in laboratory tasks in psychology, it is particularly disturbing in the present case. It is possible that, in the very many studies of verbal responses in which information processing constructs are used, one can generalize neither to language use in ordinary situations nor to any specifiable information processes.

The interpretative problems raised by these studies seem to be a legacy from the 1950s' premises about verbal behavior studies. The investigators seem to assume that there is nothing unique about language, and also that biology is of little interest in the study of language (premises 2 and 3 above). The first assumption is suggested by the apparent lack of concern for the form of response. Language is treated as an epiphenomenon to information processing, and the emphasis seems to be on measuring behaviors that fit a model. If verbal behavior does not support the model being tested, one can always try other behaviors. For example, if experiments with verbal responses do not support a particular model, one can try size estimation measures, or depth preception, or auditory detection. This strategy suggests the assumption that biology is unimportant. If this is assumed, then one need not be concerned with issues of hemispheric differences in processing different sorts of materials, or in processing the same materials with different biases. Again, measures of verbal responses should not be substantially different from measures of pattern perception or auditory discrimination.

Finally, there is an ironic footnote to the practice of studying "verbal behavior" but ignoring questions of language use. Neale and Cromwell (1970) suggest that a major methodological problem in some studies of information processing is the lack of clear instructions. Some of the findings may be artifacts, they explain, because the language use in those studies was ambiguous.

2.2.3.2. Psycholinguistic Experiments. It is possible to distinguish between experiments on "verbal behavior" and experiments on "psycholinguistics" in the study of schizophrenic subjects. Although both use verbal tasks, the former use them to study information processing, and the latter to study language processing. The different aims are reflected in different procedures: information processing is inferred from the subject's identification or discrimination of target words that are either isolated or presented in sentence frames; language processing is inferred from the subject's recognition, recall, and, perhaps, comprehension of full sentences.

If we abide by this distinction, then psycholinguisic experiments with schizophrenic patients begin with David Gerver's (1967) attempt to replicate Miller and Isard's (1963) work with normal subjects. Gerver presented chronic schizophrenic patients and control subjects with "normal" sentences (e.g., Trains carry passengers across the country), syntactically admissible but semantically anomalous sentences (e.g., Trains steal elephants around the highways) and random strings (e.g., On trains hive elephants simplify). Subjects listened to the sentences on earphones and then repeated them aloud. The results were surprising: although the schizophrenic subjects recalled fewer words than control subjects, as expected, they showed as much improvement as the control subjects as the word strings became more like normal sentences. For all groups—schizophrenic patients, psychiatric control patients, and normal subjects—normal sentences were recalled best, and semantically anomalous sentences were recalled better than random strings. And for all groups, the rate of improvement in recall over the three sentence types was about the same.

2.2.3.2.1. Earlier Studies. What was surprising about this result was the evidence that schizophrenic subjects were able to benefit, somehow, from the syntactic and semantic structure in the three sets of sentences. This seemed to contradict the findings of a persuasive clinical report and several experimental studies which suggested that schizophrenic listeners are unable to take advantage of "the organization inherent in language" (Lawson, McGhie, & Chapman, 1964).

The clinical study summarized subjective reports from 26 young schizophrenic patients and presented some absorbing accounts, such as the following:

> When people talk to me now it's like a different kind of language. It's too much to hold at once. My head is overloaded and I can't understand what they say. It makes you forget what you've just heard because you can't get hearing it long enough. It's all in different bits which you have to put together again in your head—just words in the air unless you can figure it out from their faces. (McGhie & Chapman, 1961, p. 375)

This description and others like it were convincing demonstrations for several workers that one must extend studies of "verbal behavior" beyond the isolated word and target word analyses to become "psycholinguistic" studies of sentences and discourse. As McGhie (1970) observed later, the subjective reports suggested that the patient's difficulties in understanding speech arose "not from an inability to perceive the individual words comprising a connected discourse, but from an inability to perceive the words in meaningful relationship to each other as part of an organized pattern" (p. 12).

The problem was to find a means of demonstrating that comprehension failures were due to an inability to organize language or to an inability to use the organization that was already part of language. Lewinsohn and Elwood (1961) were the first to study the effects of language structure on behavior. They borrowed Miller and Selfridge's (1950) paradigm in which, using words as units, various orders of approximation to English passages were constructed. At the lowest approximation, words were picked at random from a dictionary. At successively higher approximations, a game was played in which one person wrote, say, two words, and these were given to another person with a request to write two more words which would follow; and then another person was requested to do the same, and so on. At higher orders of approximation, each participant wrote longer series of words.

Miller and Selfridge found that normal subjects could remember more and more words as the order of approximation to English increased from 0 to about 5 (after 5 there was essentially no increase). The results showed that, as the transitional probabilities of words increased (to some point), verbal strings were easier to retain. This suggested that the structure of language was important to its recall.

Lewinsohn and Elwood adopted the Miller and Selfridge procedure to test whether schizophrenic patients could "use structure" to recall verbal strings to the same extent as control subjects. They found no differences between acute schizophrenics and control subjects, but chronic schizophrenics recalled fewer words than other subjects in all passages. However, when the chronic patients were matched to general medical patients on verbal IQ, the differences disappeared.

In effect, the Lewinsohn and Elwood study gave no support to the notion that schizophrenic patients are impaired in their ability to "use" syntactic structure. However, the same study was repeated by three other sets of investigators. In the first and most influential of these,

Lawson *et al.* (1964) compared young schizophrenics to normal subjects. Here, though verbal IQ had been equated, the schizophrenics recalled fewer words than normals for word strings with higher approximations to English. The authors conclude that the schizophrenics' failures were "related to an inability to perceive the organization inherent in normal speech" (p. 378).

This conclusion was not, in fact, supported by the remaining two studies. However, each of the subsequent replications gave some evidence that schizophrenic listeners could not recall textlike strings so well as control subjects. Levy and Maxwell (1968) found that acute schizophrenics were impaired relative to normal subjects, just as Lawson *et al.* had reported. But they also found that acutely depressed patients were even more impaired than schizophrenic patients, suggesting that the finding was nonspecific to schizophrenia. Raeburn and Tong (1968) found that almost half of their schizophrenic subjects failed to improve their recall as approximations became increasingly textlike. This result suggested that, for some schizophrenics at least, there was evidence of impairment. Raeburn and Tong explored this result in a series of experiments and concluded that it might be due to an inefficiency in the patients' recall, perhaps reflecting psychomotor retardation and lower vocabulary skills.

Thus, of the four attempts to study schizophrenics' recall with the Miller and Selfridge paradigm, one indicated impairment in acute schizophrenics and three suggested this impairment was either not specific to schizophrenia or was due to the operation of confounding variables. Nevertheless, the interpretation of impairment was the more compelling. It fit nicely with theorizing in the mainstream of psychology, and it seemed to account for some of the most disturbing experiences encountered by young schizophrenics. Consequently, in the subsequent decade, there were many attempts to test the schizophrenic listener's ability to "perceive the structure inherent in language."

2.2.3.2.2. *The Criticisms.* There have been many direct and indirect criticisms of these early studies. Pavy (1968) has pointed out that all the studies suffer from a major confounding: orders of approximation to English were always presented from random words to sentences so that subjects would be most fatigued and stressed at higher orders of approximation. This was likely to operate selectively against schizophrenic subjects. In addition, the use of order of approximation in itself has been subjected to both methodological (e.g., Coleman, 1963; Hörmann, 1971,

Ch. 13) and formal (e.g., Miller, 1965) criticism. The essential problem here is that the notion of transitional probabilities between words is based on a view of the native speaker's verbal "habits." It is much too narrow to account for how speakers produce and listeners understand language. As noted earlier, to vary the transitional probabilities in strings of words in some way captures a kind of quantitative measure of structure in language. But what is being measured is not clear.

Finally, in addition to the particular criticisms directed at these four studies, there have been at least three more demonstrations supporting Gerver's 1967 results, in which "structure" seemed to be used to the same extent by schizophrenic and normal listeners. Truscott (1970) followed a procedure from Marks and Miller (1964) and her results showed, as Gerver's did, that schizophrenic subjects had the same pattern of improvement in recall as medical patient controls. Rochester, Harris, and Seeman (1973) used a version of the "click" experiments taken from Garrett, Bever, and Fodor (1966). In this study, some schizophrenic and normal patients were asked to recognize the location of "clicks" in a series of sentences, and others were to recall the locations. In both cases, though the performance of the schizophrenic subjects was absolutely lower than that of the controls, the pattern of performance was the same. Both groups tended to displace the clicks into the nearest syntactic boundary, suggesting that they were perceiving and recalling sentences in terms of (at least) major syntactic units.

Carpenter (1976) replicated the Rochester et al. findings and presented an experiment based on Jarvella's (1971) work. In this latter study, listeners heard narrative passages that were interrupted at various intervals. During the interruptions, they wrote down the last words they could recall. Schizophrenic listeners, like normal adults and 11-year-old children, recalled adjacent clauses better if the clauses belonged to the same sentence than if they belonged to different sentences. Carpenter concludes that: "The sensitivity to syntactic structure is left intact in schizophrenic subjects" (1976, p. 49), a conclusion that seems appropriate to the other three studies as well.

2.2.3.2.4. *The Psycholinguistic Premises.* In several respects, the studies discussed in the previous section are new. Unlike studies of "verbal behavior," these studies of sentence recall have been based on assumptions about language use as a special function that is not necessarily identical or even similar to other systems of response. The experiments performed by Gerver, Truscott, Rochester et al., and Carpenter—all of which were taken from the "new" psycholinguistics of the 1960s—can be characterized in terms of the following assumptions that generally were accepted by psycholinguists in those years:

a' Language use is a special behavior which must be studied in terms of its own, language-based variables.
b' Biological considerations are of some interest.
c' Speaking and listening are best thought of as a collection of mental operations.
d' The best way to study language is to study the ways in which characteristics of input sentences are reflected in regularities of listener's (or reader's) responses.
e' The most interesting input characteristics have to do with structural (syntactic) features of sentences.

Premise e' is too narrow to characterize psycholinguistic assumptions about normal speakers at the end of the 1970s and should be expanded to read approximately:

e'' Any features of the sentence—syntactic or propositional or lexical or phonological—are interesting, and structural features of discourse (e.g., in narratives) are interesting as well.

However, a' to e' are fair characterizations of the psycholinguistic study of schizophrenic language which, as we have seen, lags about 4–10 years behind studies of normal language.

The experiments that began with Lewinsohn and Elwood (1961), and extended to the work of Raeburn and Tong·(1968), were all based on the Miller and Selfridge work in 1950. They reflect the new notion of language as a unique behavior which must be studied systematically; but they also reflect the older view that all responses can probably be explained in the same way. As a result, these studies represent an intermediary step between studies of "verbal behavior" and psycholinguistic experiments.

All these studies—the psycholinguistic experiments, the intermediary studies, and the studies of "verbal behavior"—have similarities that are as striking as their differences. However, before we examine these, let us review the particular limitations of the "psycholinguistic" experiments. Although none of these has been criticized directly—in the sense that a major confounding could be demonstrated—they never-theless can be criticized indirectly.

2.2.3.2.5. Indirect Criticisms. Several methodological and theoretical issues have been raised about the original studies from which the studies of schizophrenic listeners are derived. As with studies of verbal behavior, one can complain justly that these studies are designed for undergraduates in laboratories. Consequently, they yield data that are unrepresentative of ordinary language use (see especially Fillenbaum's 1970 paper). Moreover, they may require special skills from the subjects that are not part of normal language use. And finally, one must ask for more developed variables. In what sense does the listener use syntax—or the underlying semantic propositions—in any of the experiments? Should the interpretation of the "click" experiments be in terms of semantics or surface syntax or perceptual processes?

There will undoubtedly be modifications in the form these studies take in the next few years. If the lag still persists between the development of a psycholinguistic method and its adoption in studies of schizophrenia, these modifications will be in the direction of a greater emphasis on sentences in extended texts (as in Carpenter's second study), on presuppositions, and on efforts to make the listeners' situations more dialogic (e.g., Suchotliff, 1970). However, if these are the only changes, it will be a misfortune. If the study of schizophrenic language use continues to borrow its total methodology from mainstream psycholinguistics, it will mean that experimenters studying schizophrenic language have once again neglected their data, ignoring what their patients are doing and saying in order, once more, to make their awkward stepchild into a model one.

2.2.3.2.6. Limitations. The most cogent criticisms that can be directed toward psycholinguistic studies of schizophrenic language are criticisms derived from the data themselves. And these are several. First, although it is true that schizophrenic listeners appear to use "structure" or surface syntax to the same extent that normal subjects do in psycholinguistic experiments, it is nevertheless puzzling that many schizophrenic listeners report that they have great difficulty understanding connected discourse. What accounts for these reports? We must consider the clinical data—and not simply to dismiss these reports because we have failed to demonstrate the comparable effect in a laboratory experiment.

Second, and very critically for the role of laboratory experiments in studying schizophrenic language use, it is not clear that the response of a *listener* to a sentence or a set of sentences tells us anything useful about the aberrant productions of schizophrenic *speakers*. Lenneberg (1967) observed that it is easier to study the capacity for understanding than the capacity for speaking, because there are fewer factors affecting the former than the latter. But this does not mean, as Lenneberg seemed to imply, that by studying the listener one knows the speaker. We do not yet have any clear notion of how the capacities of the listener and speaker overlap. This is serious because it is the schizophrenic *speaker* whose behavior is so clearly aberrant. Although one would not wish to neglect studies of the listener, we must note there have been no systematic psycholinguistic studies of the schizophrenic speaker to date. If the practice of borrowing from psycholinguistics without returning anything continues, it is difficult to imagine how such studies will ever be launched. For, as Olson and Clark (1976), observe, listeners are studied by experiment and speakers by naturalistic observations. If one is committed to experiment, then it would seem that one will not study the behavior of the schizophrenic speaker for some time.

Finally, still with a focus on the data, it seems critical to try to extend the social and situational contexts of psycholinguistic experiments to approximate the contexts in which patients normally find themselves (as Del Castillo, 1970; Seeman, 1975; and Seeman and Cole, 1977 have attempted). Language is a social act and it is doubtful that we can learn much about the behavior of language users from highly controlled laboratory settings. Also, language is used in several different contexts— in interviews, in conversations that are face-to-face and over the telephone, in storytelling, and in group discussions. How can one understand the potentially profound effects of variations in contexts if one is intent on formalizing mental operations?

2.2.3.3. The Common Premises of Experimental Studies. The preceding discussion has been concerned with distinctions. The present one is concerned with similarities. The premises which experimental studies of schizophrenic language use seem to share are as follows:

1. The role of the language user is as a listener.
2. The processes of interest are the mental operations underlying perception, recall, and comprehension of words and sentences.
3. The best context for studying language is the laboratory because of the controlled conditions.
4. The best descriptions of language use are functional relations like: Treatment X has Effect Y.

5. The best things to study are response variables with an interval or at least ordinal character.

6. The goal is ultimately to characterize the mental operations underlying schizophrenia.

In 1965, Fodor commented that most experimental psychologists were still behaviorists. Perhaps it is still true, so perhaps it is apt that so many of these common premises seem to be a legacy from behaviorism. The strength of the approach that results from these premises lies in the capability of testing precisely a particular hypothesis or set of hypotheses. This is a considerable advantage. It means that one can sort through the plethora of assertions about schizophrenic deficiencies and determine to what extent any one of them can be supported. But there is also a weakness in this framework of assumptions, for it constrains the ways in which behavior may be studied. The behavior of the listener is examined in a highly controlled setting, and there are limitations in the explanations offered to account for that behavior. These limitations are discussed in more detail after the premises underlying naturalistic studies are presented.

2.2.4. Naturalistic Studies and Their Premises

To understand the schizophrenic listener, one experiments. To understand the schizophrenic speaker, one observes behavior in more or less natural settings. The goal in the latter case is ultimately to formulate the processes underlying the speaker's productions. The more immediate goal is to describe those productions. Once the speech is recorded and (perhaps) the accompanying extralinguistic context noted, the investigator must decide what to do with the utterances. With utterances from normal speakers, the immediate goal is to capture the distributional properties of the corpus—to summarize in some satisfactory way the whole collection of recorded utterances. One way to approach this problem is to formulate sets of rules that characterize the essential properties of the corpus.

The practice with schizophrenic speakers is different. Here, the aim has been to capture, not the distributional properties of the corpus, but its deviant features. That is, rather than describing the utterances as a whole, investigators of schizophrenic speech have attempted to characterize those features of the corpus that differ from normal. In effect, the effort has been to describe the failures rather than the overall performance of the schizophrenic speaker.

There have been a few exceptions to this practice. One has been the work of Laffal, discussed below. Another has been the experimental studies of Bertram Cohen and his colleagues (e.g., Cohen, 1978; Cohen, Nachmani & Rosenberg, 1974; Rosenberg & Cohen, 1964, 1966), which is reviewed in Rochester and Martin (1979), Chapters 4 and 7. A third exception has been the theoretical work of Harry Stack Sullivan (1925, 1944). Sullivan is outstanding for his early recognition of language and communication processes, rather than thought, as the interesting central phenomenon in schizophrenia. His informal observations of patients are pertinent today to many systematic efforts to study the schizophrenic speaker. For example, his conception of a normal speaker's process of pretesting utterances before producing them for actual listeners is one model used by Cohen and his colleagues in their study of reference processes in schizophrenia. Sullivan's description of the changing course of the schizophrenic speaker's awareness of disturbed speech, from initial painful chagrin to a lack of concern, predates this issue in the experimental literature (see Maher's 1972 discussion). However, for the most part, naturalistic studies of schizophrenic speakers have aimed to describe deviant features. As a consequence, they have developed a peculiarly one-sided understanding of the schizophrenic speaker. Events or behaviors that seem somehow aberrant have been described in excellent detail, but there have been no broad descriptions of the schizophrenic speaker's corpus. Lacking this description, one only knows that in some schizophrenic speakers certain categories of deviant behavior occur on some occasions.

The narrow focus of naturalistic studies of the schizophrenic speaker is easy to understand. The studies were designed primarily by those who treat patients, rather than by those who conduct experiments. The clinicians needed to identify the problems of new patients and to trace their progress through treatment. The concern was therefore on distinctive features of the utterances. Experimentalists, as we have seen, were very rarely interested in schizophrenic listeners' use of language. They were probably even less interested in schizophrenic *speakers* since there was little hope of studying speakers through controlled experiments. Finally linguists, like experimentalists, were uninterested in non-normal speakers in the early parts of this century and then for some time were concerned with idealized rather than actual speakers.

Two theoretical problems result from a focus on deviant features in a corpus. First, workable theory about schizophrenic speakers cannot be developed because one knows only what speakers *cannot* do and not what they can do. Second, even the speakers' failures are difficult to formulate without a baseline of overall behavior. Thus, the construction of a general model of the speaker is precluded, and the notion of deviant features is left rather undefined.

These theoretical problems may not seem serious because naturalistic studies, after all, are primarily initial data collection procedures. They are largely pretheoretical. However, the theoretical problems affect the data collection in some very concrete ways. Essentially, the problem is a theoretical one. The only basis for choosing "distinctive" or "deviant" behaviors is some version of what normal behavior is. But if this normal version is not based on a principled analysis, there will be no systematic basis for categorizing behavior. As a result, one may expect to be plagued by overlapping categories; by categories that include many different kinds of events; by categories that differ markedly from each other, requiring diverse kinds of judgments from coders; and by categories that are difficult to justify theoretically.

The last point is especially troublesome. Most investigators have not derived their categories from general principles that are independent of their choice procedures. Instead, categories have been made up from sets of events that will potentially discriminate schizophrenics from control speakers. The categories are refined so that the sharpest possible discriminations can be made. But their development and refinement has been entirely with a practical aim: What will separate schizophrenic speakers from others: Then on an *ad hoc* basis, the categories are vindicated (cf. Feigl, 1952) by showing that the procedures lead to accurate predictions about the speakers' identities. However, the categories are not justified in a theoretical sense from this demonstration, for it has not been shown that they can be derived from some principles or rules of language use. As a result, the constructs developed to account for the speaker's behavior are only weakly connected to that behavior.

These comments are made as an introduction to the resourceful studies that have been attempted since about 1960 in an effort to describe the distinctive features of the schizophrenic speaker's production. The studies are divided into content analyses and clinical studies.

2.2.4.1. Content Analyses. Content analysis is a method for making inferences from texts (not necessarily language-based) to the source of the texts. It is "the use of replicable and valid methods for making specific inferences from text to other states or properties of its source" (Krippendorff cited by Gerbner, 1969, p. xiv). In the present discussion, studies are considered content analyses if they use some methodological procedure to make inferences about schizophrenic speakers from their spoken or written productions. This means that the investigators must establish reliability and some validity for their categories. Clinical studies discussed in Section 2.2.4.2., omit these steps. In general, content analyses are refined procedures for categorizing schizophrenic language use; and clinical studies are initial descriptions of the schizophrenic speaker which can be developed into content analyses. Table 2.1. gives examples of the procedural differences between the two sorts of studies.

Since 1960, there have been about five or six efforts to analyze methodically the productions of the schizophrenic speaker. We will summarize these briefly since they are frequently neglected in reviews of the experimental studies.

2.2.4.1.1. Laffal's Work. Laffal (1960, 1965) analyzed the productions of schizophrenic speakers in an effort to understand "the subject's core conflicts and significant psychological configurations" (1965, p. 148). In one extensive study based on the autobiography of a famous psychiatric patient, Daniel Paul Schreber, Laffal transcribed texts that contained certain key words. The text words were categorized, and the frequency of cooccurrence of text words and key words was computed. From the correlations, inferences were made about the psychological significance of the key words for the subject.

Laffal's work provides a valuable counterpoint to most studies of schizophrenic speakers. His primary interest has been to develop a lexicon to describe the experience of all native English speakers—a kind of psychological thesaurus. This makes his analyses among the few in the literature based on a conception of general language use. However, since they are directed toward the personal dynamics of the speaker, they do not provide a model of language use for the schizophrenic speaker.

2.2.4.1.2. Gottschalk and Gleser. Gottschalk and Gleser (e.g., 1964, 1969; Gottschalk, Winget, & Gleser, 1969) developed a series of scales to serve as "verbal behavior measures" that would discriminate between groups of speakers and within individual speakers over time. Their scale for schizophrenic patients is designed to describe the "relative severity of social alienation and personal disorganization of schizophrenic persons" (Gottschalk & Gleser, 1964, p. 400). Patients are asked to talk

Table 2.1.
Procedures for Taking Speech Samples in a Range of Naturalistic Studies

	Content analyses	Clinical studies	
	(Wynne & Singer, 1963)	(Reilly et al., 1975)	(Lecours & Vanier Clément, 1976)
1. Situation			
(a) Location	Testing room in hospital (?)	Testing room in hospital (?)	Clinic or ward
(b) Formality (status relationship)	Experimenter with parents of patients or volunteer parents	Doctor with patient	Doctor with patient
(c) Mode (channel)	Spoken; attention on Rorschach cards	Spoken; conversation ("free interview")	Spoken; conversation ("clinical interview")
(d) Role (purpose)	Description of Rorschach cards	Relate personal experience	Relate personal experience
(e) Field (topic)	Rorschach cards	Personal experience	Personal experience
2. Speakers			
(a) Groups	Parents of sz, borderline, neurotic and normals	Sz and non-sz patients	Aphasic and sz patients
(b) n =	10–20	25	?
(c) Similar on age	Yes	Yes	?
education	Yes	Yes	?
social class	Yes	?	?
hospitalization	N/A[a]	Yes	Yes
medication	N/A	No	No (?)
3. Analysis			
(a) Sample size	Full utterance for first card	Total utterance (4–7 min segments)	(?)
(b) Categories	Coding manual	Coding manual	*Post hoc*
(c) Reliability between raters	82% agreement	?	?
n =	2–6	1(?)	1(?)
(d) Blind scoring	Yes	No (?)	No
4. Results			
(a) Between groups	t tests	t tests	Estimates
(b) Within a subject	No	No	Estimates

Note. For register categories (i.e., "formality," "mode," "role," and "field") see Ellis and Ure (1969). Gregory (1967) and Benson and Greaves (1973) refer to "formality" as "personal tenor," and "role" as "functional tenor."
[a]N/A = not applicable.

about some personal life experience for five minutes, and their tape-recorded speech is divided into clauses. The clauses are coded "whenever a theme or verbal act occurs which . . . can discriminate the severity of the schizophrenic syndrome" (1964, p. 40). The categories are weighted according to the discriminative power each has shown in validation experiments. Typical categories (from Gottschalk *et al.*, 1969) are as follows: others avoiding self (e.g., "She didn't want to go hunting with me."); disorientation (e.g., "I don't know what this place is—a police station?"); and incomplete sentences, clauses, phrases and blocking (e.g., "I had good spectacles./I just uh that fine print.").

These analyses demonstrate some of the difficulties of naturalistic studies discussed in the introduction to this section. Their purpose is to describe the deviant features in the productions of potentially schizophrenic speakers. In this case, the features are largely aspects of the content. The categories for describing content seem to overlap in some instances. They include a diversity of phenomena that seem to require very different kinds of judgment from coders, and are difficult to justify theoretically.

The theoretical justification of the content analysis categories is difficult for two reasons. First, the categories are not independently derivable from principles. They have been developed on grounds that whatever discriminates the productions of schizophrenic speakers is a potential item for the scales. Since items chosen for their discriminability have no necessary relation to "social alienation and personal disorganization," the constructs and the categories also have no necessary relation. Second, this technique for performing the content analysis intuits content rather than analyzing it. In the late 1950s, when these scales were developed, the accepted approach in content analysis required that "the judges' intuitions be constrained by explicit coding instructions while the critical process of semantic interpretation was left entirely implicit" (Krippendorff, 1969, p. 6).

The development of computer techniques for analyzing texts has made the distinction between the intuition of content and the analysis of content very clear. In the early 1960s, the only techniques available were dictionary look-ups in which words, precoded for form class (grammatical) membership, could be categorized. Gottschalk and Gleser and their colleagues rejected this approach for the greater sensitivity to be gained with human coders. But what was gained in sensitivity—in the judges' familiarity with the language, in their expertise with the subject matter, and in their pragmatic knowledge of speech acts—was lost in explanatory power. One simply cannot state how much of the application of categories depends on the human coder's knowledge of the world and language, and how much is due to the putative measurement of the categories.

Recently, Gottschalk and his colleagues have attempted to computerize their content analysis scales. They have not yet met with success, possibly because so much of the semantic and pragmatic decision process has been left up to human coders. As Gottschalk, Hausmann, and Brown (1975) observe in their report of efforts to computerize one of the simpler scales, "perhaps the most fascinating aspect of this research is the discovery of the amount of inferencing that a human scorer does—something that present-day computers are ill-equiped to handle" (p. 87).

2.2.4.1.3. Singer and Wynne. Singer and Wynne (e.g., Singer & Wynne, 1963, 1965; Wynne & Singer, 1963a,b) present a sensitive approach to language use in the parents of schizophrenic patients. Although their work is not addressed to the schizophrenic speaker *per se,* it provides a very interesting technique which will be reviewed briefly here.

Like Gottschalk and Gleser, Singer and Wynne developed a set of categories for discriminating deviant productions of, in this case, schizophrenics' parents from the parents of other groups of subjects. But unlike the content-based categories of Gottschalk and Gleser, the categories of Singer and Wynne have a strong language base. For example, among their most sensitive categories (cf. Singer, Wynne & Toohey, 1978, Table 1) are the following: unintelligible remarks; ordinary words or phrases used oddly or out of context; uncorrected speech fragments; inconsistent and ambiguous references; and odd, tangential, and inappropriate remarks. Moreover, these language-based categories are relatively closely tied to an etiological hypothesis, as follows:

> Parental communication, if characterized by disruptions, vagueness, irrelevance, and lack of closure, can impair the child's ability to focus attention.

Singer and Wynne argue that the impairment that results from such communication forms a basis for schizophrenia in the child.

In their original studies, Singer and Wynne gave each parent to be tested a series of Rorschach cards, asked for the parent's first impression of the card, and later asked for an elaboration of that impression. Responses to the first card were analyzed in terms of "deviances." These are summarized in Table 2.2.

The accomplishments of this program of study have been summarized by Hirsch and Leff (1975). Ten years of research, they observe, have produced results "consistently in the same direction using increasingly more objective techniques." Singer and Wynne have been able to use their technique with such discrimination that "no pair of parents of schizophrenics has been found to score within the range of parents of normals . . ., and taken individually, only 32.5 per cent of parents

Table 2.2.
Categories of Communication Defects and Deviances: Some Examples[a]

I. Closure problems

Speech fragments
Unintelligible remarks
Unstable percepts
Gross indefiniteness and tentativeness
Responses in negative form
Subjunctive, "if," "might-response"
Disqualifications
  "Derogatory," disparaging, critical remarks, if "disqualifying"
  Nihilistic remarks
  Failures to verify own responses or perception

II. Disruptive behavior

Odd, tangential, inappropriate remarks or answers to questions
Nonverbal, disruptive behavior
Humor
Swearing
Hopping around among responses

III. Peculiar language and logic

A. Peculiar word usages, constructions and pronunciations
      Ordinary words or phrases used oddly or out of context
      Odd sentence construction
      Peculiar or quaint, private terms or phrases. Neologisms
      Euphemisms
      Slips of tongue
      Mispronounced words
      Clang associations, rhymed phrases, and word play
      Abstract or global terms
B. Peculiar logic
      Illogical combinations of percepts and categories. Failure to keep incompatible or alternative percepts, images, or concepts distinct

[a]From Hirsch and Leff, 1975; adapted from Singer, 1967.

of non-schizophrenics have scored above the lowest scoring schizophrenic parent" (Hirsch & Leff, 1975, p. 113).

In a painstaking attempt to replicate this last finding, Hirsch and
Leff studied a sample of English parents of schizophrenic and neurotic
hospitalized patients. Although they found reliable differences between
groups in the direction which reproduced the Singer and Wynne finding, there was considerable overlap in the performance of the two
groups. Several thoughtful statistical techniques were tried in an effort
to improve the discrimination, but no strong differences could be found
between the parent groups.

Wynne (1977) and Singer (Singer et al., 1978) have criticized Hirsch
and Leff's procedures for administering and scoring the Rorschachs. They
suggest that insensitive or hasty techniques during initial viewing and
subsequent elaboration of the cards might have restricted or seriously
biased the corpus. Although this may be so, one must also acknowledge
that not only Hirsch and Leff but also Singer and Wynne appear to have
gone to great lengths to ensure that every important procedural detail
was followed, and that any coding difficulties were discussed before
decisions were made (cf. Hirsch & Leff, 1975, Appendix i). The failure
of the second pair of investigators to replicate the first pair's work would
seem to say more about the complexity of the procedure itself than about
the conduct of the inquiry.

One possible source of difficulty, though not necessarily the one
which accounts for Hirsch and Leff's failure to replicate, is the status
of the descriptive categories. As we mentioned, there are two major
methodological problems with content analysis categories for schizophrenic speakers: (a) the categories are very weakly connected to the
theoretical constructs, and (b) the categories are based on inferential
procedures so that one does not know the extent to which different
analyses are applied.

With regard to (a), there is some basis for believing Singer and
Wynne's categories to be motivated independently by theory. Wynne
(1977) reports that he and Singer "used a certain face validity" in selecting events that seemed to require the maintenance of a shared task
set and a common focus of attention. And indeed some of the categories
offer a strong face validity. One can imagine that, say, "unintelligible
remarks" and "forgetting responses" and "nihilistic remarks" might
well have an impact on how families share their experiences. However,
it is difficult to imagine that certain other items could be chosen simply

on the basis of their presumed negative impact on communication (e.g., slips of the tongue, mispronounced words, humor, and swearing). These categories seem better explained by the remark that, in constructing the coding manual, the authors "sought to identify features in Rorschach communication which we had found especially frequent in the Rorschach protocols of our initial samples of parents of schizophrenics" (Singer *et al.*, 1978, p. 9).

With regard to (b), the inferential procedures on which category coding is based, the problems are evident. Even though the categories in this work seem less intuitive and more solidly based in language use than those used by Gottschalk and Gleser, one must still ask: "What is it in fact that they are scoring?" (Hirsch & Leff, 1975, p. 114). In particular, the following problems exist:

1. The categories seem to require various sorts of judgments from coders and presumably would require many different sorts of decision-making models to account for the coders' decisions.
2. Categories overlap (cf. Hirsch & Leff, 1975, p. 139) and it is difficult to score global categories. These problems are especially acute because the units of measurement are not divided into easily distinguishable sets like words or clauses but are "deviances" which can cooccur and overlap without restriction.
3. The categories call extensively on the intuitions of the coders, on their familiarity with the language, and on their pragmatic skills. Wynne (1977) acknowledges this: "Raters differ in the degree to which they are willing or able to give sustained, consistent attention to this quite arduous task," he observes, and he outlines some of the knowledge which the human coder must bring to bear: "Testers and raters should be very familiar with the range of ordinary and deviant behavior shown by subjects on Rorschach, including varieties of idiomatic language used by persons of a given social class, educational and cultural background" (p. 268).

2.2.4.1.4. Summary. The content analyses proposed by Gottschalk and Gleser and by Singer and Wynne have shown great promise in discriminating between groups of schizophrenic patients or groups of schizophrenic parents and control groups. However, the dimensions on which these discriminations have been made are not well understood.

The Singer and Wynne procedures have a more highly developed language base, and the results produced by these procedures provide valuable hints as to distinctive features of language use. Nevertheless, the coding procedures in both cases rely so strongly on human coders' decisions that it is not clear how one could use these procedures to construct a language-based model of the schizophrenic speaker.

2.2.4.1.5. *The General Inquirer Studies*. Two groups of investigators, Maher, McKean, and McLaughlin (1966) and Tucker & Rosenberg (1975; Rosenberg & Tucker, 1976) have used content analyses based on the General Inquirer computer system developed by Stone, Bales, Namenworth, and Ogilvie (1962; and cf. Stone, Dunphy, Smith, & Ogilvie, 1966). The General Inquirer was one of the early attempts to develop formalized procedures for dealing with texts. It was designed as an "aid to the investigator" in organizing and making explicit text-analytic procedures, but was not intended to "completely simulate or otherwise substitute for the inspections, analyses, and insights of the investigator" (Stone *et al.*, 1962, p. 485). The system has a dictionary look-up which can categorize words and an ability to examine sentences under various conditions. The major unit of analysis is the "sentence" which "so far as possible . . . should be self-contained and not depend upon a larger context for its meaning." Any vagueness or ambiguity in the sentence would "cause confusion for the reader and hinder further work with the retrieved data" (p. 490). In addition, all words entered must be tagged for their individual form class memberships.

In about 1965, The General Inquirer was the most sophisticated alternative to intuitive category systems like those offered by Gottschalk and Gleser and Singer and Wynne. Its capacities were extremely modest, compared to the capacities of the human coder, but it did have the advantage of objective techniques. One could be sure, as Krippendorff claimed, that "no part of the procedure [would] be delegated to the inexplicable process of intuition" (1969, p. 6). About all that the system would do was categorize words in a text according to some predetermined categories, so a fruitful use of the system depended strongly on an investigator's resourcefulness.

Maher's Work. Maher *et al*. present an outstanding series of studies using this system. They used the General Inquirer to analyze written texts from over 100 schizophrenic patients in hospitals. In one study, 50-word samples were analyzed in terms of words falling into various form class categories (e.g., subject, subject modifier, verb, verb modifier) and thematic categories (e.g., natural-world, legal, political). In a replication, similar sorting procedures were used with 100-word samples.

These studies are remarkable in many respects. First, Maher and his colleagues recognized the critical problem which "thought disorder" poses for the study of schizophrenic language. They pointed out that, since many samples of schizophrenics' speech are not aberrant, it is necessary to find samples which are. But if judges are used to distinguish thought disordered from normal samples, one may simply be studying "the judging habits of raters rather than any independently consistent attribute of psychotic pathology" (Maher et al., 1966, p. 471). This is especially true where the judges are mental health professionals. Their common training in descriptive diagnosis could lead them to agreement but might have little or nothing to with the patient's state.

Next, having posed the problem of judges' evaluations of thought disorder, Maher et al. attempted to identify the cues that judges use in their assessments of thought disorder. The primary aim was "to discover explicitly the rules the judges use implicitly when diagnosing thought disorder from language samples" (p. 472). They determined assessments for various documents from the original hospital clinician, from three clinical judges unacquainted with the writers, and from two undergraduates.

Along with the original study, a replication is reported that uses longer (100-word) samples, new lay judges, and new samples of 60 documents. The results of the studies are presented not simply in terms of differences between groups, but in terms of likelihood-ratios, which indicate the proportion of individuals in a group who are described by that measure. For example, the authors found that writers who were judged thought-disordered tended to use more objects than subjects in their sentences. What is new and useful is that they report the likelihood that a given subject-to-object ratio will result in a writer being judged thought-disordered. For example, where writers used 3 objects per subject, 8 out of 8 documents were judged thought-disordered; and where writers used 2 objects per subject, 5 out of 6 cases were judged thought-disordered.

Maher et al. return to their data to try to account for their findings and to develop hypotheses to describe the possible language use of the schizophrenic speakers. The hypotheses they offer are speculations about information processing and attentional mechanisms, but they are based on observations that bear rather closely on the hypotheses. The authors note that high ratios of objects to subjects occur often at the ends of sentences: "Doctor, I have pains in my chest and hope and wonder if my box is broken and heart is beaten for my soul and salvation and heaven, Amen" (Maher, 1968, pp. 32–33). They speculate that "the attentional mechanisms that are necessary to the maintenance of coherent language are weaker at the end of the the sentence than elsewhere" (Maher et al., 1966, p. 489).

Finally, it is noteworthy that these investigators present a failure of their own hypothesis in their third experiment. Records from 90 patients were examined, and they found no significant differences between schizophrenic and nonschizophrenic patients in the use of high object-to-subject ratios. Their conclusion is a model for other such studies where failures in predictions seem not to occur: "where high ratios exist [schizophrenic patients] are likely to be judged thought-disordered, but the absolute probability that [such ratios] will be found in a randomly selected document from a schizophrenic patient is not high" (Maher et al., 1966, p. 497).

There are some limitations, too. For one thing, as the authors themselves point out, their observations do not allow one to identify most documents which would be called thought-disordered. However, they are able to identify some events (e.g., more objects that subjects) which, when they occur, almost always signal evaluations of thought disorder. Next, no model is presented which might describe how much weight particular events have in judges' decision-making. For example, judges are likely to assess thought disorder where there are references to political themes and religion. How important are these? Do they depend on the object-to-subject ratio or other factors of language use? This is not specified. Finally, because the analyses are restricted to words, the authors are not in a position to offer a model of the schizophrenic speaker's production of discourse.

Tucker and Rosenberg. Tucker and Rosenberg (1975) also used the General Inquirer system. In a pilot study they took 600-word samples from acute schizophrenic patients and from two control groups of patients and normal subjects. The patients' samples were taken from 15-min interviews collected during their first week in hospital; the normals' samples were taken after they had experienced 10 min of REM sleep and were awakened and asked to describe their dreams. An adaptation of the Harvard III Psychosocial Dictionary was used to sort words from the samples into 84 categories which had been "specifically selected for their psychological and sociological relevance" (Tucker & Rosenberg, 1975, p. 612). They found that 14 out of 84 categories differentiated schizophrenic from nonschizophrenic subjects.

In a replication (Rosenberg & Tucker, 1976), the authors studied larger samples (which included subjects from the original samples) and refined their procedures. The results of the replication, once gender differences were controlled, were that 3 out of 31 categories differentiated schizophrenic from nonschizophrenic patients. Thus, when the technique was refined and the sample size increased, the replication was no more promising as a discriminative procedure. The categories that discriminated the larger sample of schizophrenic patients were "Not" (schizophrenics used more words denoting negation), and two categories that schizophrenics underused relative to nonschizophrenic patients: "Pleasure" (states of gratification) and "Ascend Theme" (words associated with rising, falling, fire and water, supposed to indicate concerns relating to the Icarus complex).

These studies are developed from a series of clinical studies done in conjunction with other workers (e.g., Reilly, Harrow, & Tucker, 1973; Reilly, Harrow, Tucker, Quintan, & Siegel, 1975, Siegel, Harrow, Reilly, & Tucker, 1976). In the clinical studies, the categories were essentially based on Bleuler's observations and consequently relied very heavily on the intuitions of judges. Tucker and Rosenberg's work is a welcome attempt to analyze the schizophrenic speaker's productions objectively, and theirs is the first to use a computerized approach with *speaker*'s productions.

There are, however, some limitations to these efforts. First, it is discouraging to find no serious account taken of the similar but more developed analyses published by Maher and his colleagues some ten years earlier. Several important points made in the earlier study seem to be lost to the later workers: namely, the problems in defining and selecting "schizophrenic" or "thought disordered" speech; the need to describe results for individual subjects as well as for groups; and the significance of syntactic considerations as well as themes in assessing texts. Second, the authors' goal of providing "phenomenological" descriptions of schizophrenic speakers has, in practice, been addressed by previous workers, as indicated above. It is not clear that the categories provided by the Harvard III Dictionary adaptation are superior to the other categories, nor is it clear on which dimensions they differ from previous work. Moreover, it is not the case that the Harvard III categories are theory-free. Some, like the "Ascend Theme" mentioned above, have a powerful set of psychodynamic assumptions underlying them.

2.2.4.1.6. Summary of Content Analyses. The five sets of content analyses reviewed here offer an overview of the problem facing those who attempt to understand the schizophrenic speaker. They demonstrate a stubborn conundrum: analyses performed by human coders can produce remarkable discriminations, but the bases on which they operate are obscure, whereas analyses performed by computers are based on well-defined procedures, but the discriminations that they produce are rather weak. To exaggerate the situation a bit, it seems that when our measures are discriminating, we cannot tell what they are measuring; and when we can tell what they are measuring, they are not very discriminating.

In the next few years, it is likely that the computer systems for analyzing discourse will be applied to schizophrenic speech. Gottschalk and his colleagues (1975) have already begun this effort. But if their experience is a fair guide, even these techniques are rather far from human coders' decisions. Hirsch and Leff (1975) commented in their review of Singer and Wynne (1965): "The magnitude of Singer's accomplishment in these studies is truly remarkable" (p. 75). Those who study schizophrenic speakers are attempting to transform the clinician's truly remarkable skill into explicit criteria of judgment that describe the speaker's behavior. And this seems to be an inordinately difficult task.

2.2.4.2. Clinical Studies. Clinical studies, even more than content analyses, have been neglected in reviews of language in schizophrenia. The reason given is that the premises underlying these studies are so far from experimental studies that fruitful comparisons are not possible. This is probably true if one attempts a strict comparison, but it is too narrow a statement if one wants to understand the schizophrenic speaker. In fact, the last two decades have produced clinical studies that are at least as enlightening as experimental efforts on these problems.

The studies can be divided into (a) controlled observations by psychiatrists and (b) descriptive analyses by linguists and aphasiologists. Both categories provide insights into the schizophrenic speaker, and their separate perspectives give a valuable diversity.

2.2.4.2.1. Controlled Observations by Psychiatrists. Among the several studies of schizophrenic speakers, a few have provided welcome expansions of the Bleulerian descriptions. These expansions are important because it is primarily the Bleulerian accounts that are used in hospitals across North America for the diagnosis of thought disorder and schizophrenia.

Clinical studies are difficult to summarize because their value lies primarily in the detailed accounts they provide. However, there are some important observations which can be mentioned.

Reilly et al. In an interesting study entitled "Looseness of Associations in Acute Schizophrenia," Reilly and his colleagues (1975) interviewed acute schizophrenic patients and other psychiatric patients in 15 min "free verbalization" interviews (details of this study are given in Table 2.1.). One rater coded 10 categories of "deviant verbalizations." The rater gave scores of 0 to 4 (maximum pathology) whenever he found one of the 10 categories appropriate. Another category, "looseness of associations," was defined as "a lack of connection between ideas so that the reason for a shift in thought is questionable or incomprehensible . . . where continuity of thought and the logical development of a concept is lacking to some degree" (p. 242). Six subcategories of looseness were defined as follows: L1—mild shift in thought within a sentence; L2—slight shift from one sentence to next, same topic; L3—drastic shift from one sentence to next, same topic; L4—mild shift from one sentence to next different topic; L5—drastic shift from one sentence to next, different topic; L6—drastic shift within a sentence. The authors decided (on some unspecified basis) that L3, L5 and L6 should receive higher scores for deviance than the remaining subcategories.

Another category was "gaps in communication" in which "information essential for comprehension by the listener is missing, and the speaker behaves as if he presupposes information or knowledge on the part of the listener that he has no right to expect" (p. 242). What is interesting about these categories is (a) the recognition of the use of language as a social act in which the speaker must take some account of the listener's needs, (b) the notion that topic shifts can be "drastic" or "mild" and can occur within as well as between sentences, and (c) the idea that there is a gradient of topic shifts reflecting how well the speaker takes account of the listener's needs. By tying these categories to events within and between sentences, the authors suggest a way of rooting notions of the comprehensibility of the speaker to specific discourse events. Instead of talking only about ideas being "vague and wooly," they suggest some concrete ways in which this "wolliness" might be manifested.

There are problems in extrapolating from this study. Briefly, one must note that a single rater coded the texts (though the authors assert that interrater reliability was satisfactorily established, they give no details about this); the categories still rely to a considerable extent on the rater's intuition; and the parametric statistics used were probably not appropriate for the data. Nevertheless, what is impressive and valuable is the attempt to use categories that are rather more language-based than those used by earlier workers, and at the same time to use categories that are immediately relevant in clinical practice.

Andreasen. Andreasen (1979, a,b) has also attempted to refine Bleulerian descriptions of thought disorder. Her primary contribution has been to show the distribution of these categories in patients with various diagnoses. A summary of her preliminary findings is given in Table 2.3.

Her results provide evidence in support of several frequent clinical observations: (a) not all schizophrenic patients show signs of "formal thought disorder" in their productions; (b) some Bleulerian categories are more common than others in schizophrenic speakers ("poverty of speech content," and "tangentiality"); and (c) several Bleulerian categories describe behaviors that are as common in depression and mania as in schizophrenia (5 out of 7 categories given in Table 2.3.).

The studies by Andreasen and Reilly *et al.* demonstrate the increasing sensitivity of studies of language use in schizophrenic speakers. In both studies, there are careful attempts to show how psychiatric designations are based on the speaker's behavior. These demonstrations are necessary to the development of a baseline from which to describe and perhaps model the speaker's performance and knowledge. However, they still rely very heavily on unspecified decisions by sophisticated coders, and they provide descriptions only of what schizophrenic speakers can*not* do—there is no baseline of general performance provided.

2.2.4.2.2. Descriptive Analyses by Linguists and Aphasiologists. Since 1975, there has been a remarkable development in the study of "schizophasia." Schizophasia is "a deviant linguistic behavior observed in certain—not in all, by far—people considered to be schizophrenics" (Lecours & Vanier-Clément, 1976, p. 524). The term, and the publication of several studies by linguists and aphasiologists, reflect recent efforts to describe as objectively as possible the phenomena that characterize the deviant use of language by schizophrenic speakers.

Chaika. Elaine Chaika's description of a single schizophrenic patient

Table 2.3.
Recent Clinical Descriptions of Thought Disorder

To characterize the features of "formal thought disorder" Andreasen (1979) designed 18 categories of language use and counted the occurence of these categories in the psychiatric interviews of manic, depressed, and schizophrenic speakers. She found that seven of the categories occured in at least 25% of the schizophrenic patients' ($n=32$) interviews. Only two of these (*), however, discriminated schizophrenics from other patients.

Measure	Brief description	Percentage of schizophrenia
(a) Poverty of speech content*	Speech conveys little information; is vague, overabstract or overconcrete, repetitive and stereotyped. Information is not adequate and replies may be incomprehensible.	41
(b) Tangentiality*	Refers only to replies to questions. Replies are oblique, tangential or somewhat irrelevant, though clearly related to the question in some way. E.g., when asked for today's date, speaker replies, "I was born November 11, 1935."	41
(c) Derailment	Spontaneous speech in which ideas are clearly but obliquely related. E.g., "Yesterday we played volleyball in the afternoon. Babe Ruth and Lou Gehrig both played for the Yankees. Too bad Gehrig got sick."	53
(d) Pressure of speech	Speech is rapid and difficult to interrupt; tends to be loud and emphatic; excessive amount.	25
(e) Loss of goal	Speech begins with a particular subject, wanders away and never returns to it; failure to follow a chain of thought through to a logical conclusion.	47
(f) Perseveration	Persistent repetition of words or ideas, though words are used appropriately.	25
(g) Poverty of speech	Restriction in amount of speech so replies are brief, concrete, and unelaborated; unprompted talk is rare.	34

Note. All the above measures have high positive intercorrelations (r typically yields $p < .001$) except for (g) poverty of speech, which is typically negatively, though not reliably, correlated with the other measures.

(1974a), and her discussions of this and other work (1974b, 1977), and Victoria Fromkin's (1975) discussions of Chaika's work, mark efforts by linguists to describe "schizophrenic language" in terms of a small number of definable features. Chaika (1974a) analyzed a tape-recorded interview from a 37-year-old patient "who had been repeatedly diagnosed as schizophrenic." The interview was virtually a monologue, Chaika reports, and "the patient's intonation was usually not amenable to intrusion." Indeed, the patient "often seemed to be speaking to herself" (1974a, p. 259).

Chaika examined the corpus using a variety of linguistic approaches. She identified six characteristics as follows: (a) disrupted ability to match semantic features with sound strings; (b) preoccupation with too many of the semantic features of a word in discourse; (c) inappropriate use of phonological features of words; (d) production of sentences according to phonological and semantic features of previously uttered words, rather than according to topic; (e) disrupted ability to apply rules of syntax and discourse; and (f) failure to note speech errors when they occur. She concluded that these characteristics indicated a disruption in the ability to apply "linguistic rules which organize elements into meaningful structures," and suggested that "schizophrenic language" might be due to an intermittent aphasia over which the patient has no control.

Fromkin (1975) argued that all the behaviors described by Chaika could be found in normal productions, except for the disruption in discourse. She argues that the latter feature is nonlinguistic and that disconnected discourse is evidence of "schizophrenic thought" rather than "schizophrenic language": "Any attempt to include constraints on logical sequencing or social relevance in a model of linguistic competence would seem to me to be too ambitious and bound to fail" (1975, p. 501). Fromkin, like Roger Brown (1973), argues that there are not disruptions of *language* in schizophrenics but of disruptions of *thought*.

The Aphasiologists. The question of whether the aberrant productions of schizophrenic speakers reflect a true aphasia, that is, a failure of language production which is distinct from the patient's ability to conceptualize and to engage in social acts, has a long history. It has been of particular interest to clinicians who must decide whether a new patient has a temporary language disturbance or an imminent psychosis. Recently, the question has also been raised in connection with the etiology of schizophrenia. Benson (1973), DiSimoni, Darley, and Aronson (1977), and Gerson, Benson, and Frazier (1977) present reviews of this literature among aphasiologists.

One example of this recent work is the Lecours and Vanier-Clément (1976) description of "schizophasia," in which they summarize four characteristics as follows: (a) a normal or greater than normal speech flow; (b) a normal use of intonation and pronunciation; (c) a production in various amounts and combinations of *paraphasia* (deviant production of elements from a known target), e.g., verbal paraphasia would be "a scent of cadaver" instead of a "scent of caviar"; a syntactic paraphasia would be a replacement of one word or phrase by another of the same syntactic function, e.g., "people's opium" for "taxpayer's money"; and/ or *téléscopages* (several units are condensed into one), e.g., a verbal téléscopage would be a single word which results from borrowing phonemic or morphemic units from several conventional segments (e.g., "transformation" for "transmission of information"); and/or *neologisms* (deviant segments used as single words; these are reserved for items which cannot be identified by other categories); and (d) a *glossomania*, in which components of sentences are chosen mainly on the basis of phonological or semantic kinship to each other; *formal glossomania* would be sentences in which components are chosen mainly on the basis of phonological kinship; *semantic glossomania* would be sentences in which components are chosen mainly on the basis of conceptual associations that seem unrelated to the conversational topic.

The authors compare their conclusions to those of Chaika and note that her characteristics (a) to (e) correspond to deviations they have noted as well in schizophrenic speakers. However, they claim that all— with the possible exception of (b)—also define linguistic deviations observed in the jargonaphasias. In addition, they report that her observation (f), a failure to note speech errors, did not characterize their data for "archetypical schizophasic" patients. Chaika's (1977) response to this and to Fromkin's critique appears part of an ongoing discussion of these problems.

Summary of the Descriptive Analyses. A profound advantage of these studies is their power to describe individual patients very well. This is particularly apparent in studies such as the Lecours and Vanier- Clément report and in the work of James Chapman (1966). From these studies we can learn two very important facts: (a) not every schizophrenic patient is schizophasic; and (b) not every schizophasic patient is schizophasic all the time.

These facts have been responsible for great confusion in experimental investigations. Experimenters have behaved as if "schizophasia" could be sampled at random from unselected schizophrenic patients. It is no wonder that there have been so many failures to replicate even the simplest "verbal behavior" studies. If the phenomenon under study is episodic, then one must capture the episodes and describe them. To do otherwise by attempting unselected observations will necessarily lead to weak and often unreplicable outcomes. Although many investigators must have suspected this fact, very few have acknowledged and attempted to use it.

A profitable next step for these clinical descriptions would be to introduce some tabulations and patient characteristics of the sorts used by Andreasen (1979, a,b) and other clinical investigators. The lack of such procedures means that many essential features of the data are left unspecified (as indicated in Table 2.1.). In particular, one knows neither the characteristics of the patients being described nor the frequency of the various behaviors. Without systematic observations, we cannot know whether some sorts of patients are more likely than others to, say, show discourse failures rather than "verbal paraphasias,"; whether "phonemic téléscopages" can occur without other manifestations of schizophasia; whether phonemic aberrations always occur with aberrations at the verbal level and at the level of discourse; or whether chronic patients are more likely to show some of these behaviors and acute patients to show others.

2.2.4.3. The Common Premises of Naturalistic Studies. Although there is a very wide range of studies of schizophrenic speakers included under the general heading of "naturalistic" observations, the following premises seem common to most naturalistic studies:

1. The role of the language user is as a speaker.
2. The processes of interest are the mental and/or social and/or pathological processes underlying the production of words, sentences, and connected discourse.
3. The best context for studying language is the clinic or hospital in which interviews are given. This is best because of the diversity of conditions provided.
4. The best descriptions of language use are lists of (all) behaviors that are distinctive to schizophrenic speakers.
5. The best things to study are the distinctive characteristics of the speaker's productions.

Table 2.4.

Premises of Experimental and Naturalistic Studies of Language Use in Schizophrenia

Premises	Planned experiments	Naturalistic studies
(a) Role of language user is as ...	listener	speaker
(b) Processes of interest are ...	information processing	production
(c) Best context for study is ... because of ...	laboratory controlled conditions	clinic diversity of conditions
(d) Best descriptions of language use are	functional relations like: "treatment X has effect Y"	lists of behaviors that are distinctive to schizophrenic speakers
(e) Best things to study are ...	response variables with interval or ordinal character	distinctive speech events and uses
(f) Goal is to identify ...	cognitive/perceptual processes underlying schizophrenia	schizophrenic patients or their families; (psychosocial processes underlying schizophrenia)

6. The goal is to identify schizophrenic patients or their families, or to identify the features of productions which prompt listeners to diagnose schizophrenia.

These common premises are not a legacy from behaviorism. If they must be derived from one tradition, they are in the tradition of the clinic. The aim in these studies is essentially a practical one: How may we describe the schizophrenic patient so that he or she can be treated? The remaining premises are predicated primarily on this aim. The patient is seen as a producer, one who produces symptoms which must be diagnosed. And the effort of study is devoted primarily to a careful description of these symptoms such that differential diagnoses are facilitated—with organic syndromes, if possible, with aphasias, and with other psychiatric disorders.

Table 2.4 summarizes the premises that underlie both naturalistic and experimental studies of language use in schizophrenia. The contrasting traditions underlying the two categories of studies provide investigators with a broad range of procedures from which to approach the study of schizophrenics' language use. In the next section, I discuss the problems and advantages of the individual approaches and examine two problems that are common to both.

2.3. The Study of the Schizophrenic Speaker in Light of Prior Work

How is one to study the schizophrenic speaker? More precisely, how is one to study this speaker in a manner that is systematic and at the same time relevant to the everyday uses of language? The answer would seem to lie somewhere between the experimental and the naturalistic traditions. The experimental premises allow strong tests of particular hypotheses, but the tests are very narrow and are restricted primarily to listeners. The naturalistic premises allow broad descriptions of relevant behaviors, but the descriptions are generally unsystematic and intuitive. To find a middle way, let us examine some of the general issues associated with the two approaches. The issues we shall be discussing are summarized in Table 2.5.

2.3.1. Three Issues

Briefly, there are three issues which seem important in considering limitations in one or the other or both approaches to language use in schizophrenia.

Table 2.5.
Some Issues in the Study of Language Use in Schizophrenia

	Planned experiments	Naturalistic studies
A. 1. Settings provide unrepresentative data because of role and social class differences	Lab setting: experimenter-subject	Clinic setting:doctor–patient
2. Tasks require unrepresentative skills	Recall and recognition tasks do not measure comprehension	
3. Narrow hypotheses dictate narrow designs	Only know if subject responds more or less	

Common problems

B. 1. Theoretical constructs are adopted from other disciplines but not made relevant to language use

2. Theoretical goals are directed toward models of *deviance* so descriptions and formulations are not general for language use

2.3.1.1. Unrepresentative Data. The effect of the formal testing situation presents a general methodological problem in psychological studies and is particularly acute in studies of "deviant" language. The dangers of bias from the testing situation are revealed in a dramatic study that Labov (1970) conduced in New York. He demonstrated the unrepresentativeness of verbal behavior elicited from black children by white investigators and even by unsympathetic black investigators. Black children, who were virtually silent with white experimenters going through the formal ritual of psycholinguistic tasks, displayed great linguistic sophistication with black experimenters who understood the dialect and ways of life of the black ghetto.

Table 2.5. indicates that there is a risk of unrepresentative data in both experimental and naturalistic studies. In both cases, there are role differences between subject and experimenter, or patient and doctor (or nurse, psychologist, etc.). And in both cases, there are likely to be marked social-class differences in which the schizophrenic subject is from a lower social class than the graduate student or Ph.D. experimenter or the doctor or nurse, etc. (cf. Nuttall & Solomon, 1970; Seeman, 1970; Turner, Raymond, Zabor, & Diamond, 1969).

2.3.1.2. Special Tasks; Special Skills. Several aspects of the methodology of experimental studies limit the extent to which one can generalize from the individual studies. These are really further aspects of the problem of unrepresentative data discussed above, but in this case they pertain to the task rather than the observational setting. Two problems are outstanding.

First, all the following—the verbatim recall of sentences or lists of words, the recognition of written texts, the recall and/or recognition of the exact location of a click in a sentence—all these are tasks which are unrepresentative of ordinary comprehension processes. This has been demonstrated in several experiments. For example, Jacqueline Sachs (1967, 1974) has shown that normal subjects are very good at recognizing changes that alter the *meaning* of sentences but are very poor at recognizing changes that alter structural or lexical characteristics while preserving the meaning. Bransford, Barclay, and Franks (1972) have demonstrated that subjects remember the situation a sentence describes much better than the linguistic deep structure of the sentence. In view of these studies, it seems that the psycholinguistic and information processing studies reviewed in Section 2.2 are demanding unrepresentative kinds of language use from the subjects, language use which may require special skills not necessarily relevant to ordinary comprehension processes.

Next, Clark (1973) has demonstrated the limitations of analyses of variance in psycholinguistic research. He shows that the usual approaches to sampling and statistical analysis prohibit the experimenter from generalizing beyond the data of the immediate experiment. Clark's critique is appropriate to very many of the experimental studies of schizophrenics' language use.

2.3.1.3. Narrow Hypotheses. In the experimental studies summarized in Section 2.2., hypotheses about information processing or language comprehension are put forward. The hypotheses are frequently so narrowly conceived that the designs to test them do not permit the consideration of competing hypotheses.

2.3.2. The Common Problems

There are two theoretical issues that affect all studies of schizophrenics' language use. The first pertains to the development of theory and the second to the theoretical goals.

2.3.2.1. Development of Theory. In a discussion of the young discipline of psycholinguistics, Olson and Clark (1976) observe that there has been an adoption of theoretical constructs from other, older disciplines. The risk in this adoption, they warn, is that one may accept criteria from other theories that are irrelevant to one's own concern. For example, one could adopt the formal criteria of abstract automata, supposing that the grammars these produce are relevant to actual language production. But "to suppose that a distinction made on the basis of another metatheory will ipso facto be of use in cognitive psychology is to make a serious error" (p. 64).

This risk is especially profound in the study of schizophrenics' language use. This study, which perhaps may be considered a subdiscipline of psycholinguistics, has also adopted theories from other disciplines: from theories of perceptual processes (e.g., Shakow, 1962), from Shannon's mathematical theory of communications, from the transformational theories of Chomsky and other linguists, and, in earlier years, from the constructs of neurologists (e.g., Goldstein, Vygotsky), psychobiologists (e.g., Meyer), and psychiatrists (e.g., Freud).

The problem with these adoptions is that, although they permit easy initial approaches to schizophrenics' language use, they do not allow for development of alternative approaches when hypotheses fail. The adopted constructs have, in effect, been cut from already developed theories in other fields, but the roots of these constructs have been left behind. For example, Shakow's (1962) theory is developed from perceptual data, not from language use. To modify it for language use, one must tie the theory very carefully to the data—to the detailed behavior of speakers and listeners. This has not been done. Each of the adopted constructs has been grafted onto the language data, without troubling to ensure that the data and theory are matched.

As we saw in Section 2.1., the failures of studies of schizophrenic language users reflect the failures of psycholinguistics in general. But in recent years, there has been a great increase in the level of sophistication about language within psycholinguistics. The notion that one could study language with little or no interest in the details of language has been largely abandoned. It now appears that an ignorance of linguistic function leads one to naive experimental designs in which obvious properties of language are confounded with the effects of interest. It seems, as well, that one is able to describe and formulate behaviors more systematically and in greater detail than if one simply views language use as responses to internal and external stimuli.

Perhaps, as the study of schizophrenics' language use becomes a more self-conscious discipline, the difficulties of wholesale adoption of constructs from other fields will give way to a more considered use of those constructs. For, as Olson and Clark (1976) note, constructs from other theoretical approaches can be useful heuristics for guiding research—if they are redesigned to fit the data for which they are intended.

2.3.2.2. Goals of the Theory. To conclude this review, let us again note a decision that seems to have had profound effects on the field. This is the decision to study *deviant* behavior. As it was argued earlier, one cannot hope to provide an adequate account of behavior simply from an account of what is "deviant" about that behavior. It is worth stressing this point again because most recent studies of schizophrenic speakers have maintained this focus on deviance. I believe that this is an unproductive approach because it precludes the prediction of successes and it prevents the systematic description of failures.

2.4. A Final Comment

2.4.1. Goals

As psycholinguistics has developed into a self-conscious discipline, it has had to confront the problem of borrowed ideas. So many of its central constructs have been borrowed from neighboring disciplines, it has had to ask: How do we build a model which fits language *use* and not formal structures or machine processes or philosophical theories about speech acts? This is an important problem now in psycholin guistics, but it has a direction. Investigators are asking how to formulate the processes that concern them.

Those who study language use in schizophrenic subjects (and perhaps also in psychopathology generally) have a more troublesome question to confront: Is it important to formulate a model of language use in schizophrenia? Is it necessary to formulate a model, or at least principles of language use, in order to understand how the language processes of schizophrenic patients bear on their being schizophrenic?

This is an uncomfortable question to ask because, once posed, it can be answered in the negative. It is possible that the language processes of the schizophrenic patient tell us little or nothing that is critical to an understanding of the patient's state or to its cure. And this possibility leads us to ask another discomfiting question: Why study schizophrenics' language use? There seems to be three answers to this question in the literature: (a) because it is there; (b) because it aids in the diagnosis of schizophrenia; (c) because it offers significant clues to the origin of or cure for schizophrenia. As goals for a discipline, (a) is unacceptable and (b) is unrealistic. Answer (a) is unacceptable because, no matter how fascinating the productions of the schizophrenic speaker are, one cannot justify asking the patients' participation in a study which will be of no benefit to them. Answer (b), the promise of improved diagnostic performance, is illusory because forty years of research efforts appear to have had no effect on clinical practice. The verbal behavior scales or indicators that have been developed by researchers have simply not been adopted in the clinic (with the rare exceptions of a few teaching clinics). This may be because the procedures are too complex, or because they are troublesome to teach, or perhaps because they are too expensive to implement. Whatever the reasons, there is no evidence that clinicians have adopted such measures in the past so one cannot be optimistic that they will do so in the future.

It seems that answer (c) is the only goal which can be justified. Only if the study of a patient's language use will teach us something critical about the patient's disorder can we justify our studies. But even supposing this assertion is valid, how do we proceed? Especially, how do we discover anything apart from what we already know from some six decades of research and observation?

Is it necessary to study language use so carefully that one can build a fair model of that performance? Or is it sufficient to extract pieces of that performance, or to list instances of that performance? The former is the approach which has been used in experimental studies; the latter, in most naturalistic studies. Perhaps it is the lack of an answer to these questions which, in the end, is responsible for the great discouragement of those reviewing this field. Not knowing if it is even necessary to formulate language processes, we have had no clear direction for our efforts.

In conclusion, at the present time, it seems worth aiming for a formulation of language use by schizophrenic speakers that is as broadly based as possible while being as relevant as possible to the clinical descriptions of "thought disordered" or "schizophasic" speech.

2.5. References

Andreasen, N. C. I. Thought, language, and communication disorders: Clinical assessment, definition of terms, and evaluation of their reliability. *Archives of General Psychiatry*, 1979, *36*, 1315–1321. (a)

Andreasen, N. C. II. Thought, language, and communication disorders: Diagnostic significance. *Archives of General Psychiatry*, 1979, *36*, 1325–1330. (b)

Bär, E. S. Semiotic studies in schizophrenia and senile psychosis. *Semiotica*, 1976, *16*(3), 269–283.

Benson, D. F. Psychiatric aspects of aphasia. *British Journal of Psychiatry*, 1973, *123*, 555–556.

Bleuler, E. *Dementia praecox; or the group of schizophrenias.* New York: International Universities Press, 1950. (Originally published, 1911).

Bloomfield, L. *Language.* New York: Henry Holt, 1933.

Blumenthal, A. L. *Language and psychology: Historical aspects of psycholinguistics.* New York: Wiley, 1970.

Boland, T. B., & Chapman, L. J. Conflicting predictions from Broen's and Chapman's theories of schizophrenic thought disorder. *Journal of Abnormal Psychology*, 1971, *78*(1), 52–58.

Bransford, J. D., Barclay, J. R., & Franks, J. J. Sentence memory: A constructive versus interpretative approach. *Cognitive Psychology*, . *1972*, *3*, 193–209.

Brown, R. Schizophrenia, language and reality. *American Psychologist*, 1973, *28*, 395–403.
Cameron, N. A study of thinking in senile deterioration and schizophrenic disorganization. *American Journal of Psychology*, 1938, *51*, 650–665. (a)
Cameron, N. Reasoning, regression and communication in schizophrenics. *Psychological Monographs*, 1938 (Whole No. 221). (b)
Cameron, N. Experimental analysis of schizophrenic thinking. In J. S. Kasanin (Ed.), *Language and thought in schizophrenia*. Berkeley: University of California Press, 1944.
Carpenter, M. D. Sensitivity to syntactic structure: Good versus poor premorbid schizophrenics. *Journal of Abnormal Psychology*, 1976, *85*(1), 41–50.
Chaika, E. A linguist looks at "schizophrenic" language. *Brain and Language, 1974, 1,* 257–276. (a)
Chaika, E. *Linguistics and psychiatry*. Paper presented at the LSA Summer Meeting, Amherst, Mass., July 1974. (b)
Chaika, E. Schizophrenic speech, slips of the tongue, and jargonaphasia: A reply to Fromkin and to Lecours and Vanier-Clément. *Brain and Language*, 1977, *4*, 464–475.
Chapman, J. D. The early symptoms of schizophrenia. *British Journal of Psychiatry*, 1966, *122*, 225–251.
Chapman, L. J., & Chapman, J. P. *Disordered thought in schizophrenia*. Englewood Cliffs, N.J.: Prentice-Hall, 1973.
Chapman, L. J., Chapman, J. P., & Daut, R. L. Schizophrenic inability to disattend from strong aspects of meaning. *Journal of Abnormal Psychology*, 1976, *85*(1), 35–40.
Chomsky, N. *Syntactic structures*. The Hague: Mouton, 1957.
Chomsky, N. *Aspects of the theory of syntax*. Cambridge, Mass.: M.I.T. Press, 1965.
Chomsky, N. & Miller, G. A. Introduction to the formal analysis of natural languages. In R. D. Luc, R. R. Bush, & E. Galanter (Eds.), *Handbook of mathematical psychology* (Vol. 2). New York: Wiley, 1963.
Clark, H. H. Word associations and linguistic theory. In J. Lyons (Ed.), *New horizons in linguistics*. Baltimore, Md.: Penguin, 1970.
Clark, H. H. The language-as-fixed-effect fallacy: A critique of language statistics in psychological research. *Journal of Verbal Learning and Verbal Behavior*, 1973, *12*, 335–359.
Cohen, B. D. Referent communication disturbances in schizophrenia. In S. Schwartz (Ed.), *Language and cognition in schizophrenia*. New York: Erlbaum, 1978.
Cohen, B. D., Nachmani, G., & Rosenberg, S. Referent communication disturbances in acute schizophrenia. *Journal of Abnormal Psychology*, 1974, *83*(1;, 1–13.
Coleman, E. B. Approximations to English: Some comments on the method. *American Journal of Psychology*, 1963, *76*(2), 239–247.
Cromwell, R. L., & Dockeki, P. R. Schizophrenic language: A disattention interpretation. In S. Rosenberg & J. Koplin (Eds.), *Developments in applied psycholinguistic research*. New York: Macmillan, 1968.
Del Castillo, J. C. The influence of language upon symptomatology in foreign-born patients. *American Journal of Psychiatry*, 1970, *127*(2), 160–162.
DiSimoni, F. G., Darley, F. L., & Aronson, A. E. Patterns of dysfunction in schizophrenic patients on an aphasia test battery. *Journal of Speech and Hearing Disorders*, 1977, *42*, 498–513.
Feigl, H. Validation and vindication: An analysis of the nature and the limits of ethical arguments. In W. Sellars & H. Hospers (Eds.), *Readings in ethical theory*. New York: Appleton-Century-Crofts, 1952.
Fillenbaum, S. On the use of memorial techniques to assess syntactic structures. *Psychological Bulletin*, 1970, *73*, 231–237.
Flor-Henry, P. Lateralized temporal-limbic dysfunction and psychopathology. In S. R.

64 SHERRY ROCHESTER

Harnad, H. D. Steklis, & J. Lancaster (Eds.), *Origins and evolutions of language and speech.* Annals of the New York Academy of Sciences (Vol. 280). New York: The New York Academy of Sciences, 1976.

Fodor, J. A. Can meaning be an r_m? *Journal of Verbal Learning and Verbal Behavior,* 1965, *4,* 73–81.

Freedman, A. M., Kaplan, H. I., & Sadock, B. J. *Modern synopsis of comprehensive textbook of psychiatry* (2nd ed.). Baltimore: Williams & Wilkins, 1976.

Fromkin, V. A. A linguist looks at "A linguist looks at 'schizophrenic language' ". *Brain and Language,* 1975, *2,* 489–503.

Garrett, M., Bever, T., & Fodor, J. The active use of grammar in speech perception. *Perception and Psychophysics,* 1966, *1,* 30–32.

Gerbner, G. Preface. In G. Gerbner, O. R. Holsti, K. Krippendorff, W. J. Paisley, & P. J. Stone (Eds.), *The analysis of communication context.* New York: Wiley, 1969.

Gerson, S. N., Benson, D. F., & Frazier, S. H. Diagnosis: Schizophrenia versus posterior aphasia. *American Journal of Psychiatry,* 1977, *134*(9), 966–969.

Gerver, D. Linguistic rules and the perception and recall of speech by schizophrenic patients. *British Journal of Social and Clinical Psychology,* 1967, *6,* 204–211.

Gottschalk, L. A., & Gleser, G. C. Distinguishing characteristics of the verbal communications of schizophrenic patients. In D. McRioch & E. A. Weinstein (Eds.), *Disorders of communication.* Baltimore, Md.: Williams & Wilkins, 1964.

Gottschalk, L. A., & Gleser, G. C. *The measurement of psychological states through the content analysis of verbal behavior.* Berkeley: University of California Press, 1969.

Gottschalk, L. A., Hausmann, C., & Brown, J. S. A computerized scoring system for use with content analysis scales. *Comprehensive Psychiatry,* 1975, *16,* 77–90.

Gottschalk, L. A., Winget, C. N., & Gleser, G. C. *Manual of instructions for using the Gottschalk-Gleser content analysis scales.* Los Angeles: University of California Press, 1969.

Gruzelier, J. H. Bimodal states of arousal and lateralized dysfunction in schizophrenia: Effects of chlorpromazine. In L. C. Wynne, R. L. Cromwell, & S. Matthysse (Eds.), *The nature of schizophrenia: New approaches to research and treatment.* New York: Wiley, 1978.

Hirsch, S. R., & Leff, J. P. *Abnormalities in parents of schizophrenics.* New York: Oxford University Press, 1975.

Hörmann, H. *Psycholinguistics. An introduction to research and theory.* New York: Springer-Verlag, 1971.

Jarvella, R. J. Syntactic processing of connected speech. *Journal of Verbal Learning and Verbal Behavior,* 1971, *10,* 409–416.

Koh, S. D. Remembering of verbal materials by schizophrenic young adults. In S. Schwartz (Ed.), *Language and cognition in schizophrenia.* New York: Erlbaum, 1978.

Kraepelin, E. *Dementia praecox and paraphrenia* (R. M. Barclay, trans.). Edinburgh: E & S Livingstone, 1919.

Krippendorff, K. Introduction. In G. Gerbner, O. R. Holsti, K. Krippendorff, W. J. Paisley, & P. J. Stone (Eds.), *The analysis of communication content.* New York: Wiley, 1969.

Labov, W. The study of language in its social context. *Studium Generale,* 1970, *23,* 30–87.

Laffal, J. The contextual associates of sun and god in Schreber's autobiography. *Journal of Abnormal and Social Psychology,* 1960, *61,* 474–479.

Laffal, J. *Pathological and normal language.* New York: Atherton, 1965.

Lawson, J. S., McGhie, A., & Chapman, J. Perception of speech in schizophrenia. *British Journal of Psychiatry,* 1964, *110,* 375–380.

Lecours, A. R., & Vanier-Clément, M. Schizophasia and jargonaphasia: A comparative description with comments on Chaika's and Fromkin's respective looks at "schizophrenic" language. *Brain and Language*, 1976, *3*, 516–565.

Lenneberg, E. H. *Biological foundations of language*. New York: Wiley, 1967.

Levy, R., & Maxwell, A. E. The effect of verbal context on the recall of schizophrenics and other psychiatric patients. *British Journal of Psychiatry*, 1968, *114*, 311–316.

Lewinsohn, P. M., & Elwood, D. L. The role of contextual constraint in the learning of language samples in schizophrenia. *Journal of Nervous and Mental Disease*, 1961, *133*, 79–81.

Lockard, R. B. Reflections on the fall of comparative psychology: Is there a message for us all? *American Psychologist*, 1971, *26*, 168–179.

Lorenz, M., & Cobb, S. Language patterns in psychotic and psychoneurotic subjects. *Archives of Neurology and Psychiatry*, 1954, *72*(6), 665–673.

Maher, B. A. Schizophrenia: Language and thought. In B. A. Maher (Ed.), *Principles of psychopathology*. New York: McGraw-Hill, 1966.

Maher, B. A. Schizophrenia. *Psychology Today*, 1968, *1*, 30–33.

Maher, B. A. The language of schizophrenia: A review and interpretation. *British Journal of Psychiatry*, 1972, *120*, 3–17.

Maher, B. A. McKean, K. O., & McLaughlin, B. Studies in psychotic language. In P. J. Stone, R. F. Bales, Z. Namenworth, & D. M. Ogilvie (Eds.), *The general inquirer: A computer approach to content analysis*. Cambridge, Mass.: M.I.T. Press, 1966.

Marks, L. E., & Miller, G. A. The role of semantic and syntactic constraints in the memorization of English sentences. *Journal of Verbal Learning and Verbal Behavior*, 1964, *3*, 1–5.

McGhie, A. Attention and perception in schizophrenia. In B. A. Maher (Ed.), *Progress in experimental personality research* (Vol. 5). New York: Academic, 1970.

McGhie, A., & Chapman, J. Disorders of attention and perception in early schizophrenia. *British Journal of Psychiatry*, 1961, *34*, 103–116.

Miller, G. A. Some psychological studies of grammar. *American Psychologist*, 1962, *17*, 748–762.

Miller, G. A. Some preliminaries to psycholinguistics. *American Psychologist*, 1965, *20*, 15–20.

Miller, G. A., & Chomsky, N. Finitary models of language users. In R. D. Luce, R. R. Bush, & E. Galanter (Eds.), *Handbook of mathematical psychology* Vol. 2). New York: Wiley, 1963.

Miller, G. A., & Isard, S. Some perceptual consequences of linguistic rules. *Journal of Verbal Learning and Verbal Behavior*, 1963, *3*, 217–228.

Miller, G. A., & Selfridge, J. A. Verbal context and the recall of meaningful material. *American Journal of Psychology*, 1950, *63*(2), 176–185.

Neale, J. M., & Cromwell, R. L. Attention and schizophrenia. In B. A. Maher (Ed.), *Progress in experimental psychology* (Vol. 5). New York: Academic, 1970.

Nuttall, R. L., & Solomon, L. F. Prognosis in schizophrenia: The role of premorbid social class, and demographic factors. *Behavioral Science*, 1970, *15*, 255–264.

Olson, G. M., & Clark, H. H. Research methods in psycholinguistics. In E. C. Carterette & M. P. Friedman (Eds.), *Handbook of perception (Vol. 7): Language and Speech*. New York: Academic, 1976.

Pavy, D. Verbal behavior in schizophrenia: A review of recent studies. *Psychological Bulletin*, 1968, *70*, 164–178.

Rattan, R. B., & Chapman, L. G. Associative intrusions in schizophrenic verbal behavior. *Journal of Abnormal Psychology*, 1973, *82*, 169–173.

Raeburn, K. M., & Tong, J. E. Experiments on contextual constraint in schizophrenia. *British Journal of Psychiatry*, 1968, *114*, 43–52.

Reber, A. S. On psycho-linguistic paradigms. *Journal of Psycholinguistic Research*, 1973, *2*, 289–320.

Reed, J. L. Schizophrenic thought-disorder: A review and hypothesis. *Comprehensive Psychiatry*, 1970, *11*, 403–432.

Reilly, F. E., Harrow, M., & Tucker, G. J. Language and thought content in acute psychosis. *American Journal of Psychiatry*, 1973, *130*, 411–417.

Reilly, F., Harrow, M., Tucker, G., Quinlan, D., & Siegel, A. Looseness of associations in acute schizophrenia. *British Journal of Psychiatry*, 1975, *127*, 240–246.

Rochester, S. R. & Martin, J. R. Crazy talk: *A study of the discourse of schizophrenic speakers.* New York: Plenum, 1979.

Rochester, S. R., Harris, J., & Seeman, M. V. Sentence processing in schizophrenic listeners. *Journal of Abnormal Psychology*, 1973, *3*, 350–356.

Rosenberg, S. D., & Cohen, B. D. Speakers' and listeners' processes in a word-communication task. *Science*, 1964, *145*, 1201–1203.

Rosenberg, S. D., & Cohen, B. D. Referential processes of speakers and listeners. *Psychological Review*, 1966, *73*, 208–231.

Rosenberg, S. D., & Tucker, G. J. *Verbal content and the diagnosis of schizophrenia.* Paper presented at the 129th Annual Meeting of the American Psychiatric Association, Florida, May 1976.

Sachs, J. S. Recognition and memory for syntactic and semantic aspects of connected discourse. *Perception and Psychophysics*, 1967, *2*, 437–442.

Sachs, J. S. Memory in reading and listening to discourse. *Memory and Cognition*, 1974, *2*, 95–100.

Seeman, M. V. Analysis of psychotic language—A review. *Diseases of the Nervous System*, 1970, *31*, 92–99.

Seeman, M. V. Therapist-induced speech disorder. *Psychotherapy Theory, Research and Practice*, 1975, *12*, 175–178.

Seeman, M. V., & Cole, H. J. The effect of increasing personal contact in schizophrenia. *Comprehensive Psychiatry*, 1977, *18*, 283–293.

Shakow, D. Segmental set: A theory of formal psychological deficit in schizophrenia. *Archives of General Psychiatry*, 1962, *6*, 17–33.

Siegel, A., Harrow, M., Reilly, F., & Tucker, G. Loose associations and disordered speech patterns in chronic schizophrenia. *Journal of Nervous and Mental Disease*, 1976, *162(2)*, 105–112.

Singer, M. T., Wynne, L. C. Differentiating characteristics of parents of childhood schizophrenics, childhood autistics, and young adult schizophrenics. *American Journal of Psychiatry*, 1963, *120*, 234–243.

Singer, M. T., & Wynne, L. C. Thought disorder and family relations of schizophrenics. IV. Results and implications. *Archives of General Psychiatry*, 1965, *12*, 201–212.

Singer, M. T., Wynne, L. C., & Toohey, M. L. Communication disorders and the families of schizophrenics. In L. C. Wynne, R. L. Cromwell, & S. Matthysse (Eds.), *Nature of schizophrenia: New approaches to research and treatment.* New York: Wiley, 1978.

Stolz, W., & Tiffany, J. The production of "child-like" word associations by adults to unfamiliar adjectives. *Journal of Verbal Learning and Verbal Behavior*, 1972, *11*, 38–46.

Stone, P. J., Bales, R. F., Namenworth, Z., & Ogilvie, D. M. The General Inquirer: A computer system for content analysis and retrieval based on the sentence as a unit of information. *Behavior Science*, 1962, *7*, 484–498.

Stone, P. J., Dunphy, D. C., Smith, M. S., & Ogilvie, D. M. *The General Inquirer: A computer approach to content analysis.* Cambridge, Mass.: M.I.T. Press, 1966.

Storch, A. The primitive archaic forms of inner experiences and thought in schizophrenia. *Nervous and Mental Diseases Monograph,* 1924 (36).

Suchotliff, L. C. Relations of formal thought disorder to the communication deficit in schizophrenia. *Journal of Abnormal Psychology,* 1970, 76(2), 250–257.

Sullivan, H. S. Peculiarity of thought in schizophrenia. *American Journal of Psychiatry,* 1925, 82, 21–86.

Sullivan, H. S. The language of schizophrenia. In J. S. Kasanin (Ed.), *Language and thought in schizophrenia.* New York: W. W. Norton, 1964. (Originally published in 1944).

Taylor, W. L. "Cloze procedure": A new tool for measuring readability. *Journalism Quarterly,* 1953, 30, 415–433.

Titchener, E. B. *Experimental psychology* (Vol. 2). New York: Macmillan, 1905.

Traupmann, K. L. Effects of categorization and imagery on recognition and recall by process and reactive schizophrenics. *Journal of Abnormal Psychology,* 1975, 85(4), 307–314.

Truscott, I. P. Contextual constraint and schizophrenic language. *Journal of Consulting and Clinical Psychology,* 1970, 35, 189–194.

Tucker, G. J., & Rosenberg, S. D. Computer content analysis of schizophrenic speech: A preliminary report. *American Journal of Psychiatry,* 1975, 132(6), 611–616.

Turner, R. J., Raymond, J., Zabo, L. J., & Diamond, J. Field survey methods in psychiatry. *Journal of Health and Social Behavior,* 1969, 10(4), 289–297.

Vetter, H. J. *Language behavior in schizophrenia: Selected readings in research and theory.* Springfield, Ill.: Charles C Thomas, 1968.

Weckowicz, T. E., & Blewett, D. B. Size constancy and abstract thinking in schizophrenic patients. *Journal of Mental Science,* 1959, 105, 909–934.

Whitehorn, J. C., & Zipf, G. K. Schizophrenic language. *Archives of Neurology and Psychiatry,* 1943, 49, 831–851.

Wynne, L. C. Schizophrenics and their families: Research on parental communication. In J. M. Tanner (Ed.), *Developments in psychiatric research.* London: Hodder & Stoughton, 1977.

Wynne, L. C., & Singer, M. T. Thought disorders and the family relations of schizophrenics: I. A research strategy. *Archives of General Psychiatry,* 1963, 9, 191. (a)

Wynne, L. C., & Singer, M. T. Thought disorders and the family relations of schizophrenics: II. Classification of forms of thinking. *Archives of General Psychiatry,* 1963, 9, 199–206. (b)

3

Peter Ostwald and Valentina Zavarin

STUDIES OF LANGUAGE AND SCHIZOPHRENIA IN THE USSR

Psychiatry in the Soviet Union has the status of a branch of medicine, and most of the diagnostic, therapeutic, and preventative work is carried out in local dispensaries serving populations between 300,000 and 400,000 persons (Rome, 1979). There are numerous mental hospitals in the USSR. Schizophrenia is one of the major psychiatric problems, but there is considerable theoretical divergence between the Moscow school, which uses very broad diagnostic categories, and the Leningrad school, with its emphasis on specific and more limited syndromes. Theoretical interest in the language and communication problems of schizophrenic patients is much more common among psychologists than among psychiatrists, who tend to regard the disease as an organic disorder with an inherited predisposition, triggered off by environmental stress. Many theories about schizophrenia that have been popularized in the West, especially those stemming from psychoanalysis, are either poorly understood or rejected in the Soviet Union. In terms of an international view, coexistence between a typically Russian psychological theory (that of Lev S. Vygotsky, 1896–1932) and a typically American one (that of Harry

Peter Ostwald and *Valentina Zavarin* ● Langley Porter Institute, University of California, San Francisco, California 94143. Research on this paper was partially supported by the National Institute of Mental Health Biomedical Research Grant RR-05755 and the University of California Medical School Committee MSC Trevy Fund. We gratefully acknowledge the support of grant 1-R01-MH-31360-01 from the Department of Health, Education, and Welfare, Public Health Service.

S. Sullivan, 1892–1949) can be found only in the pre-World War II psychiatric literature (Kasanin, 1954).

A recent publication about the problems schizophrenic patients have with language and communication (Ostwald, 1978) reviewed the psychiatric literature available in the English language. We now turn to Soviet contributions, focusing mainly on those studies that have appeared in the psychiatric literature.

3.1. Historical Background of the Schizophrenia Concept in the USSR

Since the 1860s, Russian psychiatry has been heavily dominated by biological theories, and two Russian contemporaries of Emil Kraepelin (1855–1926), Sergei S. Korsakov (1854–1900) and Viktor Kh. Kandinsky (1849–1899), incorporated the concept of *dementia praecox* into their own formulations about mental disease. On the whole, Soviet psychiatry, especially in its early period, was closely tied to German thinking about schizophrenia, with its heavy emphasis on heredity, organic factors, and poor prognosis. This seemed consistent with the important neurophysiologic contributions of two outstanding Russian scientists, Ivan P. Pavlov (1849–1936) and Vladimir M. Bekhterev (1857–1927), which, when applied to schizophrenia, led to the idea that the disease results from cortical inhibition. Catatonic stupor, for example, was thought by Pavlov to be caused by a total inhibition of the cerebral cortex, whereas other forms of schizophrenia, especially those involving abnormal speech, resulted from partial inhibition, with subsequent release of subcortical mechanisms. Bekhterev was a skillful neuroanatomist, who contributed to improved understanding of these brain mechanisms. He described several nuclei and pathways in the subcortical system and spinal cord.

Piotr B. Gannushkin (1875–1933), a student of Korsakov, was a leading figure during the first period of the Soviet regime. One of his early works is devoted to the postulation of a "schizophrenic constitution" (1933). Although he himself wavered between his early hypothesis and those of Kraepelin, he is considered to be a forerunner of the contemporary directions in research on schizophrenia in Russia.

In the early 1930s, G. E. Sukhareva, a child psychiatrist, rejected the Kraepelinian classification and suggested that schizophrenic illnesses be separated into two types: a *sluggish* form with early onset and poor prognosis, and an *acute* form with later onset and better outcome. Some patients who showed manifestations of both sluggish and acute schizophrenia were said to have a *mixed* form of the disease. D. E. Melekhov and his colleagues (1936) found that the same forms could be identified in adults. Those patients whose illness ran a slow (sluggish) course, as well as those whose illness ran rapidly downhill, were said to have a *continuous* form of schizophrenia. Acute attacks followed by full remissions were called *periodic* or *recurrent* schizophrenia, while so-called mixed cases were called *shiftlike* schizophrenia. In addition to its clinical usefulness in distinguishing between different groups of schizophrenic patients, this division has led to considerable research into biological factors responsible for the disease.

Much of today's psychiatric literature in the Soviet Union focuses on the search for a primary schizophrenic process that might account for the myriad of symptoms found in the different syndromes of this disease. For example, the patient's thoughts, feelings, and actions are presumed to be undermined by "an ataxic antagonism" or "mental disautomatization . . . expressed as a disruption of the coordination of activities between the hemispheres" (Snezhnevsky, 1968). The emphasis is quite unmistakably organic, and psychodynamic considerations are not considered of etiologic significance. No psychosexual history is taken, whereas detailed clinical descriptions of each patient's appearance, behavior, and symptomatic expressions are subjected to careful analysis. Thus nine syndromes of schizophrenia have been deduced, on the basis of over 5,000 case histories reviewed by Snezhnevsky and his colleagues: (1) asthenic, (2) affective, (3) pseudoneurotic, (4) paranoial, (5) hallucinatory, (6) hallucinatory-paranoid, (7) paraphrenic, (8) catatonic, and (9) a terminal, polymorphic state. Over a long period of time, one sees "a continuous, ever-changing succession" of these patterns. Symptoms are classified as "positive," i.e., delusions, obsessions, hallucinations, stereotyped behavior, etc., or "negative," referring to the loss of adaptive behavior, apathy, social withdrawal, mutism, etc. In malignant, *continuous* cases of schizophrenia, the positive symptoms are said to disappear as the patient gets older and his psychosis "disintegrates into a ruin." According to one Soviet position, such cases can be explained on the basis of a drastic reduction of "energy potential" in the central nervous system. The psychopathology may actually resemble organic dementias because of cellular destruction of the brain.

Independently functioning "autonomous organs," such as those responsible for speech, as well as other finely organized behavior patterns, obviously would be very profoundly disturbed in such cases.

A cardinal tenet of Soviet psychiatry is that schizophrenic disorders cannot be neatly separated from the other forms of mental disease. Thus, as Holland (Holland & Shakhmatova-Pavlova, 1977; Holland, 1978) points out, the idea of a "spectrum" of illnesses predominates. Schizophrenia merges with the neuroses at one extreme and with manic-depressive diseases at the other. "Neither the study of the static clinical picture nor the course of the disease can assist the diagnosis," writes Snezhnevsky (1968), Russia's most influential psychiatrist today. However, in a given number of schizophrenic patients, there is always a greater percentage of "undeniably typical cases of the disease" compared to "atypical, transitional, or mixed forms." Thus, when in doubt, Soviet psychiatrists tend to diagnose schizophrenia sooner rather than later and to maintain patients in hospital for considerable lengths of time.

3.2. The Study of Language and Visualization

In spite of historical fluctuations, certain themes seem to recur in the Russian approach to schizophrenia. One of these is an interest in the relationship between language and visual forms. A good example is Giliarovsky's study of language and painting by schizophrenics. This study appeared in 1957, when Russian research on schizophrenia was still almost entirely dominated by theories of Pavlov and Ivan M. Sechenov (1829–1905) (see review by Lynn, 1963). Pavlov put forward the theory that schizophrenia results from the generation of protective inhibitions after intense or prolonged stimulation of nerve cells. He also suggested that inhibition of one region of the brain may induce excitation in other areas (Pavlov, 1941). In Pavlov's work, language is part of the secondary signaling system. The disturbances of the secondary signaling system are directly related to disturbances of the primary signaling system. Schizophrenia is explained in terms of the following assumptions. The continuous flow of proprioceptive and interoceptive stimuli provides the organism with an awareness of the body. This awareness constitutes the permanent basis of consciousness. The destruction of somatic sensations, as in toxicosis for example, leads to symptoms of dissociation. When somatic sensations drop out of the perceptual process, a patient's experiences will seem to belong not to him but to someone else. Dissociation at the level of sensations explains the feelings of unreality, depersonalization, and altered consciousness in schizophrenia. Giliarovsky exemplifies this by discussing the weakness of visual perception in schizophrenia. As a result, the capacity for color vision and visual perception of form are seriously diminished.

Language and other sign systems serve to summarize and generalize the informational input from the environment. Giliarovsky considers the analysis of speech, writing, and drawing in schizophrenia to be particularly important since each function reveals the thought processes of the patient. He exemplified schizophrenic speech by the following quotation: "Pulsation, darkening occurred, thoughts flow, in the head little sticks are stuck, grabbed my pulse, dashed promptly to lie down, heart goes hu-hu-hu, the taste in my blood is magnified, in my mouth feel cadaverousness."

Giliarovsky describes schizophrenic language peculiarities without, however, relating them to any theoretical linguistic construct. He singles out the following features. Schizophrenic speech is characterized by omission of adverbs and prepositions with an overabundance of adjectives. Sequences of closely related or synonym adjectives may characterize one phenomenon: "There it is the heavy, monotonous, boring note." Elision of the object modified by a series of adjectives is common: "Protest against the gray—dull—despondent—suffocating—is a matter of utmost importance." Antonyms or statements contradicting one another ("I found out. I didn't find out.") alternate with assertions followed by "but" that partially cancel the previous statement. Intrusion of lateral associations or unrelated associations to stimulus words are frequent ("nose—forever will remain insane"). Giliarovsky further notes the frequent use of private symbolic meanings assigned to linguistic or nonlinguistic signs ("to knock with a finger" means to accuse the scoundrel). He then notes general dullness in use of color terms which makes black and white rendering of perceptions and impressions most favored with this group of subjects. ("I guessed it—memory is a sphere—with—three 'colorsensings'—white, gray, black.")

Giliarovsky is one of the few authors who has given concrete examples of schizophrenic paintings. For example, he presents a painting with two faces: "one is a stern mask which conceals the enemy, the pseudo-person, the deceiver. Upside down in the lower half of the painting is the true face, distorted, huge, and ugly, with eyes as black holes, and a piercing penetrating gaze." Another drawing is described as follows, again said to depict antonyms: the upper part represents a concept of "glittering creativity elevated to dizzying heights." In the lower part the patient conceptualizes "the threatening downfall of the dazzling creativity into a thundering abyss." The two parts are connected with the inscribed word "or". The same patient related his sense of what constitutes "catastrophe for the world" in the verbal expression "The world today—is an indignant scandal in gray muddy tones."

Illustrations of schizophrenic art are not found in Soviet literature after the official denouncement of "modernism" and "abstractness" in contemporary painting. "Socialist realism" was reinstated in the 1960s as the "only true art form," useful for building a Communist society. Only very primitive designs are reproduced in a study by Longinova (1972). A Polish monograph on schizophrenia by Kepiński (1972) gives additional examples.

Longinova's article (1972) is of importance in that it uses the Vygotsky-Luria test to determine thought disorder. Subjects were asked to memorize a long list of abstract words, with the help of pictograms or designs. She found "inadequacy, sterility, emptiness in content" on the one hand, and "fragmentation" on the other. "Hope," represented by a park bench, was explained as follows: "When you are full of hope you inevitably wait; to wait standing up is very bothersome." Concreteness and diffuseness in schizophrenic thinking is exemplified as follows. The word to be remembered is "parting." The patient explains that "a wall, a trash can, and a man sitting on the trash can, holding his head, and thinking that once again he is alone. Man, as a superfluous being, and the uselessness of his existence, may be associated with trash, refuse, which is also useless. A wall is a symbol of solitude, a symbol of man's enclosure of himself. Walls are ordinarly represented as very tall." Although such a statement might pass for an expression of existentialist Weltschmerz in a critique of Sartre, it is called "inadequate, concrete, diffuse" by Longinova.

Examples of schizophrenic linguistic production are not frequent in Soviet literature. Possibly this has to do with a fear of subversive content. Particularly in the 1960s it was fashionable among young intellectuals and artists to seek to be labeled with "sluggish schizophrenia" and to request dispensary treatment in order to gain the privilege of relatively free speech. Thematic characterization of schizophrenic speech was done by Gabrial. He notes that 54% of the patients studied had a tendency toward "fruitless intellectualizing," "philosophizing," and "pseudo-abstract reasoning" (Gabrial, 1974).

Few studies report on Rorschach and TAT results. Kontridze, Mestiashvili, and Puladze (1975) from the Georgian Institute of Psychiatry, describe inertness (in a continuous course), lability (in acute and recurrent forms), and a variability (in cases of child and adolescent schizophrenia). A Polish study by Szafraniec (1976) analyzes the verbal content of Rorschach tests. Marginal expressions, excessive associations, and intruding themes are connected with the concept of the leaf, with sex, the flower, and blood.

3.3. *Language and Verbalization*

The relationship between language and inner speech is another enduring topic for Russian psychologists (A. N. Sokolov, 1972; Žinkin, 1968). Leontiev, Rokhlin, Savitskaia, and Shakhnarovich (1973) describe what they call "ruptured speech" in schizophrenics, based on a model of "phase structure of speech activity" advanced by Vygotsky. There are two stages in the model: (1) the prespeech or orienting activity (motif, speech intention, image of achievement in the speaker, and stage of inner programming of the speech activity), and (2) the actual generation of speech (realization of inner programming: semantic, grammatical, acoustic, articulatory and motor realization of the program, and vocal realization of the expression).

Leontiev shows that the second stage in the model (grammatical, morphological or phonetic level) does not essentially deviate from the norm. References are made to statistical analyses of parts of speech in schizophrenic discourse to demonstrate this point. The essential deviance is in the first nonverbal stage, termed "psychological predicative inner speech." Predication was defined as the "correlation of content of speech with reality." Unfortunately, Leontiev devotes his study mostly to a programmatic enumeration of essential parts of the first stage, such as goal directedness and motivation, and he does not illustrate his theory by quoting from normal or schizophrenic speech.

3.4. Hallucinations and Neologisms

Generally speaking, one finds little in the way of thematic description or direct rendering of hallucinations in the Soviet psychiatric literature. Some topics are enumerated in papers by Kontsevoy and Druzhinina (1973) and Volkova (1974). Verbal hallucinations in delusional states are described as "continuous hallucinatory monologue." A "command" monologue alternates with a "commentating" monologue. There are expressions of fear and premonitions of oncoming danger. Ideas of persecution, jealousy, and poisoning are frequent and are classified under paranoidlike states. Hallucinations in depressive states in schizophrenia contain accusations (of being a thief, murderer, traitor), disapprovals, and threats. The role of persecutors is most commonly attributed to neighbors and to police officials. Hallucinatory reminiscences appear often.

Hallucinatory scenes are said to include multiple participants. "Scenes of trials, judgment, preparation for execution, etc.," alternate with accusations and self-accusations. This may reflect the frequency of public self-accusation and public penitence as a typical ingredient of trial situations in the Soviet Union. "Accusing voices" are most common, but defending voices are also mentioned. Imperative voices, which may be commands of suicide, are also common. In oneiroid states, verbal hallucinations describe illusionlike fantastic distortions of reality. These hallucinations are particularly vivid and contain striking imagery. Voices talk about fantastic events in which the patients take part. Rich sound and orchestration is typical of this state, with screaming voices, battlefield noises, whistling bullets, etc. Scenery may include cosmic space, the ocean bottom, and even space flights. It was noted that verbal hallucinations are more common among women, particularly in the depressive hallucinatory group, where over three-fourths of the patients were women (Kontsevoy & Druzhinina, 1973). Another study of hallucinations and false recognitions done in the city of Tomsk also revealed a very high preponderance of women: 47 of 53 patients (Lavretskaia, 1970). In addition, this study reports that, in schizophrenia, false recognition and metamorphosis pertain only to human faces and not to objects. For example, there may be a preoccupation with visions of "the dead" or "returning from the other world," and the appearance of "the monster." These monster recognitions are described as distorted faces, flat or square, in trapezelike form, elongated, ugly, etc.

Concrete examples of language production during hallucinatory states were cited in a study by Savitskaia and Sizov (1973), and two types of linguistic deviances are classified under neologisms. "Occasional morphological formations" are new sound formations that cannot be correlated with any word in the language. They remind us of abbreviations such as in English, R.S.V.P., spoken as "aresvipi." These formations may have an exotic sound in Russian, e.g., "katessa, vatera, kenetta". Other formations may sound Greek, Spanish, French, etc., supposedly without the patient having a knowledge of the foreign language. Upon demand, a patient may interpret the neologism. Thus "vatas" stands for doctor. The formations may become as short as "te," or "fa," and are then reminiscent of exclamations. The authors note the occurrence of synonyms when two formations stand for the same thing ("aku" or "kure" for book). Polysemy may be present when the same formation stands for three different things or individuals, one of them being the patient himself. Rhyming of syllables and words, also variation in pitch when pronouncing neologisms, suggest abandonment of the semantic level for the phonetic one. Another group of neologisms, said to be used mainly by delusional paranoid schizophrenics, represents constructions on the basis of the morphemes of the language. Here we encounter prefix additions, suffix additions, combinations and blends as in "hydromology," "predisarmament," "lifeman," "whitecoater" (doctor), etc.

3.5. Vocal Expression of Emotional Language and Mimicry: The Leningrad School

It is characteristic of the Leningrad school to pay special attention to the emotional and nonverbal components of spoken language. Two scholars, Balonov and Deglin (1976), have been particularly influential, having published a number of studies about hemispheric specialization in sound and speech production. Particularly interesting are the distinctions which they make in the role of the emotional component in language production. Their work on hemispheric specialization was recently used for a novel classification of linguistic behavior in general by Ivanov (1978, 1979).

Balonov and Deglin used the results of unilaterally induced electroshock therapy in attempting to explain the neurophysiology of each cerebral hemisphere. They report that inactivation of the right hemisphere does not appear to influence the recognition of verbal material, but seriously affects the recognition of vocal intonational components of speech presented to both ears. Inactivation of the left hemisphere is said always to affect the recognition and perception of articulated speech sounds presented to both ears.

The left hemisphere is responsible for orientation to the environment, for interpretation of phenomena, and for generalization of information. Classification of objects on the basis of concepts, stabilized by language and reasoning processes, is also attributed to the left hemisphere. The right hemisphere is said to guarantee the perception of concrete, individual attributes of objects and to partake in the formation of a gestalt that organizes the momentary analysis of complex signals during the act of sensory perception. The right hemisphere is also said to guarantee an intuitive orientation to phenomena in the outside world. In other words, to the left hemisphere are attributed the mechanisms of abstract thinking, whereas the right hemisphere is accredited with concrete, image-forming processes of thought. The left hemisphere takes care of the analysis of sound signals, systematizes these signals into symbols, and evolves signs through an act of generalization. The right hemisphere attributes to the acoustical phenomena their actual "meanings," adequate to a given moment and a given situation. It is claimed that the right hemisphere coordinates intonational vocal components (including the subject's own speech) and the fundamental frequency.

In a 1977 study, Balonov, Deglin, Kaufman, and Nikolaenko extended their discussion to emotional states of hemispheric specialization. They indicated that inactivation of the right hemisphere results in a shift toward better mood, euphoria, and submissiveness. Inactivation of the left hemisphere produces a shift toward gloomy moods, dysphoria, and inner discomfort. Inactivation of the right hemisphere is also said to produce an impoverishment of facial and vocal expressiveness. The voice becomes monotonous and loses its intonational richness. Recognition of other people's vocal cues is also reduced. When the left hemisphere is inactivated, no impoverishment of mimicry and vocal emotional expression was observed.

Bazhin, Korneva, and Lomachenko (1978) studied 160 schizophrenics in terms of their ability to identify emotional states from samples of speech. A tape-recorded voice expressed various emotional states, such as anger, apathy, elevated mood, normal stable mood, and fear. Degrees and combinations of shades of moods were also included in the test schema. The sentences had a variety of syntactic structures and phonematic combinations, but were devoid of semantic content indicative of the particular emotional state of the speaker. By trial and error, the research group discovered that only paranoid schizophrenics performed very poorly as compared to normals.

The nonparanoid group included subjects having extreme emotional poverty or emotional coldness and seclusiveness. Still, the experiment showed that these patients could identify emotional states from the sound of language. Paradoxical results of this test are that schizophrenics who appear from the outside to be detached and were characterized by emotional flatness can and do analyze carefully and subtly the emotions of other people. These findings were supported by observations of patients with terminal illness, showing remissions in their schizophrenia during which they suddenly manifested the most refined nuances in emotional reactions. Patients in psychotherapy also were said to be extremely sensitive, so that "negative" attitudes by the therapist doom the outcome of the therapy. Bazhin proposed the hypothesis that even in the premorbid state, paranoid schizophrenics have a defect or a difficulty in identifying the feelings of others. Evidently, emotional factors in contacts with other people are perceived with a lack of precision. This may point to a depressed auditory capacity and an imprecise emotional tone perception.

Bespalko (1976) proposes a method of studying certain aspects of mimicry from photographs. Schizophrenics and normal subjects were asked to classify photographs of the same face according to similarities in facial expression. Schizophrenics made choices that were never or rarely made by normals. Statistical analysis showed that improbable judgments correlate with the severity of the clinical picture. However, another parameter was discovered. Seven percent of the control group repeatedly gave answers similar to those of schizophrenics. The author conjectures that a section of the population belongs to a normal variation group, rather than to a group with latent pathology, and that these people probably process information in a unique manner. The author looks critically at the many Soviet studies that attribute improbable information processing only to the relatives of schizophrenics. He proposes the hypothesis that improbable information processing is a constitutional factor in a certain percentage of the normal population.

3.6. Probability Prognosis: The Moscow School

The work on schizophrenia done by a group of clinical psychologists at the Laboratory of Pathopsychology, directed by Jury Poliakov will now be considered. This laboratory is part of the Institute of Psychiatry of the Academy of Medical Sciences in Moscow, chaired by A. V. Snezhnevsky. The Poliakov group works in parallel with the Laboratory of Psychophysiology, headed by I. M. Feigenberg.

Kritskaia (1973), surveyed the field, and in a paper entitled, "Characteristics of the speech of schizophrenics and their relatives," reported: "We were unable to find in the (Russian) literature specialized studies devoted to the investigation of the linguistic activity of schizophrenic patients which are connected with negative symptoms of this illness." Since then, a number of papers about language problems in schizophrenia, as well as cognitive processes in general, have been published by the Poliakov group. This group defines the schizophrenic defect as a "probability prognosis" defect. The probability prognosis hypothesis can be traced to the teaching of Pavlov (1957). Budashevsky writes:

> In 1935, Pavlov advanced the hypothesis that certain depressive states might be traceable to the subject's incorrect assessment of the probability that some threatening event, for example, a bolt of lighting, would occur. Recent attempts to verify this hypothesis empirically and to apply it clinically by distinguishing the interacting influences of the real probability and the biological significance of an event have encountered considerable difficulties of a methodological nature. (Budashevsky & Menitsky, 1974)

Studies of probability prognosis are based on the assumption that normal human behavior has a probability structure. This structure depends on an adequate reflection of the statistical characteristics of the environment in past experience, and on the individuals' use of this experience in formulating behavioral strategies (Feigenberg, 1963). Probability programs are involved in all selection activities of the brain and determine purposeful behavior. These programs are acquired from experience (Anokhin, 1974; Bernshtein, cited in Payne, 1968). The functioning of the probability mechanism is particularly vital in verbal communication. One can assume that word usage in speech is based on subconscious information about the frequency of words and the frequency of other patterns in verbal communication. A study of those regularities is particularly interesting in disturbed speech (Zaitseva, Liberman, & Minkin, 1974).

3.7. *Probability Prognosis in Perception*

A number of research projects tested characteristics of perception in schizophrenia along the dimension of probability prognosis. For example, Feigenberg (1974) described the absence of normal illusions acquired by experience. In tests that require estimating the weight of large and small cylinders of equal weight, normals judge larger objects to be heavier. Schizophrenics were free of this illusion (illusion of Charpentier), and arrived at correct answers better than normals. Again, when a blurred picture of a light bulb in a basket of pears is brought into focus, schizophrenics identified the improbable object earlier than normals. Reaching out to latent and highly improbable features may be illustrated by the following example: Schizophrenics locate a parameter such as "velocity" to characterize a "spoon" and see similarity in "spoon" and "automobile" along this parameter. They pick out the feature of "noiselessness" in a "beret" while characterizing "trumpet, umbrella, and whistle" as "noise-producing objects" (Zeigarnik, 1972). This highly eclectic processing is not considered illogical; rather it is said to be highly improbable.

3.8. *Probability Prognosis in Cognitive Processes*

Recent research of the Poliakov group and the Feigenberg group supports the hypothesis that schizophrenics exhibit a deficiency in ordering information according to a scale of probable importance or usefulness based on previous experience, and that a "probability prognosis" is not carried out efficiently in their behavior. All cognitive processes, including linguistic behavior, are shown to be affected by this defect (Dobrovich & Frumkina, 1974; Poliakov, 1966, 1972; Zaitseva *et al.*, 1974).

The Poliakov Institute carried out a large-scale project to analyze different forms of cognitive activity in schizophrenics and their relatives, including family members from several generations and branches. Twenty-two different tests were designed to study identification of visual and auditory stimuli. Various mental tasks of comparison and classification were also included. Two types of tasks formed the basis of all the tests. First, there was the requirement to select particular information without there being a predetermined system of selection. No guidelines were given for dealing with indeterminacy, and patients had to rely on their past experience for selection criteria. The second type of task involved classification and comparison, again without a predetermined format. The tests were so designed as to allow equal use of a wide range of properties and relations as the basis for generalization.

Results showed that schizophrenics and their relatives employ search strategies characterized by "an extended range of attracted knowledge." They make use of "latent information." There appears to be a failure in recognizing those qualities of objects and phenomena that had been of greatest consequence in past experience. Such focusing on subdominant properties testifies to an "effacement of hierarchical organization of knowledge," it suggests a difficulty in identifying highly probable, canonic properties of objects and a lack of "economical and optimal" processing technique.

3.9. Probability Prognosis in Language and Communication

A number of experiments were conducted to test this hypothesis in schizophrenic speech. Dobrovich and Frumkina (1974) compared the frequency of word usage among normal subjects and schizophrenics afflicted with a continuous progressive course of illness. A set of test words was presented on cards. Each subject was instructed to distribute the cards into a box with seven labeled compartments according to how frequently they used these words: never, very seldom, seldom rather than frequent, neither seldom nor frequent, frequent rather than seldom, very frequent, always. The test yielded results that were abnormal for half of the patients and seemed to correlate with the degree of severity of the symptoms. In a more refined study, Frumkina (1974) asked 200 normals and 50 schizophrenics to fill in the gaps for the set of masked Russian infinitives. The results showed that schizophrenics responded with words that occur with a low probability in normal usage. Frumkina found correlations between the severity of the clinical state and the patient's deviance from the normal word-frequency distribution. Poliakov's results, on the other hand, indicated that no correlation was shown with the clinical picture. Moreover, relatives of schizophrenics processed information similarly to schizophrenics, and a hypothesis was proposed by Poliakov that the peculiar information processing must be related to a genetically determined constitutional factor, not modified by the clinical picture and present in the premorbid state.

V. P. Kritskaia is the most prominent member of Poliakov's group to do research on language problems with schizophrenics and their relatives. In 1971, she designed a number of experiments in which continuous schizophrenics and normal controls were asked to complete sentences by guessing a word that was masked with noise interference during the presentation (Kritskaia, 1971). Several meanings could be achieved from each sentence, depending on the obscured word. For example, "under the tree lay a *fruit*" (Russian: *plod*) could also be heard as "under the tree lay a *raft*" (Russian: *plot*). Depending on the choice of the filled-in word, test sentences acquired an ordinary or an unusual meaning. Only 19% of normals selected the unusual variant, whereas 83% of schizophrenics did so. In another test, the subjects were asked to listen to a series of masked words: "apple, pear, orange, margarine, banana, peach, apricot," etc. Although normals replaced the word "margarine" with "mandarin," schizophrenics did not do this. When a second presentation of the same material was made, normals still scored lower for correct answering than schizophrenics (33% to 52%), and only in the third presentation did the scores come close (63% to 64%).

In her 1973 study, Kritskaia also tested the relatives of schizophrenics (100 patients, 50 parents, 20 siblings, 35 close relatives) matched with normal controls. The results showed that the relatives of schizophrenics did not employ highly probable hypotheses. Patients used predictable hypotheses only 35% of the time, relatives 40%, and normals 75%. Kritskaia conjectures that the unusual selection of verbal hypotheses by schizophrenics is not part of the active process of the illness but represents a constitutional trait.

Three years later, Kritskaia and Gefter (1975) retested her patients and only two showed a change in processing. All other subjects confirmed the previous patterns. To test the "coefficient of standardness," a new sample was now added, consisting of patients with periodic schizophrenia, their relatives, and normal controls. No differences were found between the relatives of the two groups. The schizophrenics belonging to the continuous group, however, processed information in the most nonstandard way, whereas the periodic schizophrenics showed the greatest variability in giving answers, greatest number of hypotheses, and an inability to narrow down the fields from which hypotheses are selected. However, it was shown that experience acquired during the test situation brings the two groups of schizophrenics, their relatives, and normals much closer together. Kritskaia makes the point that experience acquired socially in life differs from experience acquired during a test situation. So far as these tests were concerned only in the use of experience acquired socially in life did the schizophrenics deviate from the normals.

A comment should be made here. It would be relevant to know what kind of similarity patterns the schizophrenics did select when guessing the masked words. Were they lexical similarities or acoustical paradigms, or yet others? It seems clear that patients did not give preference to contextual choices in their search strategies. Kritskaia's paper does not clarify this important point.

Parallel studies were conducted by Meleshko and Filippova (1971), and Meleshko (1972) on arithmetic problems and object classification problems. Results were similar to Kritskaia in showing that the search strategies of schizophrenics were not dependent on previous life situations, or test situations.

Filippova (1974) studied object-sorting to show that categorization of objects is done differently by two groups of schizophrenics. Continuous schizophrenics compared objects more along standard categories, whereas periodic schizophrenics used fewer standard categories and relied more heavily on external visual cues. They also used feelings, concrete criteria (I like, I dislike) for classification. Such differences could not be demonstrated among the relatives of the two groups.

Serious questions about the "probability prognosis" hypothesis are raised in a study done at the Moscow Institute of Forensic Psychiatry, by Guldian (1978), who compared the tactics of behavior by imprisoned schizophrenics with other types of prisoners. Guldian postulates that, with schizophrenia, these tactics are "unpliable," reflecting a defect in adaptation to external conditions.

Additional challenges to Poliakov's theories come from the work of Aminev, Traugott, Trachenko, and Belich (1974), at Kazan University. They conjecture that, in schizophrenia, the mechanisms of speech perception and prediction may be intact while higher brain mechanism of regulation are affected. As a result, schizophrenic language is said to contain too many original formations and thus to be "insufficiently stereotyped."

3.10. Schizophrenic Speech of Childhood and Adolescence

Although language acquisition is a very important topic for psychology and education in the Soviet Union, the psychiatric literature does not show anything approaching the richness and controversiality encountered in Anglo-American schizophrenia research. Studies are mainly descriptive: Lebedinsky and Novikova (1975) used a Piaget test to demonstrate that schizophrenic children refuse to distinguish between the properties of objects, substitute perceptual for measuring responses, and have "difficulties in the narration of personal activity in well developed speech." No reference is made to the parents of the children, their social background, or educational histories. Rather, the emphasis is on careful differential diagnosis of slowly progressive schizophrenia versus autism, retardation, neurosis, and illness in childhood (Vrono, 1974). Few examples are given of specific speech anomalies. Bashina (1978) described a disturbance of self-awareness among schizophrenic children of early preschool age and noted "loss of 'I' consciousness and regression of speech." There is no discussion of pronominal relationships, nor are the speech regressions depicted phonetically or spectrographically. One does not find any attempts to relate the language disturbance to maternal influence, as is characteristic of certain American studies (Goldfarb, Yudkovitz, & Goldfart, 1973).

Because of the high frequency of onset of schizophrenia in adolescence, this period of development is given very serious attention, but again the topic of linguistic and communicative behavior is handled more along the lines of inner, cognitive processes than outward speech. For example, in a study of 60 teenagers with "sluggish" schizophrenia, Mestiashvili and Rukhadze (1972) focused on their disordered thinking in connection with psychological tests of "fixed sets." Shcherbakova (1976) compared 61 adolescent schizophrenics with 114 normals in terms of their "actualization of knowledge." She found that patients were less adept in organizing their knowledge according to the "system of social experience." Sex differences are recognized to be relevant to prognosis. Voronkov (1978) compared 100 male and 100 female adolescents and found the age of onset to be earlier and the indices of affectivity to be greater among girls, whereas the boys showed more "psychopath-like behavior." No data is given about different rates of language development or distinctive communicative styles between the two sexes, nor is the problem of incomplete sexual differentiation in adolescence discussed. According to Holland (1978), clinicians still feel a certain amount of "reluctance and embarrassment" in taking a sexual history, and, to date, we have been unable to find any studies of obscenities, profanities, or other speech phenomena that might be expected in adolescence.

3.11. Memory and Retrieval Mechanisms in Language Use

As the individual matures and accumulates more information, mechanisms of memory and retrieval become an increasingly important concern. In this regard, the contributions of Aleksandr R. Luria (1902–1977) and Evgeny N. Sokolov are especially important for our understanding of the Soviet view of schizophrenia and language.

Central to the discussion of Poliakov's hypotheses about "probability prognosis" is the question of "selectivity." The manifestation of defect in "probability prognosis" pointed to the possibility that something may be wrong or different in the way schizophrenics select information from memory. Luria has commented extensively on the processes of differentiation, selection, filtration, and blocking of information, as part of the system of higher mental functions participating in the production of discourse. He used the metaphor "kinetic melodies," since music, like speech, calls for efficient selection, smooth movements, and overall coordination of the many subsidiary components of output behavior. If any of the components—phonetic, semantic, grammatical, vocal, prosodic, etc.—are trapped by the predicament of "equalization of meaning," no selection is possible and discourse is swamped by innumerable alternatives. A complementary phenomenon described by Luria is fragmentation—e.g., the word "contentment" might dissolve into "content" "men" and "t" (tea). Blending of lexical items also occurs, as exemplified by the formation of neologisms—"psychology" + "geography" = "psychogeography." (Detailed discussion may be found in a study by Zavarin, 1980).

Sokolov (1976) in his paper on "Learning and Memory," proposed an habituation model for learning "not to respond." He interpreted responses to novelty, and subsequent habituation, in the following way: during repeated stimulus presentations a "neuronal model of the stimulus" is elaborated that selectively filters (blocks) those responses to stimuli that coincide with the elaborated model. Sokolov sees the nervous system as an elaborate system of "self-adjustable filters," tuned for the particular repeated stimuli.

In this context, it should be mentioned that Smirnov (1972) has attempted to clarify the selection problem underlying the phenomenology of "jamais vu" and "déjà vu" in schizophrenia. He has analyzed the subjective feeling of things being recognized as similar or dissimilar and noted that, in false recognitions, only parts or certain features of the images appeared to be similar. For example, in a false recognition of the hospital ward, only impersonal details in it appeared to be familiar to the patient but the people in it did not. Particularly interesting is the false identification of similarities in the juxtaposition of past and present events, a phenomenon that Singer and Wynne (1966) in the American literature on schizophrenia call a disturbance in the "conservation of meaning."

Another example given by Smirnov (1972) pertains to the misidentification of persons, based on only a partial similarity between them. This could explain a patient's false perception of a "double." He concludes that in recognitions connecting the present to some past experience, whether during hallucinations or other altered states of consciousness, there is no evidence of true memory failure. Thus, "jamais vu" is eliminated as part of schizophrenic symptomatology.

Livshits and Teplitskaia (1978), in Kiev, have also been concerned with this problem, and come to the conclusion that schizophrenics do not "encapsulate" past experiences in retrievable forms adapted for dealing with present reailty.

3.12. Summary and Conclusion

In this survey of the Soviet contributions to language and schizophrenia, we have mentioned the traditional interest in visual forms, mimicry, emotional vocalization, hallucinations, and neologism. Today there appear to be important new approaches in the Moscow school, with its emphasis on the basic internal cognitive problems in schizophrenia ("probability prognosis") and the Leningrad school, with its precise evaluation of the schizophrenic's outward communicative behavior.

A comparison of the results of these studies with research done in Western countries would be highly desirable. The efforts of Poliakov (1972), specifically his evaluation of the work of Kurt Goldstein, Norman Cameron, Lyman Wynne, and other theoreticians, were a courageous first step in this direction.

One notes the apparent absence of research utilizing some of the newer technologies, e.g., acoustic phonetics, sound spectrography, cinematographic methods, in the psychiatric literature. Most of the reported studies are descriptive, with little in the way of statistical analysis.

Within the last decade there has been a renewed vigor of interest in schizophrenia and language, and one eagerly awaits the results of the newer neurophysiological investigations on language in general by N. P. Bekhtereva (Bekhtereva, Bundzen, & Gogolitsin, 1977; Bechtereva, Bundzen, Gogolitsin, Malyshev, & Perepelkin, 1979).

There appear to be relatively few direct quotations of what patients say during psychotherapy, which in the Soviet Union is generally done in groups. This may be a reflection of the prevailing attitude that schizophrenia is essentially an organic disease of the brain, running a predictable course. Also very noticeable is the tendency to attribute adult deviations from normal behavior to the influence of "constitution," without considering the influence of intervening life events—childhood, parenting, education, social experience, etc.

In assessing the general direction of psycholinguistic research in the USSR, one cannot help but be impressed with the profound influence of such leaders as A. A. Leontiev (1976/1977), who have persistently challenged the concepts derived from structural and transformational linguistics, when applied to psychopathological phenomena. Textual studies of oral and written language occupy the forefront of Russian psycholinguistic research today, and the focus of investigation is definitely switching toward the pragmatic dimension of communicative behavior.

ACKNOWLEDGMENT

In the preparation of this paper, the advice of Jurgen Ruesch has been of great value and is most warmly appreciated.

3.13. References

A Note about the Translation of Names and Titles

Transliteration in the references follows the Library of Congress system. Spelling of Russian names in the text follows common English usage. The reader should note slight differences in spelling of Russian names in the text and in transliterated entries of Russian references.

Aminev, G. A., Traugott, N. N., Trachenko, O. P., & Belich, A. I. Nekotorye elektrofiziologicheskie proiavleniia narusheniia rechevogo predskazaniia pri shizofrenii [Certain electrophysiological manifestations of disturbances in speech prediction in schizophrenia]. *Zhurnal nevropatologii i psikhiatrii im. S. S. Korsakova*, 1974, 5, 707–710.

Anokhin, P. K. *Biology and neurophysiology of the conditioned reflex and its role in adaptive behavior*. New York: Pergamon, 1974.

Balonov, L. IA., & Deglin, V. L. *Slukh i rech' dominantnogo i nedominantnogo polusharii* [Hearing and speech of the dominant and the nondominant hemispheres]. Leningrad: Nauka, 1976.

Balonov, L. IA., Deglin, V. L., Kaufman, D. A., & Nikolaenko, N. N. Ob emotsional' noi spetsializatsii bol'shikh polusharii mozga cheloveka [Emotional specialization of the major hemispheres of the human brain]. *Problemy izmeneniia i vosstanovleniia psikhicheskoi deiatel'nosti. Tezisy dokladov k V Vsesoiuzonomu s"ezdu psikhologov SSSR*. Moscow, 1977, pp. 6–7.

Bashina, V. M. Osobennosti depersonalizatsionnykh rasstroistv u bol'nykh shizofrenii detei [Characteristics of a depersonalization disturbance in children affected by schizophrenia]. *Zhurnal nevropatologii i psikhiatrii im. S. S. Korsakova*, 1978, 10, 1517–1533.

Bazhin, E. F., Korneva, T. V., & Lomachenko, A. S. O sostoianii impressivnoi sposobnosti u bol'nykh shizofrenii [The ability of emotional perception in schizophrenic patients]. *Zhurnal nevropatologii i psikhiatrii im. S. S. Korsakova*, 1978, 1, 711–715.

Bechtereva, N. P., Bundzen, P. V., Gogolitsin, IU. L., Malyshev, V. N., & Perepelkin, P. D. Neurophysiological codes of words in subcortical structures of the human brain. *Brain and Language*, 1979, 7, 145–163.

Bekhtereva, N. P., Bundzen, P. V., & Gogolitsin, IU. L. *Mozgovye kody psikhicheskoi deiatel'nosti* [Brain codes of psychic activity]. Leningrad: Nauka, 1977.

Bespal'ko, I. G. Ob osobennostiakh vospriiatiia mimiki bol'nymi shizofrenii v sviazi s narusheniem u nikh veroiatnostnykh otsenok [Peculiarities in the perception of mimicry in schizophrenic patients connected with the disturbance of probable evaluations]. *Zhurnal nevropatologii i psikhiatrii im. S. S. Korsakova*, 1976, 12, 1828–1833.

Budashevskii, B. G., & Menitskii, D. N. Characteristics of the internal representation of the probability structure of the environment in certain mental illnesses. *Soviet Psychology*, 1974, 4, 32–43.

Dobrovich, A. B., & Frumkina, R. M. Disorders in the probability organization of speech behavior in schizophrenia. *Soviet Psychology*, 1974, 4, 54–66.

Feigenberg, I. M. Veroiatnostnoe prognozirovanie v deiatel'nosti mozga. [Probability prognosis in cerebral activity]. *Voprosy psikhologii*, 1963, 2, 59–67.

Feigenberg, I. M. Disorders of probability prediction in schizophrenia. *Soviet Psychology*, 1974, 4, 3–22.

Filippova, V. A. Sravnitel'naia kharakteristika osobennostei myshleniia bol'nykh nepreryvno tekushchei i periodicheskoi shizofreniei [Comparative characterization of peculiarities in thinking among patients with periodic and continuous schizophrenia]. *Zhurnal nevropatologii i psikhiatrii im. S. S. Korsakova*, 1974, 12, 1847–1850.

Frumkina, R. M. *Prognoz v rechevoi deiatel'nosti* [Prognosis in linguistic activity]. Moscow: Nauka, 1974.

Gabriial, T. M. Patopsikhologicheskii analiz narushenii myshleniia [Pathopsychological analysis of mental disturbance]. *Novye issledovaniia v psikhologii*, 1974, 2, 63–65.

Gannushkin, P. B. Shizofrennyi simptomokompleks kak ekho-psikhogennyi tip reaktsii [Schizophrenic complex of symptoms—its psychogenic type of reactions]. In P. B. Gannushkin, V. A. Giliarovskii, & M. O. Gurevich (Eds.), *Sovremennye problemy shizofrenii. Doklady na konferentsii po shizofrenii v iune 1932 g*. Moscow-Leningrad: Medgi, 1933.

Giliarovskii, V. A. Rech' i myshlenie bolnykh shizofreniei [Speech and thinking of schizophrenic patients]. *Zhurnal nevropatologii i psikhiatrii im. S. S. Korsakova*, 1957, *57*, 1348–1357.

Goldfarb, W., Yudkovitz, E., & Goldfart, N., Verbal symbols to designate objects: An experimental study of communication in mothers of schizophrenic children. *Journal of Autism and Childhood Schizophrenia*, 1973, *3*, 281–298.

Gul'dan, V. V. Taktiki povedeniia bol'nykh shizofreniei i psikhopaticheskikh lichnostei v veroiatnostnoi srede [Behavioral tactics of schizophrenic patients and psychopathic personalities in probable situations]. *Zhurnal nevropatologii i psikhiatrii im. S. S. Korsakova*, 1978, *12*, 1845–1850.

Holland, J. Schizophrenia in the Soviet Union: Concepts and treatment. In R. Cancro (Ed.), *Annual review of the schizophrenic syndrome 1976–1977*. New York: Brunner/Mazel, 1978.

Holland, J., & Shakhmatova-Pavlova, I. V. Concept and classification of schizophrenia in the Soviet Union. *Schizophrenia Bulletin*, 1977, *3*, 277–287.

Ivanov, V. V. *Chet i nechet. Asimmetriia mozga i znakovykh sistem* [Even and uneven. Asymmetry of the brain and of sign systems]. Moscow: Sovetskoe radio, 1978.

Ivanov, V. V. Neirosemiotika ustnoi rechi i funktsional'naiia asimmetriia mozga [Neurosemiotics of oral speech and functional asymmetry of the brain]. *Uchenye Zapiski Tartuskogo Gosudarstvennogo Universiteta*, vyp. 481, Tartu, 1979, pp. 121–142.

Kasanin, J. S. (Ed.), *Language and thought in schizophrenia*. Berkeley: University of California Press, 1954.

Kepiński, A. *Schizofrenia*. Warsaw: Pánstwowy Zakład Wydawnictw Lekarskich, 1972.

Kontridze, F. M., Mestiashvili, M. G., & Puladze, S. V. O svoeobrazii nekotorykh strukturnykh predposylok lichnosti u bol'nykh shizofreniei [Peculiarity of certain structural traits in the constitution of schizophrenic patients]. *Zhurnal nevropatologii i psikhiatrii im. S. S. Korsakova*, 1975, *2*, 1365–1368.

Kontsevoi, V. A., & Druzhinina, T. A. Kliniko-psikhopatologicheskie osobennosti shizofrenii, protekaiushchei pristupami s verbal'nym galliutsinozom [Clinical psychopathological peculiarities of schizophrenia with verbal hallucinations]. *Zhurnal nevropatologii i psikhiatrii im. S. S. Korsakova*, 1973, *6*, 902–908.

Kritskaia, V. P. Osobennosti vospriiatiia rechi bol'nymi shizofreniei [Characteristics in perception of speech in schizophrenic patients]. *Zhurnal nevropatologii i psikhiatrii im. S. S. Korsakova*, 1971, *1*, 867–871.

Kritskaya, V. P. Characteristics of the speech of schizophrenics and their relatives. *Soviet Psychology*, 1973, *1*, 9–19.

Kritskaia, V. P., & Gefter, V. M. Vospriiatie elementarnykh rechevykh struktur bol'nymi shizofreniei [Perception of elementary linguistic structures by schizophrenic patients]. *Zhurnal nevropatologii i psikhiatrii im. S. S. Korsakova*, 1975, *2*, 1677–1680.

Lavretskaia, E. F. O sindrome lozhnogo uznavaniia pri shizofrenii [The syndrome of false recognition in schizophrenia]. *Zhurnal nevropatologii i psikhiatrii im. S. S. Korsakova*, 1970, *4*, 560–564.

Lebedinskii, V. V., & Novikov, E. IU. O formirovanii poniatii u detei, bol'nykh shizofreniei [On the formation of concepts in children affected by schizophrenia]. *Zhurnal nevropatologii i psikhiatrii im. S. S. Korsakova*, 1975, *11*, 1673–1680.

Leont'ev, A. A. Some new trends in Soviet psycholinguistics. *Soviet Psychology*, 1976/1977, *2*, 15–25.

Leont'ev, A. A., Rokhlin, L. L., Savitskaia, L. B., & Shakhnarovich, A. M. Kliniko-psikholingvisticheskoe issledovanie razorvannosti rechi u bol'nykh paranoidnoi formoi shizofrenii [Clinical psycholinguistic investigation of ruptured speech in patients afflicted by paranoid schizophrenia]. *Zhurnal nevropatologii i psikhiatrii im. S. S. Korsakova*, 1973, *12*, 1858–1863.

Livshits, S. M., & Teplitskaia, E. I. Vzaimootnosheniia soznatel'nogo i bessoznatel'nogo pri shizofrenii [Relation between the conscious and the unconscious in schizophrenia]. In A. S. Prangishvili, A. E. Sherozia, & F. V. Bassin (Eds.), *Bessoznatel'noe: priroda, funktsii, metody issledovaniia* [The unconscious: Nature, functions, methods of study]. Tbilisi: Metsniereba Publishing House, 1978.

Longinova, S. V. "Piktogramma" kak metod issledovaniia rasstroistv myshleniia pri shizofrenii ["Pictogram" as a method of investigation of mental disturbances]. *Zhurnal nevropatologii i psikhiatrii im. S. S. Korsakova*, 1972, *11*, 1679–1684.

Luria, A. R. *Neuropsychology of memory*. New York: Halsted, 1976.

Lynn, R. Russian theory and research on schizophrenia. *Psychological Bulletin*, 1963, *60*, 486–498.

Melekhov, D. E., Shubina, S. A., & Kogan, S. E. (Eds.). Shizophreniia s istericheskimi proiavleniiami [Schizophrenia with hysterical manifestations]. *Moscow. Nauchno issledovatel'skii institut psikhiatrii im. P. B. Gannushkina. Trudy.* Vol. 1. 1936.

Meleshko, T. K. Izmenenie izbiratel'nosti myshleniia pri shizofrenii i problema ispol'zovaniia proshlogo opyta [Modification of selective thinking in schizophrenia and the problem of utilization of past experience]. *Zhurnal nevropatologii i psikhiatrii im. S. S. Korsakova*, 1972, *11*, 1675–1679.

Meleshko, T. K., & Filippova, V. A. K voprosu ob obuslovlennosti nekotorykh osobennostei myshleniia pri shizofrenii [Question of determinateness of certain peculiarities in thinking processes in schizophrenia]. *Zhurnal nevropatologii i psikhiatrii im. S. S. Korsakova*, 1971, *6*, 864–867.

Mestiashvili, M. G., & Rukhadze, N. V. Issledovaniia lichnosti stradaiushchikh vialotekushchei shizofreniei podrostkov po metodu fiksirovannoi ustanovki [Investigation of personality features in adolescents with sluggish schizophrenia using the "fixed set" technique (by D. N. Uznadze)]. *Zhurnal nevropatologii i psikhiatrii im. S. S. Korsakova*, 1972, *10*, 1547–1550.

Ostwald, P. F., Language and communication problems with schizophrenic patients—a review, commentary, and synthesis. In W. E. Fann, I. Karacan, A. D. Pokorny, & R. L. Williams (Eds.), *Phenomenology and treatment of schizophrenia*. New York: Spectrum, 1978.

Pavlov, I. P. *Lectures on conditioned reflexes*. New York: International Universities Press, 1941.

Pavlov, I. P. Moscow. Vsesoiuznyi institut eksperimental'noi meditsiny. Leningradskii filial (redaktsionnaia kollegiia: K. M. Bykov i dr.). *Pavlovskie klinicheskie sredy; stenogrammy zasedanii v nervnoi i psikhiatricheskoi klinikakh* [Pavlovian clinical Wednesdays; recorded conferences in the nervous and psychiatric clinics]. Moscow: Izd. Akad. Nauk SSSR, Vol. 3. 1957.

Payne, T. R. *S. L. Rubinstein and the philosophical foundations of Soviet psychology*. New York: Humanities Press, 1968.

Poliakov, IU. F. Patologiia poznavatel'nykh protsessov [Pathology of cognitive processes]. In A. V. Snezhnevskii, *Shizofreniia*. Moscow: Meditsina, 1972.

Poliakov, IU. F. The use of pathopsychological data in the investigations of structure of cognitive processes. In B. V. Zeigarnik & O. Zangwill. *Pathological psychology and psychological processes. XVIII International Congress of Psychology*, Symposium 26. Moscow, 1966.

Rome, H. P. The Union of Soviet Socialist Republics. *World Studies in Psychiatry*, 1979, *3*, 5–44.

Savitskaia, A. B., & Sizov, M. M. Kliniko-lingvisticheskii analiz neologizmov v ustnoi rechi bol'nykh shizofreniei [Clinical-linguistic analysis of neologisms in oral speech of schizophrenic patients]. *Zhurnal nevropatologii i psikhiatrii im. S. S. Korsakova*, 1973, *12*, 1863–1869.

Sechenov, I. M. *Selected physiological and psychological works*. Moscow: Foreign Languages Publishing House, 1956.

Shcherbakova, N. P. Sravnitel'noe izuchenie osobennostei myshleniia u podrostkov, zdorovykh i bol'nykh shizofreniei [Comparative study of characteristics in thought processes in normal and schizophrenic adolescents]. *Zhurnal nevropatologii i psikhiatrii im. S. S. Korsakova*, 1976, *12*, 1834–1839.

Singer, M. T., & Wynne, L. C. Principles for scoring communication defects and deviances in parents of schizophrenics: Rorschach and TAT manuals. *Psychiatry*, 1966, *29*, 260–288.

Smirnov, V. K. O psikhopatologii uznavaniia pri shizofrenii [Psychopathology of recognition]. *Zhurnal nevropatologii i psikhiatrii im. S. S. Korsakova*, 1972, *5*, 721–729.

Snezhnevskii, A. V. The symptomatology, clinical forms and nosology of schizophrenia. In J. G. Howells (Ed.), *Modern perspectives in world psychiatry*. Edinburg and London: Oliver & Boyd, 1968.

Sokolov, A. N. *Inner speech and thought*. New York: Plenum, 1972.

Sokolov, E. N. Learning and memory: habituation as negative learning. In M. R. Rosenzweig & E. L. Bennett (Eds.), *Neuro mechanisms of learning and memory*. Cambridge, Mass.: M.I.T. Press, 1976.

Sukhareva, G. E. *Klinika schizofrenii u detei i podrostkov* [Clinical picture of schizophrenia in children and adolescents], Part 1. Kharkov, 1937.

Szafraniec, J. Analiza tresci wypowiedzi v metodzie Rorschacha u chorych na schizofrenie [Analysis of the verbal content of Rorschach's test in schizophrenics]. *Psychiatria Polska*, 1976, *3*, 275–281.

Volkova, R. P. K voprosu o galliutsinatornykh remissiiakh pri blagopriiatno protekaiushchei shizofrenii [Hallucinatory remissions in non-malignant schizophrenia]. *Zhurnal nevrapatologii i psikhiatrii im. S. S. Korsakova*, 1974, *5*, 716–722.

Voronkov, B. V. O nekotorykh osobennostiakh kliniki shizofrenii u podrostkov v zavisimosti ot pola [Sex dependent clinical picture of schizophrenia in adolescents]. *Zhurnal nevropatologii i psikhiatrii im. S. S. Korsakova*, 1978, *10*, 1528–1566.

Vrono, M. S. Schizophrenia in childhood and adolescence: Clinical features and course. *International Journal of Mental Health*, 1974, *2*, 7–116.

Zaitseva, Z. M., Liberman, A. E., & Minkin, L. M. The information structure of a proposition and a psychophysiological analysis of normal and pathological speech. *Soviet Psychology*, 1974, *4*, 67–75.

Zavarin, V. Modification of goal directed behavior in discourse. In Richard F. Thompson, Leslie H. Hicks, and V. B. Shvyrkov (Eds.), *Neural mechanisms of goal-directed behavior and learning*. New York: Academic, 1980.

Zeigarnik, B. V. *Experimental abnormal psychology*. New York: Plenum, 1972.

Žinkin, N. I. *Mechanisms of speech*. The Hague: Mouton, 1968.

4

Kurt Salzinger,[1] *Stephanie Portnoy,*
Richard S. Feldman, and Jeanne Patenaude-Lane

FROM METHOD TO MADNESS

THE CLOZE PROCEDURE IN THE STUDY OF PSYCHOPATHOLOGY

The philosphers of science have it that scientists ponder theories for long periods of time, and then, by the use of the method of deduction, come up with testable hypotheses that they then carefully subject to experimentation in order to vote the theory up or down. But life being what it is, and scientists being human beings first and scientists second, if not third or fourth, theory usually gets dragged in screaming, if at all, only after the scientists have had their fun in the laboratory. Now, presumably, if one searched far and long enough, one would find a scientist who obeyed the laws set down by the philosophers of science, but much more likely, a search for the philosopher's scientist would turn up those who simply bring the theory to bear after the fact, who keep the theory alive only in the backs of their minds, or who (we hestitate to mention) pay theory no heed at all but have their ideas for experiments come fully formed from their heads, rushing out to collect their data before the opportunity to do so escapes them.

[1] On leave from the New York State Psychiatric Institute and the Polytechnic Institute of New York.

Kurt Salzinger ● National Science Foundation, Washington, D.C. 20550. *Stephanie Portnoy, Richard S. Feldman,* and *Jeanne Patenaude-Lane* ● New York State Psychiatric Institute, New York, New York 10032. A portion of the work reported here was supported by Basic Research Science Grant No. E 378L from the Research Foundation for Mental Hygiene, Inc. New York State Psychiatric Institute Division.

To all of these transgressions of the philosophers' dicta, we would like to add still another, the use of method as a source of inspiration for the scientist's work. Put baldly as we have here, this approach sounds like the most arid of dustbowl empirical approaches. Let us therefore imbue it with the current day's mot juste: the validation study. Being inspired by a desire to validate the measurement of a concept is much more admired in the science of psychology than being stimulated by a wish to exploit a method that "measures well." Whichever way the reader wishes to interpret it, we will present here the growth and nurturance of a method of measuring what we first named *comprehensibility* and then extended to *communicability*.

4.1. Conditioning of Verbal Behavior

Our interest in the study of the verbal behavior of schizophrenic patients was first pursued in a series of experiments within a conditioning framework (Salzinger & Pisoni, 1958, 1960, 1961; Salzinger & Portnoy, 1964; Salzinger, Portnoy, & Feldman, 1964a). Taking what is basically another method, that of conditioning, we demonstrated that the verbal behavior of schizophrenic patients, like that of normal individuals, could be conditioned by merely having the interviewer utter certain remarks such as, "yeah," "yes," "mmhm," and, when the speaker hesitated long enough, "I see" or "I can understand that." These remarks, which proved to be positive reinforcers, were applied to speech in general in some subjects and to a response class we called "self-referred affect" in others. Our results allowed us to arrive at a number of conclusions:

1. There is the possibility of control or bias in the effect of the interviewer on the patient. Interviewers either unaware of their reinforcing behavior or unwilling to control (or even record) it are likely to bias what the patients tell them and, as a consequence, the data they obtain— whether for diagnosis, prognosis, plans for treatment, or evaluation for termination of treatment—cannot and should not be relied on for an understanding of what is troubling the patient. Although this conclusion might be described as "merely" methodological, our current disputes over diagnosis (e.g., Salzinger, 1978) can be a least partially attributed to this methodological problem.

2. The reinforcing behavior of the interviewer can be used as a way

of increasing a patient's verbal behavior, either in general by making reinforcement contingent on speech in general, or specifically for a particular class by making it contingent on a response class such as self-referred affect. These effects open up two possibilities—the possibility of increasing speech sample size either for diagnostic purposes or for research analysis (such as we shall show below could be used in the case of cloze procedure), and the possibility of increasing speech in terms of a specific response class, either for therapeutic purposes or for research analysis (such as determining schizophrenic patients' responses to external stimuli).

3. Although the behavior of schizophrenic patients conditions, in the case of self-referred affect statements, at the same rate as that of normal subjects, it extinguishes significantly more rapidly than in normals. These results suggest that the sustained presence of external stimuli is more important in maintaining the behavior of schizophrenic patients than of normals and open up the possibility that affect is important for schizophrenics only in the context of extinction. Later, this finding was interpreted as still another instance of the Immediacy Hypothesis of Schizophrenia (Salzinger, 1973; Salzinger, Portnoy, & Feldman, 1978), about which more below.

The conditioning studies were inspired by the desire to apply a well-known method, one honed in the study of animals, to a complicated social situation (the interview) and to determine whether such basic principles as those of conditioning and extinction could apply equally well there. Here we have a clear instance of method giving rise not only to clarification of the methodology of the interview, but to substantive result, and eventually to confirmation of theory (see Section 4.3.).

4.2. The Cloze Procedure

The method under consideration began as a way of measuring readability that went beyond the counting methods in which the frequency of individual words was considered to reflect that function. Taylor (1953) took continuous text material, deleted every fifth word, asked subjects to read the material and fill in the missing words, and found, using the number of guesses that matched the missing words, that the method distinguished between such authors as Gertrude Stein and Erskine Caldwell.

To us, the method seemed to be singularly well suited as a measure of communicability in schizophrenia. For years clinical lore as well as some experimental data called attention to people's difficulty in understanding what schizophrenic patients had to say. It is in fact fair to say that one of the important ways in which schizophrenics come to the attention of psychologists and psychiatrists is through their speech and writing behaviors. "I don't get it" is a frequent reaction to a schizophrenic's verbal behavior. The cloze procedure assumes that language is basically redundant, that is, the same message is transmitted repeatedly within any given utterance, and that therefore the recipient of the message ought to be able to guess one version of a message from the other versions as long as the communication is clear. Thus, the idea of having normal subjects guess words that have been systematically deleted from samples of speech seemed most appropriate as a measure of what we eventually called communicability.

The cloze procedure had, it seemed to us, all the earmarks of a good psychological measure: It is objective in that a series of straightforward instructions given together with transcripts having blanks substituted for every fifth word gives rise in normal subjects to responses (guesses of the deleted words) that can be scored simply by calling them correct if they match the original word uttered, and incorrect, if they are different. The procedure is socially significant in that it measures how well one individual understands another. There is no doubt that, second only to violence, the way people get into trouble in our society is by what they say. Finally, the measure also provides information on the way that subjects respond to their own response-generated stimuli. Using a modification of the cloze procedure, we were able to examine the number of successive words over which verbal responses controlled one another.

Let us now look at some data. Our first published study on the cloze procedure made use of the statistical approximations to English (Salzinger, Portnoy, & Feldman, 1962). Those approximations had been generated by Miller and Selfridge (1950) to obtain a better understanding of the role of context—defined in terms of the length of the chains of words emitted together in a continuous speech situation—in memory studies. The statistical approximations provided us with exactly the kind of material we needed to determine whether the cloze procedure is sensitive to response-produced stimulus control. The results were quite clear. The cloze procedure score (the number of words correctly guessed) varied as a direct function of the statistical approximation to English: The longer the chain of connected words, the higher the cloze procedure score. Thus, we had our first step in the validation of the cloze procedure. The same study also indicated that, when two groups of subjects were given the same passage to "cloze," they replicated one another. Furthermore, generally the same results were achieved when every seventh word, as compared to every fifth word, was deleted. The results are shown in Figure 4.1.

Before we proceed to our studies of schizophrenic patients, we would do well to describe the studies that showed the social significance of the cloze procedure (Hammer, Polgar, & Salzinger, 1969; Salzinger, Hammer, Portnoy, & Polgar, 1970). If the cloze procedure has social significance, then people who know the person whose language behavior they are predicting ought to have higher cloze scores that those who do not know the author. We were able to confirm that result. We also found that, in a small group, many of whose members know each other well and most at least somewhat, those people observed to be central (found in conversation with others) in their interactions with the

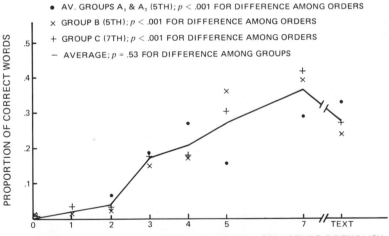

Figure 4.1. Proportion of words guessed correctly (in the cloze procedure) as a function of order of approximation to English. Groups A, B, and C are different groups of clozers responding to the same passages with every fifth or every seventh word deleted as indicated. From Salzinger, Portnoy, and Feldman (1962); copyright 1962, by the American Psychological Association, reprinted with permission.

rest of the group had speech that was better predicted than those who were less central in the group. The correlation between cloze score and observed centrality was $+.66$ ($p < .01$). When the correlation was calculated between reported centrality (based on reported degree of acquaintance) and cloze score, it was not statistically significant ($r = +.34$, $p > .05$). This finding is particularly meaningful because it shows that cloze procedure reflects actual interactions rather than people's reports about them. Further results indicated that particular individuals better predicted the speech of those who were observed talking to them than the speech of others. In general, these studies showed that subjects who spend time together have higher communicability scores for each other's language behavior.

We were ready then to try the application of the cloze procedure to schizophrenic speech. As already mentioned, we studied the effect of verbal reinforcement on the schizophrenic patient in the course of the interview. Having shown that reinforcement works in that situation, we felt obliged to test the effect of reinforcement on monologues (Salzinger *et al.*, 1964a), that is, on continuous verbal behavior uninfluenced by questions which, though we had kept them general in nature and found them not to relate to the conditioning effect, we still wanted to exclude to show a purer conditioning effect. The conditioning results were as clear here as in the interview studies. Since our experimental design included a no-reinforcement control group, in which we merely gave general instructions to the patients to continue to speak without waiting for any questions, the study supplied us with a group of uninterrupted monologues from schizophrenic patients who, in addition, were undergoing no somatic treatment whatsoever. Those speech samples, free of whatever artifacts an interviewer's questions or comments introduce, are rare indeed. They were rare in the past because investigators assumed that monologues could not be elicited from such patients. For that reason, older studies resorted to speech samples elicited in response to leading questions in interviews, to written material from diaries and letters, or to speech of patients who happened to be talking at a high rate at that time. None of these could obviously be considered to be representative of schizophrenic patients as a whole or any subset homogeneous with respect to psychopathology.

Taking a number of schizophrenic speech samples collected under conditions where a screen prevented the patient from seeing the experimenter, and matching them to speech samples collected in the same way from hospitalized physically ill patients in terms of age, sex, education, and speech community of the speakers, we examined normal-schizophrenic differences in communicability. Since we dealt with people who were confined in both the normal and the schizophrenic cases and since both groups were asked to speak about what brought them to the hospital, we went as far as possible to match even the topic of their speech samples.

The results were, to begin with, perhaps not surprising (Salzinger, Portnoy, & Feldman, 1964b). The speech of schizophrenics gave rise to fewer correct guesses when submitted to a cloze procedure than the speech of the matched normals. That result serves to validate the cloze procedure further, in that it confirms our intuitions about the difficulty we have in understanding schizophrenics. More interesting perhaps is the fact that the difference between the two groups increases from the first to the second 100 words of the monologues. Figure 4.2. shows clearly that the normal speech communicability remains at approximately the same level, whereas the schizophrenic speech—less communicable to start with—becomes worse as the patient continues to talk. One interpretation of this result is that as the schizophrenic speech con-

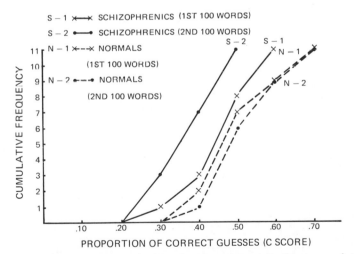

Figure 4.2. Cumulative frequency of schizophrenic and normal subjects as a function of proportion of correct guesses to total guesses in the cloze procedure. S-1 and S-2, and N-1 and N-2, refer, respectively, to the first and second 100 words of the schizophrenic and normal passages. From Salzinger, Portnoy, and Feldman (1964b), reprinted by permission of The New York Academy of Sciences.

tinues, it is further and further removed from the external stimulus of the original instructions, thus resulting in the speech's being increasingly dependent on response-produced stimulus control. If the speech that is more determined by response-produced stimulus control shows a greater communicability deficit, then we know that it is a likely place to contain a behavioral mechanism to explain at least one of the schizophrenic difficulties.

In a further attempt to validate the cloze procedure, we related it to outcome of illness (Salzinger, Portnoy, & Feldman, 1966). The monologues described above were obtained from patients approximately one week after admission to a state hospital. The speech samples so obtained were then the basis for the cloze procedure. In a follow up of the patients for a period of six months, we related the cloze score of the first 200 words of speech to the number of days spent in the hospital after the interview. Patients whose speech samples gave rise to lower cloze scores remained in the hospital for a larger number of days then those whose speech produced higher cloze scores ($r = -.47, p < .05$). In other words, patients whose speech was more communicable recovered faster—at least sufficiently so as to be released earlier from a state hospital—than those who had the greater communicability deficit. By following up the difference in deficit between the first and second 100 words, we calculated the correlation coefficients separately for the first and second 100 words. The cloze score of the first 100 words resulted in an r of $-.29$ ($p > .05$), whereas the second 100 words produced an r of $-.48$ ($p < .05$). The fact that the second 100 words manifest the schizophrenic communicability deficit more clearly than the first again emphasizes that an external stimulus fades faster in controlling schizophrenic responses than normal ones. This stimulus-fading we shall return to when we consider the "Immediacy Hypothesis of Schizophrenia." For now, suffice it to say, there is evidence that external stimuli control schizophrenic verbal behavior only as long as they are close to it.

If external stimuli have to be immediate to be effective in controlling schizophrenic verbal behavior, what about the immediacy of the response-produced stimuli generated by successive words? Do they also have to be immediate to be effective? Obviously, if words do not influence other words unless they are hard by, we have here a mechanism with which to explain the tangential nature of schizophrenic verbal behavior. We decided that the best way to test the importance of immediate versus remote response-produced stimuli in controlling the verbal behavior of schizophrenics was to modify the cloze procedure. Beginning with the blanks (deleted words), we provided different groups of "clozers" with varying numbers of words surrounding them (Salzinger, Portnoy, Pisoni, & Feldman, 1970). This time we matched both the schizophrenic and normal speakers for the regular cloze procedure, and the deleted words in terms of both their predictability (cloze scores in continuous text) and the grammatical parts of speech to which they belonged. Figure 4.3. shows the percent correct guesses by normal "clozers" of the matched normal and schizophrenic speech segments as a function of 2, 4, 8, 16, and 28 words of bilateral context. Both types of speech show a negatively accelerated increase in the percentage of correct guesses. However, as the amount of context increases, so does the difference between normals and schizophrenics. Since the clozers benefit less from words increasingly further removed from the word to be guessed, we conclude that schizophrenics are more controlled by immediate response-produced stimuli than are normals. Furthermore, it is interesting to note that this effect is more notable in such function words as "and," "but," "of," "for," and "to," which is to be expected, since function words are by their nature more dependent on context.

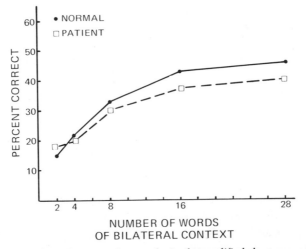

Figure 4.3. Percent of words guessed correctly (in the modified cloze procedure) to schizophrenic and normal speech segments as a function of the number of words of bilateral context. From Salzinger, Portnoy, and Feldman (1978); reprinted with permission of the authors and publisher from *Language and cognition in schizophrenia*. Hillsdale, N.J.: Lawrence Erlbaum Associates, Inc. 1978.

The use of the cloze procedure and the variant described above allowed us not only to differentiate schizophrenics from normals; it also gave rise to theory which we will describe in the next section.

4.3. *The Immediacy Hypothesis*

Given the interconnectedness of the verbal responses that constitute language behavior, it became clear to us that individuals whose responses are controlled only by nearby stimuli would have trouble communicating effectively. They would seem to go off on tangents and respond only to parts of questions; their associations would often relate to the sound of a word rather than its meaning, and they would, a surprising amount of the time, respond to words, neglecting the context in which they were embedded. Paranoid responding can be characterized as responding to stimuli out of context. The difference in rate of extinction (Salzinger & Pisoni, 1961) fits into the notion of the importance of immediate stimuli: We found no difference between normals and schizophrenics in the conditioning period, that is, as long as the reinforcing stimuli were there. However, during extinction, when no further reinforcement was forthcoming and therefore the critical stimulus became less immediate, the normals continued to show the effect of reinforcement, whereas the schizophrenics quickly reverted to their preconditioning level.

Similar effects are found in psychophysical experiments. Schizophrenic patients instructed to counteract the effect of an anchor weight preceding each stimulus weight to be judged in a method-of-single-stimuli situation respond much more to the immediate anchor stimulus than to the more remote instructions by comparison to a group of normals (Salzinger, 1957). In contrast, when the anchor stimulus is presented much earlier (more remote) than the stimulus to be judged, the anchor effect is reduced (Wurster, 1965). One can easily multiply the examples in which the schizophrenic patients' behavior is primarily controlled by stimuli immediate in their environment. We have reviewed a great many experiments providing similar evidence (Salzinger, 1973; Salzinger, 1980; Salzinger *et al.*, 1978). We have called it the *Immediacy Hypothesis*. It states that schizophrenic behavior is primarily controlled by stimuli that are immediate in the environment. Given a situation containing a number of stimuli acting on a schizophrenic patient, the controlling stimulus is the one that occurs closest to the occasion for response.

Another question remains to be answered concerning the validity of the Immediacy Hypothesis. The fact that much evidence is consonant with it does not rule out alternate theories equally in agreement with the data. This is not the place to discuss these issues in detail, as we have done so in the references above. It is of interest, however, in the context of the uses of method, to consider the lapse-of-attention hypothesis put forward by McGhie and Chapman (1961). In our search for the most appropriate method to describe schizophrenic speech, we (Salzinger *et al.*, 1966) devised the *unitization technique*. Normal subjects were asked to divide the unpunctuated transcripts of schizophrenic and normal speech samples into sentences by marking them off and crossing out any words that could not fit into the sentences. As might be expected, more such words needed to be crossed out for the schizophrenic than for the normal speech samples. These words (intrusions) seemed to us to constitute an appropriate measure of attention lapse; the fact that those words are so unrelated to what was said before or after suggests that some other short-lived stimulation produced them. We reasoned that, if the lapse-of-attention hypothesis is correct, then reconstituting the passages by leaving out the intrusions should improve the communicability of the schizophrenic passages. We (Salzinger, Portnoy, & Feldman, 1977) then compared the passages that had the intrusions excised with those that retained them by subjecting both to the cloze procedure. No significant difference was apparent between the two types of schizophrenic passages. Moreover, they both differed significantly from their normal matches. Thus, we concluded that momentary lapses of attention are inadequate as an explanation of the communicability deficit. Furthermore, we concluded that it is necessary to invoke the idea of immediacy to explain the schizophrenic deficit.

Having shown how our past research on method resulted in an accretion of meaning that eventually gave rise to a theory of schizophrenia, we are now ready to describe some more recent results from our laboratory.

4.4. Recent Results on the Cloze Procedure

4.4.1. Long-term Outcome

As already indicated, when we correlated the cloze procedure score on the speech obtained one week after admission (and without having the speaker under the influence of drugs) to the number of days spent in the hospital on a six-month follow-up, a respectable correlation ($r = -.47$, $p < .05$) was obtained. We have since been able to follow up all but one of this group—14 male and 8 female schizophrenic patients—for a period ranging from 15 to 19 years following the collection of the predictive speech sample. We calculated an outcome measure by summing the time between all admissions and discharges for each hospitalization during the follow-up period and dividing by the total follow-up period. The resulting percentages varied from 1% to 63%, with a median of 15%. The communicability measure was again the percent correct prediction of the words deleted. Overall correlation between cloze score and number of days in the hospital, on the two hundred words, had decreased from the six-month-outcome to $-.39$ ($p < .05$) but was still statistically significant. Like the six-month outcome results, the correlation based on the first 100 words was lower ($r = -.26$) than for the second 100 words ($r = -.35$). The former was clearly not statistically significant ($p \geqslant .05$), but the latter just missed reaching statistical significance at the .05 level (.359 is necessary).

Since schizophrenics as a group showed a decrease in communicability from the first to the second 100 words but not all individuals did so, we decided to see whether those who spent more time in the hospital differed from those who were hospitalized for less time, with respect to the communicability change. Examination of the cloze score changes showed that of those 11 patients whose total stay in the hospital was above the median (15.5%), 7 decreased, 1 showed no change, and 3 increased in cloze score. On the other hand, of the 11 patients whose total stay was below the median, 9 showed an increase and 2 a decrease. The Mann–Whitney U test showed that the patients who stayed longer than the median proportion of the group were significantly different in cloze score difference (from first to second 100 words) from those who stayed less than the median of the group.

In essence, these analyses show that a moderate but statistically significant relationship is to be found between a communicability score and amount of hospitalization over a period extending from 15 to 19 years follow up. Any method that results in a relationship covering that long a period of time cannot be all bad.

4.4.2. Topic

An important question to ask about the communicability deficit in schizophrenia is whether it is all-pervasive or whether it is produced by the emotional situation in which patients are asked to recount their reasons for hospitalization. This question was already answered in part, because the normal subjects were also asked to talk about something which undoubtedly had made them unhappy—a physical ailment serious enough to require hospitalization. Nevertheless, we thought it might be useful to have the same group of schizophrenic patients speak on two different topics to determine what contribution, if any, topic made to the schizophrenic communicability deficit.

Fourteen male schizophrenic patients consented to participate. Eleven had been previously hospitalized; all were receiving phenothiazines. Half were asked to speak first of their reasons for being in the hospital and then about things they enjoy or like doing; the other seven patients were given the two topics in reverse order. We then took the first 50 words of each monologue (the maximum amount of uninterrupted speech available from all the patients on both topics) and subjected them to the cloze procedure by having a group of normal college students fill in the blanks. The results showed no statistically significant difference between the two topics (paired replicates test; $p > .05$). We concluded that the communicability deficit of schizophrenics is not eliminated or even attenuated by having them speak about a topic unrelated to their hospitalization, that is, presumably pleasant things.

A number of criticisms come to mind in reference to this study. Only male subjects participated, all were receiving phenothiazine treatment, and the language sample size was small. Furthermore, when the patients are taken individually, statistically significant differences are found in most of the patients—half favoring the "hospital" topic and half the "enjoyable things" topic. The fact that the significant differences go in opposite directions for different subjects, with the remainder showing no significant difference, suggests that they all may simply reflect the overall result of no difference. Nevertheless, the possibility of an individual difference variable in explaining the difference in topic must await further research. To accept those individual subject comparisons as valid, we would first have to have the same subjects talk about those and possibly other topics repeatedly and determine whether those differences among topics can be replicated. Second, it would be useful to identify what other individual difference variable the topic differences relate to.

There is one additional set of analyses that points to a difference in topic, however. We analyzed the same 50-word passages for signs of speech disruption. Basing our analysis on a modified form of Mahl's

(1956) speech disturbance ratio, we devised a composite speech disruption score based primarily on the number of words in sentence fragments and the number of words immediately repeated, and found, using the paired replicates test, significantly ($p < .05$) more speech disruptions when the patients were discussing the "hospitalization" than the "enjoyable things" topic. This result, based on the same sample of male subjects and the same short speech samples as the cloze procedure results, provides further evidence for the conclusion first stated. The genuine difference in topic was reflected in a measure—speech disruption—sensitive to "stress" or emotion, whereas the cloze score, which measures basic communicability in the schizophrenic patient, is little affected by such transient states as are induced by the topics discussed. This result then bolsters the immediacy hypothesis, which states that the peculiar kind of stimulus control found in schizophrenics is generally characteristic of such individuals rather than being a function of momentary changes of state.

4.4.3. Stability of the Cloze Scores over Time

The study described above has shown a stability of the cloze score in schizophrenics over different topics. The question arises further as to stability over repeated speech samples. There are two ways in which one can view the degree to which two successive speech samples produce similar scores: viewed as a test, cloze scores should correlate highly; viewed as a form of behavior under the control of different discriminative stimuli, one might expect differences. To take some extreme examples, one would expect a normal person's speech to a child to be more communicable than the speech to another adult. If the communicability were the same, one might assume there is something wrong with the speaker. How does that relate to our discussion of topic invariance? To answer that question we must reconsider the immediacy hypothesis. It states that schizophrenic behavior is primarily (and generally) controlled by immediate stimuli. What is wrong with such control is not its existence, but its all-pervasiveness. Normal behavior is also at various times controlled by immediate stimuli, but it is also controlled by remote stimuli. To the extent that the occasions for such control—immediate versus remote—vary with discriminative stimuli, one might expect both normals and patients having diagnoses other than schizophrenia to vary in their cloze scores from one speech sample to the next. In other words, topic communicability invariance would be viewed as a form of psychopathology characteristic of schizophrenia. We would view a high correlation between two speech samples from the same speaker as an indication of excessive similarity of kind of stimulus control (in the face of variation in discriminative contingencies) rather than as an index of reliability, particularly if another group of subjects—not expected to be describable by the immediacy hypothesis—would show a low correlation for two speech samples.

We tested the above reasoning at a community outpatient service. Selecting a group of 16 patients who usually came to the clinic approximately once a week, we asked each to talk for five minutes on how things had been going for them for the last week. Seven to ten days later, when these patients came again, they were asked to do the same by the same interviewer. The patients had all been attending the clinic for drug treatment, group therapy, and/or simply to participate in a day program. Eight of the patients (2 female, 6 male; age range 20–55 years, median 32) were diagnosed schizophrenic with a consistent history (as shown by their case records) of the same diagnosis on previous occasions. The other eight patients (3 female, 5 male; age range 20–40 years, median 29.5) had a distribution of diagnoses including alcoholism, paranoid character disorder, acute psychotic episode-nonspecific, and schizoaffective disorder, with a history of varying diagnoses before our study. The resulting tape recorded speech samples were transcribed, and the first 100 words were then prepared as cloze procedure forms. Ten volunteer college students filled in the blanks of all the cloze procedure forms. A rank-order correlation coefficient for the schizophrenic group between the two successive monologues was $+.79$ ($p < .05$); the other group with a variety of nonschizophrenic diagnoses achieved a coefficient of $-.16$ ($p \gg .05$). The results confirm our earlier reasoning, namely, that only the schizophrenic patients—controlled as they are by the consistent immediate stimulus mechanism—would not vary in communicability. What about the general problem of reliability then? The answer would seem to lie in comparing the variation in communicability over different situations and audiences. Rather than looking for an absolute degree of correlation over a group, we must systematically control the conditions under which the speech is emitted, expecting the same amount of communicability only when those conditions are the same, with increasing variation as they are altered.

We do not have much data here yet, and more research is clearly needed. But the idea of viewing invariance of behavior over many different conditions is worth pursuing.

4.4.4. *The Effect of Marijuana on Communicability*

The use of drugs in our society has much increased and so have the resultant forms of psychopathology. Unfortunately, the use of the drugs and their alleged effects are surrounded by two mythologies— one extolling the great wonders they produce, the other warning of the horrors they induce. Clearly, what is needed is data collected systematically under double-blind conditions in which neither subject nor experimenter know who is getting the active drug at any particular time. Tapes and transcripts of 12 monologues collected from 4 subjects under such conditions were generously made available to us by Zeidenberg, Clark, Jaffe, Anderson, Chin, and Malitz (1973).[2] A detailed description of the subject population and experimental procedures is to be found in their article. Four male residents between the ages of 25 and 29 at the New York State Psychiatric Institute volunteered as subjects. They were told with each administration of both the THC (Δ^9 tetrahydrocannabinol) and matching placebo capsules that they were getting THC, the exact amount of which the experimenters did not know. They were administered a 15 mg dosage of THC for the drug condition. The collection of the first speech sample was carried out in the morning under placebo, the second around midday of the peak of the drug effect ($1\frac{1}{2}$ hours after drug ingestion in three subjects and 1 hour afterward for one subject), and the third later in the afternoon of the same day in a guest apartment of the Psychiatric Institute normally used for visiting scientists. Each subject was instructed to speak continuously for 5 minutes on one or several topics he could choose from a list provided by the experimenter. Testing of the subjects included a memory and a perception of thermal stimulation task in addition to the speech task.

The total speech samples were transcribed and converted into cloze form. They were filled in by groups of Indiana University student volunteers.[3] The results are presented in Table 4.1. All statistical compari-

---

[2] We wish to express our thanks to Drs. Phillip Zeidenberg, W. Crawford Clark, Joseph Jaffe, Samuel W. Anderson, Susan Chin, and Sidney Malitz, who did the original study (and to Dr. Michael Natale, who was working on a content analysis of the speech samples at the time we did the cloze procedure study), for allowing us to use the speech samples collected in their study.

[3] Dr. David Pisoni of Indiana University generously administered some of our cloze forms to student subjects.

Table 4.1.
Mean Cloze Scores and Paired Replicates Test Results for the Marijuana Passages

Subject[a]		Pre-drug	Drug	Post-drug	No. of pairs of clozers in comparison
A	No. of words in sample	682	790	713	
		.43(T)[b] —— $p \ll .01$ ——▶ .36(T)		——▶ .38(U)	14
			NS	NS	12
		.42(T) ◀————————	.34(T) ◀————————	.39(U)	12
B	No. of words in sample	1154	534	864	
		.31(W) ◀—— $.01 < p < .05$ ——	.26(X) ——▶	——▶ .34(X)	12
			NS		10
		.32(W) ◀————————	.27(X) ——— $p < .01$ ——▶	.33(X)	14
C	No. of words in sample	425	354	753	
		.36(Y) ◀—— $p < .01$ ——	.48(V) ——▶	——▶ .41(V)	15
			NS		15
		.36(Y) ◀————————	.47(V) ——— $p \ll .01$ ——▶	.40(V)	20
D	No. of words in sample	879	844	589	
		.42(Z) ——— NS ——▶ .47(Y)		——▶ .41(U)	14
			NS	NS	12
		.43(Z) ◀————————	.47(Y) ◀————————	.43(U)	12

[a] Letters correspond to subjects in Zeidenberg et al. (1973).
[b] T, U, . . . Z refer to different groups of clozers (Indiana University student volunteers). The length of the speech samples and the limit on clozers' time meant that only 2 speech samples could be presented to a given clozer. Where data from different clozers are compared, pairs of clozers are matched across speech samples to within no more than a one-word difference in cloze score on a standard passage given to all clozers

sons were done with the same clozers filling in the passages being compared or by groups of clozers consisting of different subjects matched
in pairs within a 1-word difference in cloze score on a Standard Passage.
All statistical comparisons made use of the paired replicates test. Table
4.1. shows that pre- and post-drug conditions (placebos) are never significantly different from one another, even when one or both are significantly different from the drug condition; in other words, communicability returns to its baseline level. With respect to the effect of THC
relative to the placebo condition, two subjects showed a lowering of
communicability, one an increase in communicability, and one no
difference. What saves this result from simply demonstrating random
effects is the pattern of direction of difference. For example, although
Subject 3 had a significantly *higher* communicability score when taking
THC, whereas Subject 2 had a significantly *lower* communicability in
the drug condition, both subjects showed the effect of post-drug return
to pre-drug level. The same kind of consistent pattern, although not
statistically significant in some instances, was also found for the other
two subjects.

The study (Zeidenberg *et al.*, 1973) from which the speech samples
were obtained often found effects consistent in direction over the four
subjects. Why then did the cloze procedure yield results that are inconsistent over subjects (although consistent within subjects)? The answer lies in the complexity of the phenomenon being measured by the
cloze procedure as opposed to such basic measures as pause, phrase,
and vowel length used in the Zeidenberg study. The more complex
communicability measure showed how subjects might characteristically
respond to THC in a social situation. It demonstrates that, even though
subjects might consistently increase in pause length, more complex phenomena—dependent not only on these basic mechanisms but also on
the responses to those changes—are differently affected because of the
different conditioning histories. Thus, one subject finding himself paus-
ing more might use those pauses to choose his words more carefully
than when speaking more fluently (thus showing an increase in communicability to THC), whereas another might respond to his difficulty
in speaking as fast as usual by saying whatever pops into his head
without considering his words as he usually does. In other words, the
same physiologically induced change acts as a discriminative stimulus
for one subject to monitor his speech and for another to largely ignore

it. Furthermore, the cloze procedure, unlike the techniques used in the Zeidenberg study, lends itself to statistical analysis for each subject and thus is especially useful for finding individual differences. Finally, the results of this study may be said to reflect the situation with respect to drugs as it is commonly experienced, with contrasting effects reported by different people. The advantage of the cloze procedure is that it provides objective quantitative evidence that could be used to identify different kinds of drug responders. Naturally, further research is needed to establish such use.

4.5. Final Comment

This brief review of our work with the cloze procedure shows the many uses to which a particular technique can be successfully put. It proves also, we hope, that inspiration for work in science comes from many sources, with the inspiration produced by method being a fruitful one. We might add that many other methods have been at least equally inspiring; see, for example, the memory drum, the pursuit rotor, the tachistoscope, the electroencephalogram, and the one-way vision screen.

The reader will note that we have carefully avoided any mention of the question which continues to come up for cognitive psychologists, namely, the relationship between language and thought. As radical behaviorists, we have no difficulty accepting the idea of private events such as thought. The importance of self-instruction in solving both intellectual and social problems, for example, is undeniable. We also assume—in the absence of any evidence to the contrary—that, generally speaking, thought does not differ qualitatively from such activities as speaking and writing (for verbal thought) or from looking and listening (for what cognitive psychologists call "imaging").

As methodological behaviorists, we believe that little is to be gained from discussing various relationships between language and thought as long as we are measuring language but merely speculating about thought.

All of which, we hope, explains why we have dealt only with language behavior in this chapter and have simply assumed that our findings probably reflect thought as much as language behavior.

ACKNOWLEDGMENTS

The authors thank Richard Sanders, Ilene Weil, Andrew Glover, George Gavora, and Seth Narrett for assistance in data collection and tabulation.

4.6. References

Hammer, M., Polgar, S., & Salzinger, K. Speech predictability and social contact patterns in an informal group. *Human Organization*, 1969, *28*, 235–242.

Mahl, G. F. Disturbances and silences in the patient's speech in psychotherapy. *Journal of Abnormal and Social Psychology*, 1956, *53*, 1–15.

McGhie, A., & Chapman, J. Disorders of attention and perception in early schizophrenia. *British Journal of Medical Psychology*, 1961, *34*,103–116.

Miller, G. A., & Selfridge, J. A. Verbal context and the recall of meaningful material. *American Journal of Psychology*, 1950, *63*, 176–185.

Salzinger, K. Shift in judgment of weights as a function of anchoring stimuli and instructions in early schizophrenics and normals. *Journal of Abnormal and Social Psychology*, 1957, *55*, 43–49.

Salzinger, K. *Schizophrenia: Behavioral aspects*. New York: Wiley, 1973.

Salzinger, K. A behavioral analysis of diagnosis. In R. L. Spitzer & D. F. Klein (Eds.), *Critical issues in psychiatric diagnosis*. New York: Raven, 1978.

Salzinger, K. Schizophrenia. In A. E. Kazdin, A. S. Bellack, & M. Herson (Eds.), *New perspectives in abnormal psychology*. New York: Oxford University Press, 1980.

Salzinger, K., Hammer, M., Portnoy, S., & Polgar, S. K. Verbal behaviour and social distance. *Language and Speech*, 1970, *13*, 25–37.

Salzinger, K., & Pisoni, S. Reinforcement of affect responses of schizophrenics during the clinical interview. *Journal of Abnormal and Social Psychology*, 1958, *57*, 84–90.

Salzinger, K., & Pisoni, S. Reinforcement of verbal affect responses of normal subjects during the interview. *Journal of Abnormal and Social Psychology*, 1960, *60*, 127–130.

Salzinger, K., & Pisoni, S. Some parameters of the conditioning of verbal affect responses in schizophrenic subjects. *Journal of Abnormal and Social Psychology*, 1961, *63*, 511–516.

Salzinger, K., & Portnoy, S. Verbal conditioning in interviews: Application to chronic schizophrenics and relationship to prognosis for acute schizophrenics. *Journal of Psychiatric Research*, 1964, *2*, 1–9.

Salzinger, K., Portnoy, S., & Feldman, R. S. The effect of order of approximation to the statistical structure of English on the emission of verbal responses. *Journal of Experimental Psychology*, 1962, *64*, 52–57.

Salzinger, K., Portnoy, S., & Feldman, R. S. Experimental manipulation of continuous speech in schizophrenic patients. *Journal of Abnormal and Social Psychology*, 1964, *68*, 508–516. (a)

Salzinger, K., Portnoy, S., & Feldman, R. S. Verbal behavior of schizophrenic and normal subjects. *Annals of the New York Academy of Sciences*, 1964, *105*, 845–860. (b)

Salzinger, K., Portnoy, S., & Feldman, R. S. Verbal behavior in schizophrenics and some comments toward a theory of schizophrenia. In P. Hoch & J. Zubin (Eds.), *Psychopathology of schizophrenia*. New York: Grune & Stratton, 1966.

Salzinger, K., Portnoy, S., & Feldman, R. S. Intrusions in schizophrenic speech: The immediacy hypothesis vs. the lapse of attention hypothesis. *Comprehensive Psychiatry*, 1977, *18*, 255–261.

Salzinger, K., Portnoy, S., & Feldman, R. S. Communicability deficit in schizophrenics resulting from a more general deficit. In S. Schwartz (Ed.), *Language and cognition in schizophrenia*. Hillsdale, N.J.: Lawrence Erlbaum, 1978.

Salzinger, K., Portnoy, S., Pisoni, D., & Feldman, R. S. The immediacy hypothesis and response-produced stimuli in schizophrenic speech. *Journal of Abnormal Psychology*, 1970, *76*, 258–264.

Taylor, W. L. Cloze procedure: A new tool for measuring readability. *Journalism Quarterly*, 1953, *30*, 415–433.

Wurster, S. A. Effects of anchoring on weight judgments of normals and schizophrenics. *Journal of Personality and Social Psychology*, 1965, *1*, 274–278.

Zeidenberg, P., Clark, W. C., Jaffe, J., Anderson, S. W., Chin, S., & Malitz, S. Effect of oral administration of Δ^9 tetrahydrocannabinol on memory, speech, and perception of thermal stimulation: Results with four normal human volunteer subjects. Preliminary Report. *Comprehensive Psychiatry*, 1973, *14*, 549–556.

Sheldon M. Frank, Mario I. Rendon, and
Gregory Siomopoulous

LANGUAGE IN HALLUCINATIONS OF ADOLESCENT SCHIZOPHRENICS[1]

5.1. Introduction

This study, which is part of Rendon, Frank, and Siomopoulous's (1977) investigations of the phenomenology of hallucinations in adolescents, relates to the rather sparse literature on language in abnormal states of consciousness. In our review of that literature, we found that these states may be classified as (1) sleep (including REM dream-stages and hypnogogic/hypnopompic states), (2) physiological alterations (secondary to brain pathology, convulsions, or drugs), and (3) alterations secondary to a mental disorder, especially schizophrenia.

With regard to dreaming, many researchers regarded Freud's (1900, 1911) conception of "primary process" organization as applying not only to the symbolic representational aspects of dreams but also to the language of the narration and of the spoken language within the dream. Examples of such organization would include the condensation and

[1] This paper was presented to the annual meeting of the American Academy of Child Psychiatry, San Diego, October 1978.

Sheldon M. Frank ● Departments of Psychiatry and Pediatrics, University of Miami, D-29, P.O. Box 016960, Miami, Florida 33101. *Mario I. Rendon* ● 333 East 30 Street, New York, New York 10016. *Gregory Siomopoulous* ● Army Medical Department, Athens, Greece.

displacement of elements, the equivalence of negated and/or denied elements or propositions with their positive counterparts, and the lack of distinction of time- and person-designation.

With regard to spoken words in dreams, Fisher (1976) assembled laboratory evidence to refine Isakower's (1954) conclusion from psychoanalytic data that they represented exclusively superego manifestations, such as commands, injunctions, and self-criticism. Baudry (1974), also cited by Fisher and also employing psychoanalytic data, found such phenomena only rarely in dreams but more commonly in hypnogogic and hypnopompic states. Both Baudry and Fisher stressed the difference between REM dreams and non-REM phenomena such as night terrors. Language in the non-REM states is more likely to be comprised of short, interjective, and affectively loaded elements, with accompanying physiological manifestations of anxiety.[2] Language in the REM dreams contains drive and defense elements as well as some superego contributions, which are rarer than Isakower believed. The interposition of waking phenomenon[3] in the preparation of the dream narrative was felt by Fisher to explain Isakower's overemphasis on superego elements.

The literature on language in physiologically abnormal states has been dominated by Jaffe, Fink, and Weinstein, all of whom emphasized semantic and lexical-statistic qualities of language, such as denial and type-token ratio as respective examples. Thus, Jaffe, Fink, and Kahn (1960) reported increased negation and the displacement of person and tense as well as decreased type-token ratio after electroconvulsive therapy. Fink, Jaffe, and Kahn (1960) had similar findings in drug-induced states, and Weinstein and Kahn (1955) found some of the same phenomena in various types of cortical pathology. In a less systematic study of a few subjects, Landon and Fisher (1970) compared written language samples in normal and hallugenogenic, drug-induced, creative states. Of some relevance to our current study are their findings of the shorter length of clauses and sentences in the abnormal states.

Language in schizophrenia, that is, the language of the *patient* with that condition, has frequently been studied. Recent investigators and reviewers include Brown (1972), Carpenter (1976), Chaika (1974), Maher (1972), Salzinger, Portnoy, and Feldman (1964), and Tucker and Rosen-

[2] But see Arkin (1966) for a review of the rarely occurring monologues and dialogues—
sometimes complex—in non-REM sleep.
[3] Includes superego elements.

berg (1975). It is difficult to summarize current opinion as a specific consensus is not apparent. Generally agreed upon aspects of relevance to the present study include:

1. Relative rarity of "word-salad" phenomena with grossly distorted semantics, syntax, and thought apparent in nearly every sentence; restriction of such phenomena to certain patients, usually in an acute phase, though subtle semantic abnormalities may be discerned clinically and by computer-assisted linguistic analysis.
2. Essentially normal parameters of syntax and sentence length by schizophrenics in an interview situation.
3. Lack of superego-like phenomena (absent also in the physiological states mentioned above) ascribed to certain states of sleep and dreaming.

The language of the voices hallucinated by patients in schizophrenia (or other mental disorders) has not been investigated to the best of our knowledge.[4] Clinical teaching, in some of our training, often included the following hypothesis: In the course of schizophrenia, auditory hallucinations follow a typical natural course, beginning as sounds, and progressing through single words (often the patient's name), and short sentences, to a final stage of more complex sentences. Auditory hallucinations are felt commonly to possess the character of superego communications: *imperatives, injunctions, self-criticisms*—often concise, authoritative, and including addressing the patient by name.

Against this background, our aim has been to survey a population of adolescent schizophrenics, who report auditory hallucinations, and to assess the linguistic structure and function of the hallucinated utterances. We have been guided by Shapiro and Fish's (1969) concept of separate analyses of *morphology* and *communicativeness* (applied by them to the study of language of childhood schizophrenics), the latter conceived of in a Piagetian fashion and assessed by assignment of an utterance into one of two communicative (*appeal speech* and *signal/symbol speech*) or three noncommunicative categories. Our structural analysis included Brown's (1973) frequently used method of measuring MLU's

---

[4] Since this chapter was written, an article has appeared by Linn (1977), in which the language of (adult and adolescent) schizophrenics was found to have the following characteristics: *multiple-voices sensed as source; mainly 2nd with some 3rd person verbs; "predominantly disparaging, call opprobious names, or are accusatory."*

(mean length of utterance) as well as sentence-type analysis as developed by Frank (Blank & Frank, 1971; Frank, Allen, Stein, & Myers, 1976) for assessing syntactic transformation rules (Chomsky, 1957, Roberts, 1964). Before turning to the specifics of our methodology, let us summarize our assumptions and hypotheses.

Included in our assumptions are the following notions, based on earlier clinical observations and on our psychoanalytic orientation:

1. Hallucination of voices is *restitutive* in function for a schizophrenic, particularly vis-à-vis his or her defects in thinking and in object relations.
2. The voices often carry the functions of the superego and, as such, may resemble a regressed view of parental commands and/or injunctions.

Our hypotheses are that the quoted language of hallucinated voices in adolescent schizophrenics, as compared with the language of the subjects themselves speaking in a nonhallucinating state, would reveal the following:

1. *Structure*
   (a) Shorter, less complex sentences
   (b) Greater proportion of imperatives and vocatives
   (c) Relative absence of "word salad" type and other "schizophrenic" language behavior
   (d) Verbs predominantly in the second person and in the present tense
2. *Communicativeness*: Greater proportion of communicative speech (Shapiro, 1969) than of noncommunicative speech, with *appeal speech* the major category

5.2. Method

All admissions to the adolescent service of Bellevue Psychiatric Hospital between October 1, 1974, and September 30, 1975, were considered for our study. Charts were reviewed following admissions, and special interviews were arranged (with Dr. Siomopoulous, except in a few cases, Dr. Rendon) within one week of admission for all patients who had auditory hallucinations as a sign or symptom. The patients were all aged 13 through 16 and of working-class or welfare-class status.

Complete demographic data, in which the subjects are typical of the inner city New York population, are given in Rendon *et al.* (1977).

Each of the 44 subjects selected in this way was asked, in the special interview, a series of 14 questions about the content, nature, history, and other aspects of his or her hallucinations (Rendon *et al.*, 1977). Their answers were transcribed verbatim for later analysis. After the routine hospitalization of the patients, including independent discharge diagnosis, the transcripts were analyzed for parameters derived from the above hypotheses by Drs. Frank and Rendon, who did not have access to the diagnosis at the time of analysis and who analyzed them independently. (Inter-rater reliability was nearly 100%, with the few discrepancies readily resolvable.) For this particular study, the 19 patients who had a diagnosis of schizophrenia and who provided analyzable data were the subjects. The linguistic data included the subjects' quotation of utterances of the hallucinated voices and their answers to two of the questions asked in the special interview, which served as control utterances.

For each group of utterances (hallucinated and control), the following parameters were scored (see Section 5.3., for definitions):

1. *Sentence structure.* Mean average MLU per subject, mean maximum MLU, total number of 1-word utterances per group, total number of ungrammatical clauses per group, total number of "schizophrenic" language features per group, mean number of transformational rules, total number of different transformations per group
2. *Transformation and verb analysis.* Different individual transformational rules and frequency of occurrence; person and tense of verbs used, with frequencies.
3. *Communicativeness.* Frequency of utterances of communicative and noncommunicative speech, with subcategories of Shapiro (1969)

5.3. Results

The 19 subjects produced a total of 38 utterances which they perceived as coming from a hallucinated voice (or, rarely, voices). The range was from 1 to 4 utterances per subject, with a mean and median of 2.

It was therefore decided to take 2 utterances per subject from the responses to questions in the special interview. The response to question No. IX[5] was used for each subject. Since, in any case, responses were shorter, less complex utterances than spontaneous utterances, and these responses contained many one-word utterances, the longest response to the other questions was taken as the second sample sentence for each subject. Thus, there were 38 control utterances.

Table 5.1., shows the length and complexity of the hallucinated and the control utterances. For each subject, the mean MLU and maximum MLU[6] of their utterances was calculated. The group of hallucinated utterances had means of 3.3 and 4.2 on these measures, respectively; the group of control utterances had means of 8.9 and 2.4. There were many more one- and two-word utterances in the hallucinated sample. *Ungrammatical kernel sentences*[7] were a minor feature in both groups, usually consisting of omitted verbs. Since several utterances had more than one kernel, the ungrammatical percentage amounted to less than 15% for both groups. Unusual structure, as described by Chaika (1974) and others, was even rarer, occurring in less than 8% of the utterances, also with no difference between the groups.

Turning to the transformations[8] that we employed, we observed first that close to 2 transformations per sentence were used in the control sample and about 1 per utterance in the hallucinated sample. The difference in repertoire of transformations was even more striking. A total of 19 different transformations were employed in the control sample versus 9 in the hallucinated sample. Table 5.2 spells out which transformations were used. The control sample contained a typical repertoire of adolescent-adult spoken English, including many complex transformations. Imperatives and vocatives, scarcely present in the control sample, constituted over three-fourths of the hallucinated sample. In examples of hallucinated utterances, there was a preponderance of simple commands: "Kill," "Wake up," "Hit the teacher," "Act nice." Two-thirds of the utterances were commands to perform violent or self-harming actions; a few were commands to behave better or not to perform such actions.

[5] "Were you in an unusual mood when you heard the voice?"
[6] Calculated as in Brown (1973).
[7] Roughly equal to a clause (see Frank & Seegmiller [1969]).
[8] Types of structure, such as negative, question, etc. (see Chomsky [1957] and Roberts [1964]).

Table 5.1.
Sentence Structure Analysis

	No. of subjects	Total no. of utterances	Mean average MLU	Mean maximum MLU	Total no. of one word utterances	Total no. of ungrammatical kernels	Total no. of "schizophrenic" language abnormalities	Mean no. of t's per utterances	Total no. of different t's
Hallucinated utterances	19	38	3.3	4.2 (range 1–10)	8	9	2	1.1	9
Control utterances	19	38	8.9	12.4 (range 6–28)	2	7	3	1.9	19
Significance (2-tailed t-test)			$p < .05$	$p < .05$				$p < .10$	$p < .05$

Table 5.2.
Transformation and Verb Analysis

Type of transformation	No. present in hallucinated utterances	No. present in control utterances
Imperative	25	1
Vocative	4	0
Interjection	4	4
Relative	0	3 (2 types)
Subordordinate	0	10
Negative	1	8
"do"	1	9
Conjunction	1	11 (2 types)
Series	1	4 (2 types)
Object	1	7
Reflexive	1	2
6 other types (to, V–NP, apposition, indirect object, "like", V–adj.)	0	10 (total)
Person of verb		
First	3	31
Second	27	2
Third	1	15
Tense of verb		
Present	30	27
Past	0	15
Future	1	1
Conditional	0	3
Subjunctive	0	2

Verb analysis is seen at the bottom of Table 5.2. Over 60% of verbs in the control sample were in the first person, about 30% in the third person, with less than 5% in the second person. The second person dominated the hallucinated sample, with just under 90% of verbs falling in that category. With regard to tense, also, the hallucinated sample was overwhelmingly in one category—the present tense (over 95%)—whereas the control sample verbs comprised only 55% of the present tense, with 29% past tense, and 10% in complex tenses (subjunctive and conditional). Interestingly, in both samples, there was only one occurrence of a future tense verb (less than 3%).

In an analysis of communicativeness (Shapiro's *functional analysis* [1969]), over 80% of the hallucinated utterances could be seen to fall into the *appeal* subcategory of communicative speech (see Table 5.3.), about

Table 5.3.
Communicativeness

	Communicative speech		Noncommunicative speech
	Appeal	Signal/symbol	
Number of hallucinated utterances	31	6	1
Number of control utterances	0	38	0

15% into the other communicative subcategory—*signal/symbol* speech, and only 1 utterance was a noncommunicative utterance. In the control utterances, 100% fell into the *signal/symbol* subcategory.

5.4. Discussion

Many of the group differences that were found support our assumption of a restitutive aspect of the hallucinations. From the standpoint of object relations, the voices "behaved" as a person relating to the subject, using language that was communicative and in the second person, with frequent use of the vocative transformation. In these ways, the voice(s) may be seen to substitute for real objects, with which relations may be minimal and/or conflict-ridden in the psychotic state of the subject; it is a language of relationship.[9] The preponderant use of the present tense added an immediacy to this hallucinated relationship, perhaps adding to the illusion of reality.

Restitution was also a way to approach the nature of thought processes seen in the language of the voices as well. With one exception ("Libras are lovers"—interpreted by the subject as a command to kill his mother), there were no gross examples of the "primary process" related language found in word salad or in loosened associations. Utterances were short, to the point, usually grammatical. What they expressed in content was often close to drive material, especially aggressive drive; the form remained remarkably "secondary process" in its manifest appearance. Thus, the "voices" may serve a purpose of cognitive and linguistic simplification and organization. However, because

[9] It is also a *self-representation*; the projection vitiates need for the first person verb.

the control utterances were also relatively free of schizophrenic-like and ungrammatical features prevented us from overemphasizing this fact. (It may be that the interview from which control data were derived was given too late and, thus, that the two groups of utterances were produced in different mental states for a comparison to be made.)

The assumption of a superego aspect in the hallucinated voices was also borne out by the linguistic data. As we have seen, commands (imperative transformation) and injunctions abounded, though there was little in the way of self-criticism in these subjects. The short, noncomplex, and well-formed nature of the hallucinated utterances was reminiscent of the specially tailored language a parent normally produces in conversation with his or her child or infant. The mean MLU level, as well as the types of transformations employed, were similar to those parameters in the language of mothers speaking to a child in the third year of life (Frank, Allen, Stein, & Myers, 1976). Again the form and content were disparate: the parent- and superego-like language were urging gratifications of drives that were usually forbidden by these agencies. The self-directed violence, of course, can be seen as punishment, and perhaps the other-directed violence as identification with the cruel, vengeful parent fantasized by the pre-oedipal child. Suffice it to say that, in this preliminary study, superego elements abounded in the hallucinated data. Further study, especially toward an indepth, individually oriented correlation of voices and psychodynamics might elucidate this further.

Some further problems that should be approached in future investigations include the role of the nature of the particular sample of subjects and the importance of the relatively early point in the developmental course of schizophrenic illness. With regard to the sample, its social class and geographical nature may have made superego issues seen unduly important. Furthermore, under current criteria of hospital admissions, it may be that patients with problems in that area would be more likely to be admitted.

As far as the time course is concerned, it may be that (as our clinical teachers told us) at this early point the hallucinated utterances are indeed short and simple but will grow more complex with time.

Our clinical impression is that there is something inherent in the phenomenon of schizophrenia that, transcending these alternative explanations, pushes hallucinated language in the directions reported in this preliminary work: toward short, simple, communicative utterances. For more of the phemomenology, course, and meaning of these findings, we must await further work by ourselves and others.

5.5. References

Arkin, A. Sleep-talking: A review. *Journal of Nervous and Mental Disorders*, 1966, *143*, 101–122.

Baudry, F. Remarks on spoken words in the dream. *Psychoanalytic Quarterly*, 1974, *43*, 581–605.

Blank, M. & Frank, S. Story recall in kindergartent children. *Child Development*, 1971, *42*, 299–312.

Brown, R. Schizophrenia, language and reality. *American Psychologist*, 1972, *28*, 395–403.

Brown, R. A first language. The early stages. Cambridge, Mass.: Harvard University, Press, 1973.

Carpenter, M. Sensitivity to syntactic structure: Good versus poor premorbid schizophrenics. *Journal of Abnormal Psychology*, 1976, *85*, 41–50.

Chaika, E. A linguist looks at "schizophrenic" language. *Brain and Language*, 1974, *1*, 257–276.

Chomsky, N. *Syntactic Structures*. The Hague: Mouton, 1957.

Fink, M., Jaffe, J., & Kahn R. Drug induced changes in interview patterns: Linguistic and neurophysiologic indices. In G. Sarwer-Foner (Ed.), *The dynamics of psychiatric drug therapy*. Springfield, Ill.: C. C. Thomas, 1960.

Fisher, C. Spoken words in dreams. A critique of the views of Otto Isakower. *Psychoanalytic Quarterly*, 1976, *45*, 100–109.

Frank, S., Allen, D., Stein, L., & Myers, B. Linguistic performance in vulnerable and autistic children and their mothers. *American Journal of Psychiatry*, 1976, *133*, 909–915.

Freud, S. The interpretation of dreams (1900). In The standard edition of the complete psychological works of Sigmund Freud, Vols. 4 and 5. London: Hogarth, 1953.

Freud, S. Formulations regarding the two principles of mental functioning (1911). In The Standard Edition of the psychological works of Sigmund Freud, Vol. 11. London: Hogarth, 1953.

Isakower, O. Spoken words in dreams: A preliminary communication. *Psychoanalytic Quarterly*, 1954, *23*, 1–6.

Jaffe, J., Fink, M., & Kahn, R. Changes in verbal transactions with induced altered brain function. *Journal of Nervous and Mental Disease*, 1960, *130*, 235–239.

Landon, G., & Fischer, R. On common features of the language of creative performance and hallucinogenic-drug-induced creative experience. In W. Keup, (Ed.), *Origins and mechanisms of hallucinations*. New York: Plenum, 1970.

Linn, E. Verbal auditory hallucinations: Mind, self, and society. *Journal of Nervous and Mental Disorders*, 1977, *164*, 1.

Maher, B. The language of schizophrenia: A review and interpretation. *British Journal of Psychiatry*, 1972, *120*, 3–17.

Rendon, M. Frank, S., & Siomopoulous, T. *Hallucinations in adolescents*. Unpublished manuscript, 1977.

Roberts, P. *English Syntax*. New York: Harcourt Brace Jovanovich, 1964.

Salzinger, K., Portnoy, S., & Feldman, R. S. Verbal behavior of schizophrenic and normal subjects. *Annals of the New York Academy of Science*, 1964, *105*, 845–860.

Shapiro, T., & Fish, B. A method of study language deviation as an aspect of ego organization in young schizophrenic children. *Journal of the Academy of Child Psychiatry*, 1969, *8*, 36–56.

Tucker, G., & Rosenberg, S. Computer content analysis of schizophrenic speech: A preliminary report. *American Journal of Psychiatry*, 1975, *132*, 611–616.

Weinstein, E. A. & Kahn, R. L. *Denial of illness: Symbolic and physiological aspects.* Springfield, Ill.: C. C Thomas, 1955.

PART III

SEMANTICS IN
PSYCHOPATHOLOGY

Luis R. Marcos and Murray Alpert

BILINGUALISM
IMPLICATIONS FOR THE EVALUATION OF PSYCHOPATHOLOGY

6.1. Introduction

Our purposes in this chapter are twofold: to contribute to the quality of mental health care delivered to bilingual patients and to add to our understanding of the psychopathology. Bilingual patients present a challenge to our mental health service delivery system because they far exceed the number of competent bilingual clinicians. Although it would be argued that communication between doctor and patient is crucial in any branch of medicine, in psychiatry it is the central issue, and there are no alternative laboratory procedures. By the same token, the bilingual patient presents a unique opportunity for study of questions concerning the role of cognition in psychopathology. Thus, two issues can be distinguished: one we have termed *the language barrier*, which inhibits communication in the language in which the patient is less proficient; the second, *language independence*, attempts to explore the implications of different language codes acquired in different pragmatic contexts.

Luis R. Marcos ● Department of Psychiatry, New York University School of Medicine, New York, New York 10016, and Department of Psychiatry, Gouverneur Hospital, New York, New York 10002. *Murray Alpert* ● Department of Psychology, New York University School of Medicine, New York, New York 10016.

For the past years at New York University School of Medicine, the psychiatric assessment of bilingual patients has been the subject of several studies. A consistent finding has been that the clinicians' frame of reference applicable to the monolingual patient is not equally appropriate for the evaluation of psychopathology in patients who are affected by cross-language factors. For example, psychiatric examinations of a group of Spanish-American bilingual schizophrenic patients disclosed more severe psychopathology when the patients were interviewed in English than when the interview was conducted in Spanish (Marcos, Alpert, Urcuyo, & Kesselman, 1973). In this study, the patients were found to exhibit higher levels of somatic concern, motor tension, mannerisms, anxiety, hostility, depressive mood, and emotional withdrawal in the English language interviews. Although several factors may have been responsible for the results (e.g., clinicians' negative or positive prejudice, the language barrier, cultural misunderstanding, or a combination of all), subsequent studies (Marcos, Urcuyo, Kesselman, & Alpert, 1973) have shown that the switch in the language of the interview had a significant effect on the content, paralinguistic, and motor components of the patients' communicative behavior. The participating patients were all subordinate bilinguals or individuals whose linguistic performance showed a differential competence in the two languages. In comparison with their dominant language, in their nondominant language these bilinguals revealed lexical, syntactic, and phonetic deficit. Therefore, this chapter will describe the effects of the patient's bilingual condition on the evaluation of specific areas of psychopathology.

6.1.1. Bilingualism

As an introductory step, let us broadly define bilingualism as the practice of speaking two languages, and bilinguals as the individuals involved (Marcos, 1976a). In this chapter we will focus on major bilingual dimensions such as the *language barrier* or linguistic deficit in the nondominant language, and the *language independence* or bilinguals' capacity to maintain two alternate experiential inner worlds associated with the languages. Also, it is important to consider the bilinguals' view of their own languages as either additive to or subtractive from their image and social status.

6.1.2. The Mental Status Examination

The Mental Status Examination is the systematic record of a range of areas of the patient's behavior relevant to the assessment of psychopathological states. These data are obtained by direct examination of the patient's spontaneous verbal and nonverbal behaviors as well as the patient's response to the specific questions of the clinician. The mental status constitutes the foundation of the psychiatric diagnostic process. It includes the descriptive evaluation of the patient's appearance, motor behavior, speech, intellectual functioning, affect, and his or her attitude and reactions to the examiner.

6.2. Bilingualism Effects on Mental Status

6.2.1. Attitude

This component of the mental status includes a range of behavioral dimensions such as patients' cooperativeness, responsiveness, alertness, and attention. We have observed that subordinate bilingual patients who struggle with the language barrier tend to behave rather passively and submissively in psychiatric interviews. This attitude is often paradoxically interpreted by the clinician as an indication of guarded behavior in the sense of "unwillingness" to cooperate with the interviewer.

Apart from the patient's frequent culturally "preset" unfavorable expectation of the English-speaking examiner, there are a number of nondominant language behaviors which can create the impression of slow and reluctant participation in the interview process. Thus, in a comparative content analysis of the speech of subordinate bilingual schizophrenic patients whose dominant language was Spanish, and who had been interviewed in both English and Spanish, there was a striking tendency by the patients to answer the English questions with short sentences, a word, or even a silent pause (Marcos, Urcuyo, Kesselman & Alpert, 1973). In fact, these patients, when interviewed in English, produced a significantly higher number of expressions such as "I don't know," "I don't think so," "No Sir," all of them easily interpreted by the clinicians as defensive reluctance to communicate.

The patient's own feelings about the language of the interview may easily permeate his or her attitude toward the interviewing clinician. In general, subordinate bilingual patients show a preference to be interviewed in their dominant language. This may be consonant with the concept of "language loyalty" proposed by Weinreich (1953) as a form of ethnocentrism. In the course of our work, however, we have studied situations in which a primarily Spanish-speaking patient has refused to speak in Spanish while expressing his preference to communicate in English. This reaction may be related to the additive-subtractive dimension of bilingualism, and the values and attributes that bilinguals associate to each of their languages (Marcos, Eisma, & Guimon, 1977).

6.2.2. Motor Behavior

The evaluation of the patient's motor activity has always been considered a fundamental part of the mental status assessment. By conceiving body movements as an expressive behavior, clinicians may interpret them as a reflection of the patient's affect (e.g., motor retardation and depression), or the patient's thinking (mannerisms and autism). Clinicians may also utilize the patient's motor behavior to infer about the quality of the interview interaction. Subordinate bilingual schizophrenic patients, when interviewed in their nondominant language, were evaluated by clinicians as exhibiting more motor tension and more mannerisms. Recent studies (Marcos, 1979) have shown that, when subordinate bilinguals communicate in their nondominant language, they produce more hand-movement activity. This extra nonverbal activity has been considered by a group of investigators (Freedman, 1972; Grand, Marcos, Freedman, & Barroso, 1977) to have a facilitatory function in the process of verbalization.

In light of these findings, the clinician assessing the motor behavior of subordinate bilingual patients faces a difficult discriminatory task. Unaware of the motoric component of the nondominant language verbalization process, clinicians may interpret some of these verbalization-related movements as reflecting tension, anxiety, mannerisms, or hyperactivity; thus, ascribing to bilingual patients' psychopathology what belongs to the adaptive task of compensating for a verbalization handicap.

6.2.3. *Speech and Stream of Thought*

The evaluation of the patient's speech and stream of associations constitutes a fundamental component of the mental status. Dimensions such as tone and rate of speech, grammatical and semantic congruency, and concatenation of ideas are evaluated from the verbal productions of the patient. As with other components of the mental status, however, the valid interpretation of these characteristics of the patient's thinking is significantly hampered by linguistic productions which are a result of the patient's bilingual condition.

Consequently, subordinate bilingual patients, when interviewed in their nondominant language, have been found to produce a significantly higher frequency of speech disturbances such as sentence correction, sentence incompletion, stuttering, repetition, omission, incoherent sound, tongue-slip, and "Ah" sound (Marcos, Urcuyo, Kesselman, & Alpert, 1973). Since these speech disturbances have been suggested to be indicators of anxiety in monolingual patients, clinicians may possibly interpret them as such without taking into account that these disturbances may be a consequence of the verbalization work in a nondominant language.

Subordinate bilingual patients, when interviewed in their nondominant language, also show a lower speech rate and longer silent pauses than when the interview is conducted in their dominant language. Thus, it appears that speaking in a second language may have a low activation effect on speech similar to what has been described in depression (Alpert, Frosch, & Fisher, 1967). If the clinician is not aware of this, he or she may interpret these vocal cues as indicators of the patient's depression despite the fact that the patient may be manifesting nondominant language-related signs.

Another related issue is the occurrence of *language mixing* during the nondominant language interviews of subordinate bilingual patients. Thus, a majority of patients utilize dominant language words during their nondominant language interviews. This language intrusion makes their stream of thought sound less logical and more confused.

We therefore see a number of vocal and paralinguistic aspects of verbal behavior which may be interpreted as having clinical significance, whereas they derive from the special problems posed for patients when they are interviewed across the language barrier.

6.2.4. Thought Content

The evaluation of patients' thought content includes the assessment of the patient's present ideation and beliefs, the responsiveness of this ideation to both internal and environmental cues, its congruence with the cultural system, and the richness of the associations.

In the content analysis of the psychiatric interviews of bilingual patients, we have found that on numerous occasions the patients give different responses to the same question in each language. Most often, the nondominant language response suggests greater psychopathology. A critical issue in the interpretation of these findings is whether the greater pathology in the nondominant language is a real one or based on the interview conditions. One might wonder which interview reflects the "true" condition of the patient. It seems reasonable, however, to assume that the interview demands contribute to the manifest level of psychopathology and that, under the lower linguistic demands of the dominant language interview, patients are in fact less sick.

Beyond these linguistic problems, the psychiatric evaluation of thought content involves the assessment of culturally bound attitudes and beliefs which permeate the patient's emotional experience and behavior. For example, the Spanish-American population is characterized by a diversity of cultural values which are often misunderstood or misdiagnosed by clinicians who are unfamiliar with the Spanish culture. Some of these attitudes include the concepts of "spiritualism," "santeria," "respeto," "dignidad," "ataque," "black magic," "visiones," and other culturally bound attitudes such as the disposition toward authority, time notion, and male dominance. We may therefore conclude that a valid evaluation of thought content in bilingual patients requires both familiarity with the effect of bilingualism and knowledge of the patient's culture.

6.2.5. Affect

Affect is the feeling tone or emotion that accompanies an idea. The clinician's task in evaluating the patient's affect is to assess the patient's articulation into words of his or her internal world. Often, however, patients suffering from psychiatric conditions are unable to verbalize their overwhelming experiences. At those times, facial expressions and other nonverbal behavior may convey to the clinician the patient's emotional state.

In general, subordinate bilingual patients are found by clinicians to be more anxious, more depressed, and more emotionally withdrawn when the interview is conducted in their nondominant language than when it is in their dominant language. Apart from the changes in the patients' stream of thought, secondary to the verbalization in a non-dominant language (e.g., longer silent pauses, lower speech rate, etc.), which are often interpreted by clinicians as indicators of depression or anxiety, it is our contention that the process of verbalization in a non-dominant language may constitute an impediment for the emotional involvement of the patient. Thus, the extra cognitive demands placed on subordinate bilinguals when speaking across the language barrier determine a deflection of affect into the task of encoding itself (Marcos, 1976b). In fact, these patients tend to invest their affect primarily in *how* they say things and not so much in *what* thay are saying. Frequently, the patient manifests this effect by verbalizing emotionally charged material without displaying the expected emotion. Furthermore, these patients tend to capitalize in the extra cognitive demands of the non-dominant-language encoding work by making supplementary use of intellectualization, repetition, and reaction formation,which determine their future evasion from emotional involvement.

Another source of distortions in the evaluation of bilingual patients' affect is the language independence condition of some bilinguals (Marcos & Alpert, 1976). In effect, some bilinguals do not simply have a duplex set of words to refer to experiences, but may have alternate and not necessarily congruent experiential inner worlds linked to each of the languages. When a patient's significant experience is verbalized in the language in which it did not take place, the patient may report it and not show the appropriate involvement.

6.3. Recommendations

Clinicians assessing psychopathology in bilingual patients ought to be sensitized to the significance of linguistic factors such as language dominance, language independence, and the patient's attitude toward the language of the interview. A clinician who is unfamiliar with the effects of these bilingual dimensions on the expression of psychopathology can easily misevaluate the patient's mental condition by neglecting the consideration of some communicative cues as bilingualism-related.

6.3.1. The Language Barrier

When a bilingual patient with a language barrier has to be interviewed in the language in which he or she is less competent, the examiner must assure that the patient understands what is being expected. The clinician should introduce redundancy to facilitate communication, and should not accept brief or laconic responses as evidence of depression or emotional withdrawal. Furthermore, cues residing in the patient's motor activity or in the vocal channel of communication should be carefully evaluated before considering them indicators of psychopathology. In addition, clinicians should be familiar with the culturally bound attitudes and beliefs of the bilingual patient.

Psychiatric clinicians should be aware that the language barrier of subordinate bilinguals often interferes with their ability to understand and derive meaning from the interviewer's use of paralinguistic cues such as voice intonation, pauses, and emotional tone. This effect tends to minimize the patient's capacity for involvement in the interview interaction and, thus, his or her motivation. Also, a patient who speaks in a poorly commanded language poses additional demands on clinicians. Apart from the possible misunderstandings of the patient's verbalizations, the clinician faces the difficult task of deciding which of the patient's verbal cues are relevant and which are mere consequences of the language deficit. This imposition upon the clinician may give rise to feelings of frustration, uncertainty about the diagnostic process, and even rejection of the patient.

A thorough language evaluation will permit the clinician to estimate the severity of the language barrier and, subsequently, to anticipate its possible distorting effects as well as to plan strategies to minimize them. Since a mental status examination across the language barrier places tremendous demands on clinicians, they should also be sensitive to their own feelings about the patient and the linguistic constrictions of such an endeavor.

6.3.2. The Language Independence

In regard to the language independence phenomenon, when evaluating the linguistic dimensions of the patient, clinicians ought to explore and look for aspects that are shared by the two languages as well as events that seem unique to either one. This language evaluation will permit assessment of the degree of language independence and help to anticipate areas that may be unavailable in a particular language. Language choice and switching, when used by a linguistically matched clinician, have been found to be useful in the exploration of areas of the bilingual patient's personality that are language specific (Pitta, Marcos, & Alpert, 1978). On a more theoretical level, language switching may also be utilized strategically during the evaluation to promote the patient's uncovering. For instance, it may be advisable to encourage an obsessive patient who uses constant intellectualization and avoidance to verbalize in his first, more emotionally charged, language. Conversely, a hysterical patient whose intense affect interferes with attempts at objectifying issues may become more revealing when encoding experiences in the second, less emotional, language.

It is also important for clinicians to keep in mind the possible defensive functions of language-related mechanisms such as the compartmentalization and repression of an acceptable past ego-identity in an attempt to establish a new one. In this regard, when the clinician and the patient are matched bilinguals, the switch from one language to the other offers the opportunity to explore directly the patient's language-specific sense of self and to analyze its cognitive and affective components.

6.4. References

Alpert, M., Frosch, W. A., & Fisher, S. H. Teaching the perception of expressive aspects of vocal communication. *American Journal of Psychiatry*, 1967, *124*, 202–211.

Freedman, N. The analysis of movement behavior during the clinical interview. In A. Siegman & B. Pope (Eds.), *Studies in Dyadic Communication*. New York: Pergamon, 1972.

Grand, S., Marcos, L. R., Freedman, N, & Barroso, F. Relation of psychopathology and bilingualism to kinesic aspects of interview behavior in schizophrenia. *Journal of Abnormal Psychology*, 1977, *5*, 492–500.

Marcos, L. R. The linguistic dimensions in the bilingual patient. *American Journal of Psychoanalysis*, 1976, *36*, 347–354. (a)

Marcos, L. R. Bilinguals in psychotherapy: Language as an emotional barrier. *The American Journal of Psychotherapy*, 1976, *30*, 552–560. (b)

Marcos, L. R. Hand movements and nondominant fluency in bilinguals. *Perceptual and Motor Skills*, 1979, *48*, 207–214.

Marcos, L. R., & Alpert, M. Strategies and risks in the psychotherapy with bilingual patients: The phenomenon of language independence. *American Journal of Psychiatry*, 1976, *133*, 1275–1278.

Marcos, L. R., Eisma, J., & Guimon, J. Bilingualism and sense of self. *American Journal of Psychoanalysis*, 1977, *37*, 285–290.

Marcos, L. R., Alpert, M., Urcuyo, L., & Kesselman, M. The effect of interview language on the evaluation of psychopathology in Spanish-American schizophrenic patients. *American Journal of Psychiatry*, 1973, *130*, 549–553.

Marcos, L. R. Urcuyo, L., Kesselman, M., & Alpert, M. The language barrier in evaluating Spanish-American patients. *Archives of General Psychiatry*, 1973, *29*, 655–659.

Pitta, P., Marcos, L. R., & Alpert, M. Language switching as a treatment strategy with bilingual patients. *American Journal of Psychoanalysis*, 1978, *38*, 255–258.

Weinreich, U. *Languages in contact.* New York: Publications of the Linguistic Circle of New York, 1953.

7

Donald P. Spence

LEXICAL LEAKAGE

On a number of occasions, Saussure made the statement that nothing is given in linguistics. He meant by this remark (see Culler, 1977) that meaning was largely carried by the relation between words rather than by the words themselves. Unlike sign language which has a certain fixed, iconic quality—the sign for a lie in Plains Indian, for example, is two fingers extended across the lips, or two tongues—signs in written and spoken language are largely arbitrary. Because they are not isomorphic with the signified, they can change with each utterance, and Culler (1977) makes clear how the meaning of any given word is always constrained by the surrounding features in the sentence.

7.1. *Syntagmatic and Paradigmatic Constraints*

Saussure identified two fundamental constraints which operate at all levels of language. Their formal names are paradigmatic and syntagmatic; we can also think of them as vertical and horizontal. Consider the sentence:

(1)   Napoleon lost the battle of Waterloo.

Each word in this sentence enters into a paradigmatic (vertical) relation with other words of the same grammatical class, and a syntagmatic (horizontal) relation with other words in the sentence. Thus, the word

Donald P. Spence ● College of Medicine and Dentistry of New Jersey, Rutgers Medical School, Piscataway, New Jersey 08854.

Napoleon is in opposition to *Wellington, lost* is in opposition to *won,* and *Waterloo* is in opposition to *Egypt.* We can say that words like *Napoleon* and *Wellington,* or *lost* and *won,* belong to the same paradigmatic axis, and that in the process of writing or speaking, we search a series of such axes for the proper words to put in the sentence.

By using a word like *lost,* we are also saying that he did not *win;* the meaning gains by contrast. By choosing any particular word from a given axis to fill the frame of a sentence, we automatically exclude all other words in the axis; thus every time we choose a word we are making at least two assertions. The meaning of the word chosen is reinforced by all the words not chosen.

Syntagmatic (horizontal) relationships define the way in which individual elements may combine in a sequence. In the example just given, *battle* is the object of *lost* in part because it follows the verb; the word order of subject-verb-object in English is one kind of syntagmatic sequence. Syntagmatic relationships acquire particular force in English because English depends so heavily on word order; other languages like Latin, that are more heavily inflected, can often ignore word order and depend on declension to distinguish subject from object—thus, *Brutus necavit Caesarem* is equivalent to *Caesarem necavit Brutus,* although it should be pointed out that even Latin does not tolerate completely random ordering.

Another way to appreciate the impact of the syntagmatic relationship is to omit one word in our specimen sentence and consider what possibilities might be allowed. There are certain constraints on word choice. Suppose we omit *lost;* if we disregarded historical fact we could substitute *won;* we could certainly substitute *fought;* but we could hardly substitute *stole, admonished* or *painted.* Because all words in a sentence belong to a particular syntagmatic relationship, each imposes constraints on the other. Culler (1977) puts the issue this way: "Our knowledge of syntagmatic relations enables us to define [for a given part of a sentence] . . . a particular class of items which can follow it. These items are in paradigmatic contrast with one another" (p. 46).

The more complex the sentence, the more complex the syntagmatic structure. Because of the linear interdependence of all words in the sentence, the meaning of each is modified by the others. At times, the meaning may be amplified, at other times attentuated; it is almost never equivalent to the meaning of the same word in isolation. Because new sentences are always being created, new meanings are always being formed, and we can begin to see that the dictionary definition is, at best, only a crude approximation of how a word can be used. (This is one reason why dictionaries must be constantly brought up-to-date.)

7.2. Speech Faults

Almost all of the classical errors of speech can be generated by relaxing either the syntagmatic or paradigmatic constraints. Each of the mistakes usually found in spoken language—slips of the tongue, spoonerisms, tip-of-the-tongue errors, and the like—can, in fact, be related to a disturbance in either the syntagmatic or paradigmatic code. We now consider each of these errors in turn, first giving examples and then analyzing the source of the disturbance. We begin with the syntagmatic errors.

7.2.1. Syntagmatic Errors

7.2.1.1. Spoonerisms. The classical spoonerism consists of a transposition of the consonant sounds of two words; the following example is attributed to the Reverend Spooner himself:

(2)   You have tasted your worm, hissed my mystery lectures, and you must catch
        the first town drain. (Cited in Cuddon, 1977, p. 636)

The syntagmatic constraint is not sufficiently strong to withstand the transposition of consonants, but it does not give way altogether; thus, the ghosts of the original words can be sensed and, because it is both right and not right at the same time, the sentence becomes funny. Furthermore, we usually find that the errors in a spoonerism usually conform to syntactic principles (as in the first two phrases of the specimen just quoted); in fact, it is this syntagmatic agreement which most probably allows it to be spoken in the first place. What makes it primarily a syntagmatic dislocation is the fact that the ingredients for the errors can all be found within the frame of the presumably intended sentence: "tasted your worm" is a transposition of "wasted your term"; "hissed my mystery lectures" a transpose of "missed my history lectures"; and "town drain" a transpose of "down train" (the train from Oxford to London). Because all the ingredients are present in the sentence, paradigmatic alternatives (word choices that lie outside the sentence frame) are not relevant to this particular speech fault.

Further evidence that a spoonerism is a syntagmatic dislocation comes from a series of experiments by Motley and Baars (1976) and Baars and Motley (1976). In the typical case, a pair of target words (e.g., *sat feet*) is preceded by a cueing pair (e.g., *large rear*); when the subject tries to pronounce the target words following the cueing words under somewhat speeded conditions, he will frequently produce the spoonerism *fat seat*. Were this a paradigmatic mistake, we would get errors like *large feet*; the fact that a spoonerism is produced instead, composed of interchanged consonants taken from the original target sentence, suggests a syntagmatic dislocation. In this experiment, the cueing stimulus seems to promote the transposition of initial consonants.

7.2.1.2. Inversions. Consider the following sentences:

(3)   I came upon the face of the boulder and saw many stones run through the crack.

Now suppose that the speaker intended to say

(4)   I came upon the face of the boulder and saw many cracks run through the stone.

We can assume that the frame of the sentence was already formed at the time the error was made. This type of speech fault can be considered a syntagmatic error because the ingredients for the inversion—*cracks* and *stone*—can both be found within the original sentence; thus, they need not be imported from other parts of the paradigmatic axis that cuts vertically across each word. A momentary lapse of attention apparently relaxed the intended syntax of the sentence and permitted *stones* to appear before *crack*. The inversion works because both words are nouns. Errors of this kind frequently occur without the speaker being aware of the mistake.

A more clinical example is provided by Freud (1901/1960, p. 65). A lady said to him

(5)   If you want to buy carpets you must go to Kaufmann in the Matthausgasse [Matthew Street]. I think I can give you a recommendation there.

Freud replied:

(6)   At Matthaus . . . I mean Kaufmann's.

This mistake qualified as an inversion because he used one word instead of another and both words come from the intended sentence. The reason Freud gives is that, when his wife was his fiancée, she also lived on Matthausgasse. Thus, the word Matthaus took on personal meaning as a result of this association; these personal meanings may have forced it into the sentence frame in place of Kaufmann. As in the first example, the inversion works because both words share the same grammatical form.

7.2.2. Paradigmatic Errors

7.2.2.1. *Slips.* We turn now to the first of four kinds of paradigmatic dislocations. The *slip*, in contrast to the *inversion*, is formed by the intrusion of words from outside the frame. They belong to the same word class as the (intended) target word and satisfy all syntagmatic constraints of the intended sentence. For example:

(7)   The doctor felt the patient's purse and felt there was nothing he could do.

The slip, *purse*, is similar in many respects to the target word, *pulse*; they are both nouns, both five letters long, and have four out of five letters in common and in the same position. One can think of varying degrees of what might be called paradigmatic congruence and *purse/pulse* share a high degree of commonality. In a corpus of 234 slips collected by Tweney, Tkacz, and Zaruba (1975), the authors found that a certain fraction of the slips had the same meaning as the target word; another fraction was related in sound alone (e.g., *mittens* for *muffins*); and a third group was related in both sound and meaning (e.g., *increase* for *decrease*). Slips with similar sound tended to use the same number of syllables as the target word, although this was significantly less frequent with slips showing similarity in meaning. A very strong serial-position effect was found for slips with similar sound; for example, the probability of a letter match at either end of the word was greater than the probability of a match one letter away. For slips with similar meaning, there was no evident serial-position effect.

These findings suggest (a) that the slip may occur relatively late in sentence production, as suggested by the fact that the syntagmatic frame is relatively well defined by the time the error occurs; and (b) that there may be an interaction between the insistence of the intrusive word and the local syntagmatic constraints. If the intrusive word is only faintly "clamoring" to enter the sentence, it conforms to the structural code of the target word—thus, *mittens* for *muffins* (assuming that *mittens* had some dynamic significance). If the demand for entry is higher, structural requirements are ignored—thus, *blanket* for *pillow*; but even here, the slip conforms to the same word class. We might therefore conclude that, when intrusive pressure is low, all syntagmatic constraints are obeyed; when the pressure is somewhat greater, some constraints are relaxed (there may be a change in the structural features) but other constraints are maintained (the word class remains the same). At high levels of intrusive pressure, all syntagmatic constraints may be violated and the error cripples the sentence. Under these conditions, it stands a good chance of coming to the immediate attention of both speaker and listener, whereas when syntagmatic rules are not affected or only partially violated, the slip may well remain unnoticed.

If we assume that the error occurs relatively late in sentence production, it is not surprising that slips are relatively common in spoken language. As the speaker is uttering one sentence, he is beginning to frame the next; as more attention is withdrawn from the sentence being uttered, it becomes all the easier to fill in the frame with mistaken choices. Because attention is directed forward, it is often not surprising that the slip goes unnoticed.

7.2.2.2. Tip-of-the-Tongue Errors. Tweney *et al.* (1975) have pointed to the similarities between slips and tip-of-the-tongue errors (TOTs). The TOT is defined as the failure to retrieve a word from memory when it is felt to be "known" (and therefore in the subject's lexicon); instead, it is replaced by a near-equivalent substitute. Both slips and TOTs tend to resemble the target word in number of syllables, stress assignment, letter matches, and (to some degree) meaning. In the classic study of TOT (Brown & McNeill, 1966), a subject was given the definition of a low-frequency English word and asked to produce the word defined. If the definition were

(8)   A navigation instrument used in measuring angular distances, especially the altitude of sun, moon, and stars at sea

the subject might say that he knew the word, could not remember it, and offer "secant" as a substitute (the target word in this case is *sextant*). Both *secant* and *sextant* are nouns, they both have two syllables, and they have the same letters in first and last position.

The similarity between slips and TOTs suggests that the two errors may be different expressions of the same phenomenon. In trying to complete the definition of the rare word, the subject in the TOT study is, in effect, trying to complete a sentence frame; in the definition just given, he knows that a noun is required rather than a verb or an adjective; thus his search is restricted to a single paradigmatic vector. Why the similarity in structural features? Tweney *et al.* (1975) argue that

> the fact that number of syllables and stress assignment was nearly always identical for slips, together with the fact that a serial position effect was observed, suggests that the portions of a phonological entry corresponding to the overall shape of the word and its ends are more likely to be retrieved than other aspects of the word. (p. 395)

This argument suggests that paradigmatic relationships hold more strongly on the phonetic level than on the semantic level; that structural property is marked more clearly than meaning; and that this difference may stem from the fact that structural properties are relatively unambiguous and tightly grouped, whereas meaning clusters are notoriously overlapping.

7.2.2.3. Momentary Forgetting. This error might be thought as the clinical analogue to the TOT. As defined by Luborsky in a series of trailblazing papers (Luborsky, 1967, 1973), momentary forgetting occurs when the subject (usually a patient in a psychotherapy session) makes the statement that he forgot what he was going to say (sometimes using the words "on the tip of my tongue"). Some of the memories are recovered; others are not. The forgetting seems to be triggered by some kind of stress which is frequently related to some issue in the therapist-patient relationship. Here is a typical example; the patient is speaking:

(9)   Yes, but I seem not to have the key to the keyhole. I feel here like I can't go into things here because I can't do anything outside if I do. I feel that I can't get into things because I can go ahead with things outside. I'm "directed," as you put it. I seem to have my life going the way I want it. [*long pause*] I forgot what I was going to say. I forgot what I just said, I think [*pause*]. [*She could not recall the missing thought.*] (Luborsky, 1967, p. 187)

Momentary forgetting, in contrast to the other errors we have been discussing, represents a substantial disturbance in sentence production. When it occurs in mid-sentence, we see a notable relaxation in syntagmatic constraints with the result that the complete sentence frame disappears, making it impossible to supply paradigmatic substitutes. Although no systematic linguistic analysis of Luborsky's samples has been carried out, it would be reasonable to expect that momentary forgetting is most likely to occur in sentences with relatively few degrees of freedom; that is, in frames that offer relatively few alternatives for individual words. The only way to avoid producing such a sentence would be to forget it and skip on to the next. We might also hypothesize that the target sentences may not be fully recovered (despite the subjective impression of the patient to the contrary), but that the recovery attempts contain subtle paradigmatic variations on the original target sentence which serve to attenuate its meaning. More research is needed.

7.2.2.4. Lexical Leakage. Errors of this kind leave very faint traces. In contrast to the parapraxes we have been discussing up to this point, lexical leakages are mostly silent and do not result in obvious dislocations of the surface structure. Lexical leakage can be defined as the choice of words which is influenced by unconscious and preconscious background factors, but which conforms to *both* syntagmatic and paradigmatic constraints. This speech fault is included in this section because the background factors influence paradigmatic choice.

The influence of background factors can range from the obvious, as when a farmer, applying for drought relief, says

(10)   We're drowning in red tape

to the subtle, as when Shakespeare speaks of the

(11)   Flinty and steel couch of war

with the allusion to flint and steel for firing a gun. We can also make a distinction between intended leakage, as found in newspaper headlines such as

(12)   Hostility of Icelanders to American base melts a bit

and unintended, as in the following classified advertisement:

(13)   Radiation oncology
                                 Growth position
                                 Edward W. Sparrow Hospital

If it conforms to all local constraints, how can we identify lexical leakage? First (and this procedure is illustrated in some of the examples just given) by sensing a semantic overlap between the choice of word in the target sentence and the surrounding context. Of the different verbs in (12) which might describe a reduction in hostility, *melts* is suspiciously close to Iceland; it is this closeness which makes us suspect leakage. A semantic overlap, unless it is very obvious, does not prove the existence of leakage but it begins to alert our suspicions. Second (and this procedure is more straightforward), we can detect leakage by statistical means and later in this chapter we will give an illustration of this approach. This way of defining lexical leakage assumes that if certain words are overdetermined by background factors, they will appear with a greater frequency in all contexts. Thus, a simple word count of specific markers will prove the hypothesis. Third, we can look for subtle errors in usage. If certain words are being forced into the syntagmatic frame, they will probably displace other, more appropriate choices; a careful reading of the passage, asking at every point is this the one and only word to be used, might uncover subtle mistakes which may sometimes be examples of lexical leakage. Unnecessary repetition is a useful clue, as in

(14)   I have already said that Britain holds the key to this key-problem of Franco
German relations. (Graves & Hodge, 1979, p. 169)

When the same word recurs in the same sentence or paragraph, it tends to appear as a grammatical error and careful reading will detect it; when the repetition occurs after a longer lapse of time, a statistical approach must be used.

In the second and third of these approaches, the overuse of a certain word or group of words must be related to a significant background theme before it can be defined as lexical leakage. Significant changes in frequency or errors of usage alert us to the possibility of leakage, but before overdetermination (in the psychological sense) can be established, we must establish the background link. Because it conforms to all local restraints, lexical leakage is frequently hard to identify; by the same token, it probably occurs much more frequently than is generally recognized, and of all the speech faults discussed in this chapter, it is probably far and away the most frequent. The converse is probably true of momentary forgetting; because it is such an obvious disruption, it tends to be rather rare (in one sample of 19 patients, Luborsky identified only 69 instances in 2085 sessions; see Luborsky, 1973, p. 30). It could also be argued that lexical leakage is probably much more likely to occur in English (with its loose syntax and relatively large vocabulary) than in French or German which are much more logical and unambiguous languages; if it did appear in the latter languages, it would also be much easier to identify.

Lexical leakage can be thought of as the first cousin to the slip. An extraneous idea is challenging the sentence frame but is brought under sufficient syntagmatic and paradigmatic control so that it does not violate the surface structure of the sentence. But we can see that whether or not a particular entry is appropriate depends on who is listening; a slip violates everyone's expectations, whereas lexical leakage will be noticed by only a few—the psychoanalyst, the diplomat, the grammarian, and one or two other lovers of language. We can assume that leakage may become a slip when the background forces become stronger, when the language changes from written to spoken, and when the speaker is under some kind of time pressure, interpersonal pressure, etc. The two kinds of errors may be related in time, with the result that a series of early leakages may anticipate a later slip. In a typical sequence, the early leakages may become more and more intrusive until they give way to a clear disruption. Several slips, in turn, may give way to momentary forgetting or perhaps severe stage fright and blocking. Systematic sequential analysis of natural language under stress would answer many of these questions.

7.3. *Lexical Leakage and Somatic Constraints*

Signals from the body, triggered by hunger, thirst, or disease processes of various kinds, have been a significant cause of lexical leakage and studies of this domain have provided us with some of the best examples of this kind of error. Body states and changes in these states provide an ideal background influence because they are continuously active (although not necessarily conscious) and therefore have the potential for influencing a wide range of spoken discourse.

It is necessary at this point to emphasize the importance of speech as a response measure. Because of the looseness of expressive syntax in natural language, the choice of specific words is much less constrained than is the case with prose or poetry (consider the constraints on the classical sonnet, for example, where certain rules of meter and rhyme must be observed). This syntactical freedom allows other factors to play a much larger role than would be the case in the more restricted genres. There is the second point that size of vocabulary is much less important as a constraint on word choice. This idea follows from the fact that natural language shows a strong preference for the most frequent words; thus, only a small proportion of the speaker's vocabulary is ever being used, and therefore differences in vocabulary size introduce relatively little variation. Third, since the rate of language production (an average of five words per second) is considerably higher in spoken language than in written language, it becomes impossible for a speaker to monitor each and every word, and it is a fairly frequent observation that even trained speakers make occasional mistakes.

One subset of spoken language offers us the ideal "culture" for studying lexical leakage—dreams and free associatons. Dream reports are particularly useful if they are gathered right after the dream occurred because under these conditions, the speaker is still in a sleeplike state and his control over sentence production and word choice is substantially relaxed. Free association under ideal conditions may be similarly regressed. We will begin with an analysis of the influence of thirst on dreaming, and then turn to studies of the effect of symptoms on free association.

7.3.1. Somatic Influences on Dreams

In laying out the background for his theory of dreams, Freud (1900/ 1953) concerned himself with the question of whether dreams can be influenced by various kinds of noncognitive stimuli. He listed three kinds of sources: external sensory stimuli, such as bright lights or noise; internal sensory stimuli, such as retinal excitation from outside light; and internal, organic somatic stimuli, such as hunger pangs, local symptoms, and the like. We will be concerned here with the third category. The theory of somatic sources has a long history, and complicated theories had been developed, long before Freud, to identify a specific organ as the source of a specific type of dream. Thus, heart trouble was supposed to trigger dreams of short duration with terrifying endings—the analogue of a heart attack; lung problems were supposed to trigger dreams of suffocation and crowding; gastrointestinal problems, dreams of food and nausea. We can see the kind of metaphorical reasoning that took place and have reason to be sceptical of such neat theories. Nevertheless, Freud was quite willing to admit that somatic sources can often be identified in dreams; however, he tended to minimize their importance because he saw them as a special class of a more general law. Somatic sources were simply an example of a day residue. Furthermore, somatic sources, although necessary for the formation of a dream, were not sufficient, he argued, without a related infantile wish. Thus, it would be wrong to concentrate on these stimuli alone, and they receive only brief mention in *The Interpretation of Dreams*.

But even though he tended to minimize their importance, Freud was willing to admit that a certain proportion of dreams could be explained entirely by somatic sources; one study cited a figure of 13%. Some recent supporting data is provided by a doctoral study by Bokert

(1967). Eighteen subjects spent three nights in a sleep lab; in a coun-
terbalanced design, each subject was made thirsty on two of the nights
and was sated on the third. Thirst was produced by eating a spicy meal
of spaghetti and peppers before bedtime. During one of the thirst nights,
the words "a cool delicious drink of water" were whispered while the
subject was asleep. All dreams were monitored by recording the subject's eye movements, and the subject was awakened at the end of each
eye-movement period for a full dream report. These reports were than
transcribed and content-analyzed for thirst words and thirst derivatives.

The main finding was that more thirst words appeared in dreams
following the spicy meal than following the sated condition. There was
also a significant increase in the rate of thirst words over time; more
appeared in later dreams in any given night. There was no increase in
thirst words in the whispering condition; the priming stimulus did not
seem to potentiate the effect. The fact that Bokert found a main effect
of thirst without the need to take into account its specific dynamic meaning for each subject suggests that under certain conditions, a somatic
stimulus, in and of itself, may have significant influence on dream content. The fact that the sheer frequency of thirst-related words is increased
on thirst nights can be seen as a clear example of lexical leakage.

7.3.2. Somatic Influences on Free Association

When a psychiatric patient is interviewed by a method called "associative anamnesis," it is sometimes possible to monitor the influence
of his underlying somatic and emotional disturbances on his choice of
language. Felix Deutsch pioneered this approach with psychosomatic
patients, and a close analysis of his case interviews reveals many examples of lexical leakage. In this method, the interviewer listens for the
first report of the somatic complaint, paying particular attention to its
specific wording. He then repeats the complaint, using the patient's
original words, and listens carefully to the patient's response; it will
often contain additional significant material or show a significant choice
of words. What the interviewer is doing, in effect, is building a word-
association test into the interview. As described by Deutsch and Murphy
(1955, p. 23),

> in the associative anamnesis, the word used as a stimulus . . . belongs to a
> pre-existent configuration from which it is picked up, cautiously uprooted
> and inplanted in another culture medium from where new seedlings of as-

sociations shoot up. In this new environment, it attracts and provokes other symptom associations, somatic and otherwise, and becomes attached to them.

In the first example to be considered here, the patient was admitted to the hospital complaining of pain and weakness in his right arm. The symptom developed three months before admission when he was firing on a practice range and trying to squeeze the trigger. Knifelike pain developed in his right arm and shoulder, and he was forced to leave the team. If we start with the fact that pulling the trigger was the precipitating conflict, we can assume that the word *pull* belongs to a significant configuration; it then becomes a matter of considerable interest to study the different ways in which this word appears in the interview. Consider the following interchange:

(15) PATIENT: My father is dead, though.
THERAPIST: Hm?
PATIENT: Pul . . . pul . . . pul . . . *pulled* his heart, or something. *Pulled* something and hurt his heart, you know. Working in an apple orchard.
THERAPIST: Apple orchard?
PATIENT: Well, he was *pulling* a hose, you know—one of those long hoses—*pulling* it and he *pulled* his heart, or done something to his heart. (Deutsch & Murphy, 1955, p. 96)

Two things stand out. First, the expression "pulled his heart" sounds awkward and unusual; we might say *pulled a muscle* or *strained his heart*, but the use of *pull* in connection with heart makes us suspicious that some kind of lexical leakage may be taking place. We become more suspicious when we learn that this patient suffers from an inability to *pull* the trigger, and we might argue that conflict over shooting has endowed this word with particular significance and "forced" it into sentence frames where it ordinarily would not belong. Notice, furthermore, the apparent conflict over *pull* when it is first mentioned; the patient shows difficulty in using it in the context of his father's death.

In the second example, the patient is suffering from arthritis. He was first admitted to the hospital with a history of pain in the neck, low back and right leg. His spinal flexion was limited to 30°, and there was marked limitation of flexion and external rotation of the right hip. In the subsequent interview, the word *back* seems to take on additional significance because of the patient's condition. Consider for following contexts:

(16) I pulled a muscle in my *back*.
(17) It wasn't considered good sportsmanship to fight *back*.

(18)   I did start to try to fight everybody and anybody, and I would end up on my *back*.
(19)   We had been drinking . . . and words went *back* and forth.

In contrast to the previous patient, there are no deviant usages in these examples; nevertheless, the significance of the arthritis and the continuing presence of associated rigidity and pain would suggest that the word *back* is very likely overdetermined. Because we can relate this marker to an ongoing disease process, we can consider its appearance as an example of lexical leakage.

7.4. *Language Correlates of Cervical Cancer*

The examples of lexical leakage from Deutsch and Murphy, although suggestive, are anecdotal and inconclusive. To put the hypothesis to a more severe test, we analyzed a set of 62 interviews of women who were at risk for cervical cancer and who were coming to the hospital for cone biopsy. Each woman's private physician had referred her for biopsy following one or more abnormal Pap tests. Interviews were (with one exception) all conducted by the same interviewer, and took place before the biopsy outcome had been reported (a more detailed report can be found in Spence, Scarborough, & Ginsberg, 1978).

7.4.1. *Interview Corpus*

The 62 cases ranged in age from 21 to 52 years. They were originally interviewed as part of a study (Schmale & Iker, 1971) which attempted to determine the relation between subjective hopelessness and ongoing disease process—in this case, positive cone biopsy. (Of the 68 women originally interviewed, we could use only 62.) The main finding of three separate studies by Schmale and Iker (1971) was that a patient's level of subjective hopelessness, as judged by the interviewer, was correlated with the outcome of the biopsy. The assessment of hopelessness depended on such criteria as a history of long-standing hyperactivity and devotion to causes with little or no feelings of success or pleasure, irrespective of actual accomplishment; and feelings of doom or similar thoughts, experienced in connection with a loss of gratification for which the individual assumed responsibility.

Of the 68 women in the original sample, 50 were correctly identified on the basis of the hopelessness criteria, giving a chi square of 12.18, $p < .001$. Of the 28 women with a positive diagnosis, 68% were predicted correctly on the basis of the interview; of the 40 women with a negative diagnosis, 77% were predicted correctly. Thus, it would seem that patients who project hopelessness at the time of the interview, either in their current mood or in the way they describe their past, tend to be those harboring an ongoing cancer process.

The interview was conducted in the hospital, after the biopsy had been performed and during the time the patient was waiting to hear about the outcome. Under these conditions, we would expect that each patient's awareness of her illness would "force" certain words into the surface structure of her sentences with the result that (a) a significantly greater number of marker words would appear in the speech of the positive patients; and (b) that the change in frequency would be independent of context. Just as in the two patients reported by Deutsch and Murphy, the significant word may appear in any number of different frames. If the word is overdetermined by some continuously present background factor, we would expect that it would be inserted wherever it could possibly "fit"; and as noted above, some of these insertions might be on the borderline of good usage. In this analysis, we make no attempt to pass on usage but depend entirely on a statistical test of differences in frequency.

How, exactly, is the positive patient in this sample "aware" of her illness? We can identify several sources of influence. Her personal physician, in the process of collecting and evaluating the initial Pap smears, very likely transmitted a certain amount of information in a variety of verbal and nonverbal modes. Frequency of smears is another indicator— the request to have more than one within a certain time period is very likely sensed as some kind of warning. Third, the reaction of the physician during the cone biopsy probably conveyed certain kinds of information. Even though the outcome depended on microscopic analysis, the physician doing the procedure could draw certain conclusions from the appearance of the surgical field and he might transmit some of these conclusions in a variety of ways.

Thus, the patient comes to the interview with a reservoir of conscious and preconscious information about her condition and her level of risk. But it would be an oversimplification to assume that her degree of conscious and unconscious concern is all that is needed to determine the degree of lexical leakage because this hypothesis leaves out the important variable of defensive style. We know from clinical experience that some patients are much more open and expressive of inner states than are others. We felt that the women at risk for cancer might show the same variation, with the result that the more defended patients would filter out the marker words allowed to reach the final stage of speech. Another possibility is that the more defended patients would replace words which were clearly related to the ongoing disease process with more distant associates; we know from clinical experience that displacements of this kind are a frequent corollary of denial. Since we have no way of knowing the private code of each patient using denial, we would have no way of systematically detecting this displacement and adding the appropriate correction factor.

7.4.2. Defensive Style

With this concern in mind, we first rated all patients on defensive style by giving the interviews, stripped of all diagnostic information, to two judges to rate on a seven-point scale. The scale ranged from complete denial—marked by such statements as "There is nothing wrong with me"—to open worry and concern—marked by such statements as "I'm sure I have cancer." Each of the seven scale points was defined by a set of key words or phrases to give the judge a clear sense of its referent, and to make sure that both judges used the scale in the same way. Reliability between judges was .94; they agreed on all but eight of the 62 cases, and in no instance did the judges differ by more than two scale points. Disagreements were resolved through discussion.

Ratings of defense, obtained from this scale, were uncorrelated with outcome of cone biopsy ($r = -.02$) or with the interviewer's prediction of cancer ($r = -.07$). The first finding indicates that the patient's style of reaction to the current risk had nothing to do with how sick she actually was; whatever information was conveyed by the physician during the cone biopsy or by her personal physician doing the earlier Pap smears was not contributing to her sense of her present condition. We seem, on the contrary, to be measuring a style of coping rather than a sensitivity to an ongoing cancer process; in other words, a measure of *trait* rather than *state*. The second finding suggests that the interviewer's prediction of cancer, based on his estimate of the patient's subjective hopelessness, was not influenced by her defensive style.

Because of the near-zero correlation between defensive style and diagnosis, it was possible to distribute the 62 patients into four cells by dividing them on two variables: outcome of the cone biopsy (positive or negative) and defensive style. Ratings of style were made by determining the median score on the seven-point scale; all patients who scored above the median we will call *concerned* patients and all patients scoring below the median we will call *defended* patients. About half of each group carried a positive biopsy; thus, there are roughly 15 patients in each cell.

7.4.3. Marker Words

We developed two clusters of marker words to measure hopelessness and hope. The first cluster was presumed to occur significantly more often in patients carrying a positive diagnosis; it was derived from an interview by Kübler-Ross with a patient in the terminal stages of cancer (see Chapter 6 in Kübler-Ross, 1969). Two judges independently read through the interview and listed all words which were synonyms of hopelessness (e.g., death, fail, fear, grief, sad, etc.). Thirty words were chosen by both judges; two additional words were selected by only the first and 17 by only the second. The two lists were combined (because we wanted to exhaust all possible references to hopelessness) and then further expanded by representing each verb in all possible tenses and each noun in both singular and plural endings. The final cluster contained 89 words. We assumed that some subset of this intentionally broad cluster would be overdetermined by the ongoing disease process and that a significant number of these marker words would be "leaked" into the speech of patients carrying a positive diagnosis, with the leakage mediated by defensive style. With concerned patients, we expected the leakage to be relatively clear-cut. With defended patients, we expected the leakage to be attenuated by denial and displacement; as a result, the words which discriminated between defended positive and negative cases might be more distantly related to the theme of hopelessness.

The *hope* cluster was derived from three content-analysis dictionaries. This cluster contains such words as hope, want, wish, yearn, etc.; as with the first cluster, verbs and nouns were represented in all possible forms. The final cluster consisted of 81 words. We expected that patients carrying a negative diagnosis (free of cancer) would use more words from the hope cluster than patients carrying a positive diagnosis. Would leakage be mediated by defensive style? Unlike the case with the *hopeless* cluster, there is no negative information associated words in the hope cluster and, therefore, no reason to expect that defended patients would attempt to reduce their frequency or fall back on distant associates.

7.4.4. Language Analysis

Each interview was keypunched, proofread, and stored on computer tape. All identifying information, such as place names, proper names, etc., was replaced by codes. A specially designed computer program (Spence & Dahl, 1972) sorted all words spoken by each patient and listed them alphabetically, by frequency and by case, on a second tape. Another program searched the sorted output and counted matches between each word in the corpus and the two predetermined clusters of marker words—hopelessness and hope. Two scores were generated from these matches—*rate* and *range*. The first score counts the number of words in each cluster used by each patient without regard to repetition; thus one marker word used five times gives the same score as five marker words used only once. To correct for differences in length of interview, the rate score is divided by the total number of words spoken by the patient; the resulting ratio is multiplied by 1000 (to give a rate per 1000 words) and normalized by a square-root transformation.

The second score, range, takes into account the number of *different* words from each cluster. Where rate would reflect the total amount of "leakage," range would reflect the degree of displacement, i.e., the extent to which the subject moved up and down the paradigmatic axis.

7.4.5. Lexical Leakage—Patients

Mean rates for the two sets of marker words for all patients are presented in Table 7.1. Positive cases in the concerned group use a significantly greater number of words from the hopeless cluster than do negative cases ($t = 2.13$, $p < .05$), although their rate still falls below the rate shown by Kübler-Ross's terminal patient. Positive cases from the concerned group use significantly fewer words from the hope cluster than do negative cases ($t = 2.81$, $p < .01$). Essentially, the two clusters are independent since the two sets of rates are only modestly correlated ($r = -.11$). This fact indicates that a patient who uses a high number of hopeless words will not necessarily use a low number of hope words.

Table 7.1.
Mean Rates for Marker Clusters in Patients' Speech

Biopsy	Cluster		
	Hope		Hopeless
	Concerned patients		
Positive	1.82	[a](t = −2.81)	3.94	[c](t = 2.13)
Negative	2.23		3.63
	Defended patients		
Positive	2.25		3.60
Negative	2.33		3.71
	Total sample		
Positive	2.01	[b](t = −2.57)	3.79
Negative	2.28		3.67
	Kübler-Ross patient		
	2.04		5.33

[a] $p < .01$.
[b] $p < .02$.
[c] $p < .05$.

Therefore, finding significance on both clusters is not simply a matter of saying the same thing in two different ways. One reason for the low correlation between clusters may stem from our not taking context into account. Thus, many of the marker words, although they appear in the surface structure of the patient's speech, are not necessarily reflecting the deep structure of hope and hopelessness.

Turning to the defended patients (see Table 7.1.), we find that neither cluster of marker words discriminates between positive and negative cases. One way of interpreting these findings is to say that patients who deny the risk of cancer are also more guarded in their use of specific marker words, although this explanation makes the most sense with the hopeless cluster. But negative findings of this kind are at best only suggestive; to carry any weight, the assumption that some kind of displacement is taking place must depend on other kinds of data.

To this end, we looked at the findings for range (see Table 7.2.), and these data, at least in part, are consistent with the hypothesis. Positive cases in the defended group use a significantly larger number of *different* marker words than do negative cases ($t = 2.58$, $p < .02$). This difference does not appear among patients in the concerned group. It is tempting to speculate that patients who are unconcerned about the risk of cancer use some kind of displacement mechanism which distributes the reference to hopelessness over a wide range of words, thereby keeping the theme well disguised from both the speaker and the listener. On the other hand, patients who are more concerned about the risk of cancer are less in need of such a displacement mechanism; as a result, they "allow" the marker words to emerge as necessary.

Table 7.2. also makes clear that range does not show a difference with the hope cluster. Part of the explanation for this negative finding (as noted above) may be that positive words are not expected to arouse anxiety and therefore should not trigger denial and displacement. In spite of that fact, we still have no explanation why the hope cluster did not work with the defended patients.

Further evidence for displacement comes from a separate analysis in which we inverted the matrix. In this approach, we started with a set of 181 high-frequency words and determined, for each word in turn, the degree to which it discriminated between positive and negative cases in the concerned and defended subgroups. The findings are shown in Tables 7.3. and 7.4. Listed here are all the words from the original pool which discriminate between groups with a t of better than 1.5 (to simplify the analysis, we used only positive markers; that is, words which appeared more often in the speech of positive, as compared to negative, patients). Twelve markers met this double criterion for the concerned patients and 20 for the defended patients.

The horizontal line in Tables 7.3. and 7.4. shows where the level changes from significant ($t > 2.0$) to nonsignificant ($t < 2.0$). There are significantly more words above the line in the defended group than in the concerned group, a finding which seems consistent with the greater

Table 7.2.
Mean Ranges for Marker Clusters in
Patients' Speech

	Cluster	
Biopsy	Hope	Hopeless
Concerned patients		
Positive	6.67	19.40
Negative	7.24	19.76
Defended patients		
Positive	8.75	21.75
Negative	7.28	17.67
Kübler-Ross patient		
	7	50

[a]$(t = 2.58)$

[a] $p < .02.$

Table 7.3.
Significant Marker Words for Concerned Group

Word	Discriminant level (*t*)
Cancer	2.74
Death	2.40
(Each word above this line is significant, $p < .05$, two-tailed *t* test)	
Painful	1.98
Worried	1.89
Fall	1.82
Black	1.74
Bitter	1.57
Ached	1.57
Bled	1.55
Complains	1.54
Infections	1.54
Alcoholic	1.51

use of displacement by defended patients noted above. When we look more closely at the two groups of discriminating words, we notice an interesting difference. The only significant markers for the concerned patients are *cancer* and *death*—clearly denotative, clearly related to the illness, and showing a minimum amount of transformation or disguise. On the other hand, the markers for the defended patients are largely denotative and, for the most part, only weakly associated with cancer or hopelessness. We are tempted to conclude that this set of words can be thought of as derivatives of the ongoing disease process. Defended patients, because of their greater use of denial, distribute the leakage over a greater number of different words and disguise it even further by using words which are only distantly related to the underlying theme. We now begin to see why the two original clusters of marker words were not sensitive to differences in the defended patients; they did not take account of individual transformations. We suspect that highly defended patients either censor the appearance of clearly related markers because they are too directly threatening, or minimize their impact by avoiding repetition and using a number of different words. We also have evidence that they will substitute a distant derivative for a marker word wherever possible. As a result, each positive patient codes the underlying theme in her own individual way, and the attempt to find a general code—that is, to detect lexical differences by a global cluster—will necessarily fail.

Table 7.4.
Significant Marker Words for Defended Group

Word	Discriminant level (*t*)
Dark	3.35
Disgusted	2.85
Screaming	2.84
Difficulty	2.68
Conflict	2.36
Depend	2.35
Drop	2.35
Tense	2.35
Accept	2.15
Strain	2.10
Black	2.04
Death	2.01
(Each word above this line is significant, $p < .05$, two-tailed *t* test)	
Fractured	1.83
Complains	1.83
Confused	1.80
Infections	1.76
Crying	1.71
Winter	1.70
Finish	1.55
Unhappy	1.53

How can we break the more idiosyncratic codes and find an alternative to statistical analysis? One approach might take advantage of the possibility, noted earlier, that leakage can also be detected by means of subtle deviations in usage. Such deviations might not necessarily appear more often, but a close reading of the interview might reveal a number of instances in which cluster words were used in a slightly forced manner, in a way which somehow makes the word stand out or makes the surface structure seem awkward or inappropriate. We are picking up a kind of leakage that borders on being a slip but which is sufficiently consistent with syntagmatic demands so as to escape attention. (Consider the word *pull* in the hysterical patient cited earlier: it is not clearly inappropriate but stands out as somewhat awkward.)

7.4.6. Lexical Leakage—Interviewer

Mean rates for the two clusters of marker words in the interviewer's language are presented in Table 7.5. As before, the differences between

Table 7.5.
Mean Rates for Marker Clusters in
Interviewer's Speech

Biopsy	Cluster		
	Hope	Hopeless	
	Concerned patients		
Positive	1.64	3.59	[a]$(t = 3.22)$
Negative	1.63	2.99	
	Defended patients		
Positive	1.98	3.18	
Negative	1.86	3.08	
	Total sample		
Positive	1.79	3.41	[b]$(t = 2.47)$
Negative	1.75	3.04	

[a] $p < .01$.
[b] $p < .02$.

positive and negative cases are significant only for the concerned patients. Mean rate of words from the hopeless cluster is significantly higher when the interviewer is talking to a positive patient than when he is talking to a negative patient ($t = 3.22$, $p < .01$). In other words, when a concerned positive patient is being interviewed, more words from the hopeless cluster appeared in both the patient's speech and the interviewer's speech than when a negative patient is being interviewed. But the correlation between patient and interviewer is only moderate ($r = .37$, $p < .01$) and accounts for only 14% of the variance; that is, different sets of words from the hopeless cluster are being used by interviewer and patient; the first is not simply mirroring the second.

Words from the hopeless cluster do not discriminate between positive and negative patients in the defended group, a finding which parallels the earlier data from the patients' speech. Nor do we find that the interviewer, when talking to positive defended patients, uses a greater range of different words, a finding which supports our assumption that the difference in range is triggered by denial in the patient. The interviewer has no reason to use this defense and, therefore, whether he uses the same marker word many times or many words only once is a matter more of his personal style than of the demands of the interview.

The interviewer's rate for hope words did not discriminate between positive and negative patients in either group.

How do we understand the lexical leakage on the part of the interviewer? What is its source? The data suggest that in conversation with another person, we may change our own lexical usage to match roughly that of the other speaker's, just as we modify utterance length (Welkowitz & Feldstein, 1969), pause duration (Jaffe & Feldstein, 1970), and voice intensity (Meltzer, Morris, & Hayes, 1971; Natale, 1975) to conform to the other speaker's. But convergence of that kind is only part of the answer; as noted, the correlation between patient and interviewer accounted for only 14% of the variance. It is possible that leakage is also marked along nonlexical dimensions; thus, the marker word may be uttered with slightly higher intensity or surrounded by slightly longer pauses. Since we know from other studies that speakers are sensitive to pause length and intensity, these and other indicators may attract the interviewer's attention to a significant family of words and cause him to include corresponding words in his own conversation. What we are suggesting is that the stressed marker words uttered by the patient serve to activate the interviewer's own network of associations; since both lie within the general hopeless cluster, we find differences in mean rates for both interviewer and patient, while at the same time finding that they use different sets of words.

In the original study by Schmale and Iker (1971), the interviewer made a prediction at the end of the interview as to the outcome of the cone biopsy. This prediction is, rather surprisingly, not correlated with either the number of hopeless words in the patients' speech or in his own. This negative finding points up the difference between surface structure and deep structure, and helps us to understand the limits of lexical leakage. The differences in use of hopeless words we have been discussing up to now are differences in the surface structure—in the sheer frequency of individual lexical items. There is a fair amount of evidence (e.g., Bransford & Franks, 1971; Sachs, 1967) that surface structure is ignored during comprehension; that the listener goes immediately to the deep structure and a focus on the meaning of the utterance rather than on its form. Schmale, in listening to the cancer patients, was attempting to gather information about the illness and to make an evaluation of the patient's condition; he was not trying to do a linguistic analysis. We would suppose that he would simply ignore individual markers unless they identified specific facts: proper names, for example, locations, or specific dates. To make an evaluation of the patient's hopelessness, he must necessarily pay attention to the underlying meaning;

to keep track of individual markers would so seriously interfere with the task of listening as to completely paralyze any clinical assessment.

There is a second reason why the rate of hopeless words is not correlated with his estimates of hopelessness. We have counted the marker words in all possible contexts, whether or not they were used in relation to a related theme. Thus, the marker word *death* in the sentence

(20)   The first year we were married we nearly froze to death.

does not have a particularly morbid or hopeless ring to it. Similar conclusions could be drawn from such other usages as

(21)   When they're like that, you can love them to death.

(22)   I thought I was going to scratch myself to death.

Because we included all usages in our count, we necessarily included contexts which cover a wide range of disparate meanings. The interviewer is presumably focused on a subset of these meanings in his evaluation of hopelessness; he very likely ignores contexts in which hopeless words are negated ("I am *not* sad"); and he may also include other contexts which do not use hopeless words. Because of the partial overlap between his area of interest and the presence of marker words, the correlation between his estimate of hopelessness and the appearance of hopeless words is substantially attenuated.

Nevertheless, some information is coming through. This conclusion is suggested by the fact that the surface structure of his language is significantly related to the patient's diagnosis; that is, to her conscious and preconscious sense of the ongoing risk. The information transfer is particularly significant in the case of concerned patients. The interviewer, as he speaks with these patients, is apparently accumulating more information than he is aware of at the time; even though this information is not incorporated into his clinical estimate of hopelessness, it is still influencing his choice of words. If we combine his estimate of hopelessness with the rate of hopeless words in his speech, the multiple correlation with the outcome of the cone biopsy rises to .67 ($p < .001$), or 45% of the variance.

These data suggest that we can isolate two levels of information processing. On the one hand, the interviewer is evaluating the patient's general level of hopelessness by attending to significant details in her history and current outlook; this information is extracted from the deep

structure of the patient's responses and is used to form his explicit assessment. On the other hand, he is apparently being influenced by specific words in the patient's language, alerted perhaps by slight variations
in intensity, cadence, and other paralinguistic cues, but he is apparently
not aware of this level of information; it is influencing his language but
not his evaluation. Could he be made aware? Could the speaker be made
aware of his own surface structure? Certain kinds of training in psychotherapy (see Spence, 1979) make this one of their primary goals;
particularly valuable is the ability, which some therapists seem to have,
of switching attention back and forth between deep structure and surface structure. With this ability, it might be possible to sample both
domains and still carry on a reasonable conversation. Had the interviewer listened in this manner to the women at risk for cancer, he might
have significantly increased his ability to predict the biopsy. But listening
to surface structure may have the additional effect of reducing lexical
leakage, and in a later section, we will discuss this possibility in more
detail.

7.4.7. Summary

Our statistical analysis of the cancer interviews has suggested that,
despite the apparent absence of parapraxes, there is a consistent bias
in the choice of language. The bias is most clearly established in the case
of the concerned patients. It shows itself by the fact that words related
to the underlying theme of hopelessness appear more often, in all contexts, in the speech of positive cases, whereas words related to the theme
of hope appear more often in the speech of negative cases. We can
assume that the experience with previous Pap tests, physician contacts,
and with the recently experienced cone biopsy has left each patient with
a certain residue of positive or negative information. This residue exerts
a subtle background constraint on the extent to which each patient, at
each step in sentence formation, can choose the most appropriate word
from the full range of paradigmatic and syntagmatic choices. If the background bias is particularly strong, it will cause certain words to be inserted repeatedly into the sentence frame, but as long as the bias is not
peremptory, these words will not violate local constraints, and, therefore, they will not appear as deviant choices. For these reasons, the

biasing effect of background information is largely silent and can only be detected by statistical analysis.

In spite of the fact that these leakages are largely silent, the defended patients must have sensed an even greater danger. Their sensitivity to using hopeless words, no matter what the context, appears to be so acute as to make them seek alternatives wherever possible. Two strategies seemed available: first, to use each cluster word no more than once, if at all possible; and second, to extend the bounds of the hopeless cluster and use words which were only distantly related to the underlying theme. We can assume that the patient was unaware of either mechanism; as a consequence of the extensive use of displacement, the defended patient managed to keep her denial intact and—we can assume—this denial enabled her to continue the interview, free of such obvious disruptions as blocking, slips, and similar parapraxes.

We can think of the interviewer as listening on two levels. On the one hand, he is listening to the deep structure of the patient's response in an effort to assess her underlying level of hopelessness. In this role, he must ignore individual words as much as possible; language for him is largely "transparent" and something to be listened through rather than directly examined. But we also have evidence that the interviewer is occasionally alerted by specific words, perhaps because they are given unusual stress or set off by slightly longer pauses, and although he may not be consciously attending to these markers, his language changes as a result; the hopeless words uttered by the patient trigger a partially overlapping set of hopeless words in the interview.

How does this change come about? We can assume that as the interviewer starts each new sentence, his choice of words is partly conditioned by the patient's; this influence either causes him to use a similar word (if syntagmatic constraints allow) or to restrict his paradigmatic search to a relatively close associate. Just as the background concerns of the patient seem to bias her paradigmatic search, so the accumulation of marker words in the patient's speech tend to bias the interviewer's. But because syntagmatic constraints are usually observed, the biasing effect is subtle and, in interviewer as in patient, can only be detected by statistical procedures.

What we have just described is similar to the way in which new words or phrases enter the language. They do not emerge as slips, in violation of syntactic rules; on the contrary, they emerge gradually and appropriately, obeying all necessary grammatical constraints until suddenly some critic will call our attention to the fact that everyone is now saying

(23)   Hopefully you can come

instead of the more correct

(24)   I hope you can come.

Another example of this kind of gradual change may be seen in

(25)   At this point in time . . . .

as a replacement for

(26)   At this point . . . .

That the invasion of new words or phrases takes place gradually and outside of our general awareness until it is too late is simply a consequence of both syntagmatic and paradigmatic constraints being observed. Whereas before Nixon we might simply say (26), we now feel an unspoken pressure, formed by exposure to many examples of written and spoken English, to extend the phrase and add "in time," or (25). A piece of the Nixon era has, as it were, leaked into the language. Most of us are unaware of this leakage for the (now familiar) reason that we are attending to the deep structure of the sentence and paying very little attention to how it is constructed; only the grammarian or linguist can stand back, look at the surface of the language, and call our attention to the change.

7.5. Implications for Clinical Listening

In some recent research on doctor–patient communication, Korsch and Negrete (1972) found that word borrowing could be used as an index of empathic listening. Conversations were recorded between pediatricians and mothers of sick children; in contrast to our cancer interviews where specific words were traded back and forth between speakers, doctors tended to use a highly technical vocabulary, beyond the mother's comprehension, whereas the mothers discussed anxieties that the doctors evidently did not want to share. Each party in the dialogue used his or her own domain of markers; communication suffered as a result, and as the interview progressed, the misunderstandings increased as the shared language decreased. A total of 800 interviews was studied; in only 42% of the cases did the mother carry out all of the doctor's advice, and the authors attribute this failure, in part, to the communication disturbance.

These findings suggest that good communication may have something in common with lexical leakage. The good interviewer must listen on two levels at the same time, attending to both deep and surface structure; i.e., he must listen partly for meaning and partly for words. The evidence suggests that communication flourishes to the extent that he picks up on the words. The apparent lack of empathy in the study just cited stems from the doctor's failure to listen to surface structure and pick up on the mother's language. It can also be argued that the language sharing we observed in our cancer interviews may also have contributed to greater empathy. We have noted that the interviewer was, in general, highly successful in predicting the outcome of the biopsy, and part of his clinical sensitivity may have been a consequence (consciously or preconsciously) of making use of specific words in the patient's speech.

7.5.1. Syntagmatic Listening

We can distinguish two kinds of listening that flow from Saussure's primary distinction. In syntagmatic listening, we follow the conventional mode in which language is transparent and the words in a sentence are secondary to its meaning. Listening in this mode, we allow each sentence to lay down a continuously changing concept which is always being revised as each new word is added; since the focus is on the intended meaning, the specific form of each new word is less important than its impact on the evolving message. (In a reversal of the McLuhan dictum, we would say that it is the message which counts, *not* the medium). The sentence is presumably parsed as it unfolds; specific words function primarily to extend the thought and to resolve transient ambiguities. The longer the time lapse after the sentence, the more likely it is that we may forget some of the specific words—and this phenomenon has been demonstrated with experiments by Sachs (1967).

Listening in the syntagmatic mode is our normal mode of gathering information; we are always listening *through* the words in the sentence to what the speaker is trying to convey. Listening in this mode, we are probably more aware of syntagmatic faults, such as incomplete sentences, inversions, or spoonerisms, than of paradigmatic faults, such as incorrect word choice. If a word is not exact, we may register an ambiguity and wait for subsequent words to bring about its resolution. If this resolution does not take place before the sentence ends, we may forget about the ambiguity as we begin to process the next sentence. Assisting this tolerance for poor usage is our need to keep up with the flow of speech; we cannot afford to become fixated over a particular word else we lose the thread of the sentence.

7.5.2. Paradigmatic Listening

In this mode, the medium (following McCluhan) is very much the message. At every point in the sentence frame, the paradigmatic listener has the option of searching the full range of his paradigmatic axis and asking himself such questions as "Is this word important? Is there a better choice? Does it have a particular significance?" Listening in this mode is particularly useful to the diplomat, the psychotherapist, and the lawyer, to name only three professions which might benefit. Because paradigmatic listening focuses away from the underlying meaning of the speaker, it tends to interfere with ordinary conversation. It may be the only way to pick up lexical leakage and other rather subtle speech faults. When using this mode, the listener, in effect, is trying to simulate the efforts of the speaker; he is checking each addition to the unfolding sentence for its place in the paradigmatic axis. But notice the asymmetry: what is natural for the speaker is unnatural for the listener. Most listening is carried out in the syntagmatic mode, and it is this very fact that allows lexical leakage to flourish. It is precisely because the average listener is listening *through* the language that subtle deviations in word choice—lexical leakage—are not discovered.

What we have just described is what might be called *controlled, adaptive paradigmatic listening*. Under certain conditions, however, a pathological form may appear. These conditions are not very well studied but seem to occur during extreme stress or in other situations which put limits on memory and concentration. At such times, normal grammatical parsing seems to break down, and the sentence is heard as an approximately random string of words rather than as a well-ordered syntactic structure. Individual words are heard in isolation; because grammatical functions are attenuated, each word is heard in more or less its iconic form, out of context, and unmodified by other words and other features of the sentence. Something of this kind seems to have happened with the mothers in the study by Korsch and Negrete (1972). They were sufficiently frightened by their child's illness and by the authority of the physician to give up part of their normal language competence. As a result, a sentence like

(27)   Could just be a little hole in his heart.

may have been heard as essentially two words—*hole* and *heart*. Listening in this pathological mode, the listener will probably ignore modifiers and negations; she will understand more of the early part of a sentence than the later (because a long series of individual words puts increasing strain on short-term memory); and she will gradually drop out of the conversation because, as her understanding becomes more and more impoverished, she will have progressively less to offer as a response. Careful analysis of one of the transcripts presented by Korsch and Negrete shows the mother engaging less and less actively as the interview proceeds; at the end of the session, she is reduced to an occasional "Mm-hm" and the infrequent repetition of one of the doctor's technical terms.

It should be made clear that pathological listening in the paradigmatic mode is quite different from its controlled use by a professional. In the former case, the listener is driven to this extreme by anxiety; he no longer has the option to listen in the normal manner; and as his listening becomes fragmented, meanings are distorted, adding to his anxiety which, in turn, adds to the fragmentation. Professional paradigmatic listening, by contrast, is under the listener's control, and he is always able (at least in theory) to switch back to the normal mode of syntagmatic listening.

Further examples of this pathology may be found in experiments on delayed auditory feedback and restricted feedback. Studies on delayed feedback have shown quite clearly that when the speaker hears his voice after a very short delay, his sentences begin to deteriorate, his speech begins to falter, and he may often perseverate on a single word— all symptoms of a shift from the syntagmatic to the paradigmatic mode of listening. A similar disturbance can be caused by white noise which prevents the speaker from hearing his own voice (see Klein and Wolitzky, 1970). In both of these experimental situations, the normal sentence form is disrupted and the speaker is forced to shift to a paradigmatic mode to retain any meaning whatsoever. It sometimes happens that single words become so important that they may be repeated or shouted in order to compensate for the loss of syntax.

The experience of the listener using the pathological mode is very similar to the experience of a beginning student hearing a foreign language spoken at a normal rate. Certain words are familiar and tend to stand out; other words are partly familiar, and the listener begins searching the paradigmatic axis to discover what possibilities might have been intended. The very act of concentrating more than a brief moment on any given word means that the rest of the sentence must be abandoned, along with all of its grammatical implications. The listener is left with a collection of single words in no particular sequence or hierarchy; their combined meaning under the best of arrangements can only roughly approximate the speaker's intended meaning, and communication is distorted. Fixated on individual words which just happen to be within his comprehension, the listener will probably miss most of the syntactic information being conveyed and, therefore, will very likely misunderstand even the few words he picks up.

Disorders of this kind make very clear the requirements of ordinary syntagmatic listening. We focus on individual words at our peril, and the faster the rate of speech, the greater the risk. Only by treating the language as fully transparent and ignoring individual word choices can we do justice to a complicated syntactic construction and understand the complete sense of the intended sentence. Worth noting is the fact that it is probably under conditions of concentrated syntagmatic listening that lexical leakage is most likely to occur; when the listener is functioning in a purely syntagmatic mode, we can be almost certain that individual word choice will be ignored. Going a step further, it could be argued that leakage varies inversely with syntagmatic listening; that the speaker may be able to sense, on some level, the stance of his listener and he (the speaker) may allow more leakage to develop at just those times when word choice is being ignored by the listener. Clues to the contrary—that is, signs that the listener is beginning to concentrate on individual words—may suddenly interrupt this leakage, and if the listener raises a question about a particular word, leakage may suddenly stop. It is probably no accident that the interviewer during the cancer interviews was generally information-gathering (i.e., syntagmatic) in his approach, and made almost no attempt to query individual words; we might assume that this very stance may have reinforced the leakage on the part of the patient. Had he switched to a more therapeutic (i.e., paradigmatic) mode of listening, he might have warned the patient that she must, quite literally, "watch her words," and our frequency findings might have been seriously reduced.

7.6. Toward a Theory of Lexical Leakage

Although English, with its almost boundless vocabulary and relatively relaxed syntax, offers a wide range of ways of expressing any given idea, a close analysis of spoken English would probably show that a relatively narrow range of sentence forms is used by the vast majority of speakers. Although it does not have the rigidity of a language like French, spoken English, in particular, tends to rely repeatedly on certain common constructions, just as it relies heavily on the 100 most common words.

Thus, we can assume that, in a very high proportion of utterances, the speaker is prepared to use a ready-made syntactic construction to express a high proportion of his ideas; he puts his frame to use by filling it with the appropriate words. In contrast to the listener who functions primarily, as we have argued above, in a syntagmatic mode, the speaker is faced with a series of paradigmatic choices as he fills each frame. He is, furthermore, probably more conscious of the task of finding words than of finding the proper grammatical sequence.

Although each paradigmatic axis must be searched in turn for the most appropriate word, the pace of sentence production forces the speaker to execute these searches very quickly; if he pauses too long on a single word, his sentence begins to lose its intended form, and the listener may begin to complain. Thus, word finding is a semiautonomous function, carried out in the fringes of awareness, and all the more likely to come under the influence of conscious and unconscious factors. When we say that the choice of a word is overdetermined, we mean that one or more background factors (usually unconscious), in addition to local paradigmatic and syntagmatic constraints, have played a part in its choice. We have noted how lexical leakage is produced when the background factors are subordinate to local constraints, and how the more obvious types of speech faults are produced when background factors overwhelm local constraints.

A theory of lexical leakage should be able to identify the conditions under which word finding is most likely to show the influence of background factors. We will set forth some of the more compelling conditions at this point; many more remain to be discovered.

First, the speaker must not be unnecessarily aware of choosing a particular word. This rule would suggest that leakage would occur more often in the middle than at the beginning of clauses because many studies (see, for example, Goldman Eisler, 1968) have shown that pauses—presumably a sign of word-finding difficulty—are longer at clause-junctions.

Second, we would assume that leakage would occur more frequently within a sentence frame of normal syntactic complexity because a demand for more deviant syntax would shift attention away from word-finding to grammatical construction. The best environment for leakage is probably the overused phrase or figure of speech, and it turns out that the best discriminator between positive and negative patients in the cancer study was the single word *death* in the context of rather ordinary figures of speech (see the sentences in examples 20 to 22, above).

Third, we would assume that leakage is heavily dependent on the stance of the listener. As we have indicated in the previous section, optimal leakage probably occurs when the listener is making no attempt to challenge individual words and seems to be listening in a purely syntagmatic manner. So long as the listener is listening *through* the language, the speaker is not made self-conscious about his choice of words, and background factors are more likely to influence word choice. Even though the speaker is concentrating more on word choice than on sentence construction, we can assume that he is attending more to the task of filling slots in the sentence frame than to the question of precisely what he is filling them *with*. As soon as the speaker calls attention to a specific word, however, the balance is suddenly altered, and we can assume that leakage would significantly diminish.

We can generalize this rule to say that leakage can occur only so long as the speaker is not aware that it is happening. When background factors become too insistent, leakage degenerates into a more obvious speech fault, and as these breakthroughs become more and more disruptive, the speaker will eventually come to realize what he is "saying." He may also become aware of leakage when repetition of certain words exceeds a particular threshold, or when word finding becomes such an effort that he is stopped in midsentence. Under these conditions, he is presumably no longer able to find a word which will express his thought, fulfill the local constraints of the sentence, and convey something of the background theme, and he breaks off the sentence rather than reveal more than he intended. Such a midsentence disruption can be seen as a close cousin to Luborsky's momentary forgetting.

These considerations suggest that leakage cannot continue to the point where it exhausts any particular paradigmatic axis. We have seen how our defended positive patients try to avoid repeating marker words and we can assume that, were the interview prolonged beyond a certain period of time, repetitions would be bound to occur. After this point, we can assume that sentence construction would become more and more difficult as the patient finds fewer ways of avoiding certain themes; certain sentence frames would necessarily require the use of marker words which would be too revealing, and a certain kind of aphasia might set in. As a result, word finding would fail, and the speaker would be unable to complete the sentence.

What brings about the conflict? The answer to this question leads us to the final condition necessary for lexical leakage: the background theme motivating the leakage must be somehow unsuited for direct expression. Our cancer patients were unable to express their hopelessness openly because to do so would have raised their anxiety to an intolerable level. They were, in addition, probably not fully conscious of the degree of concern generated by visits to previous doctors and were thus unable to express these thoughts directly. Had they been made aware of their thoughts (as a result, for example, of some kind of hypnotic suggestion) then we might assume that leakage would diminish because open expression of the background theme would necessarily be more complete than any amount of lexical leakage.

We can begin to see that leakage requires a nicely balanced series of opposing conditions: the speaker must be speaking in a paradigmatic mode, concentrating more on word choice than on sentence construction; the listener, on the other hand, must be listening in normal, syntagmatic fashion and not focusing on particular words. This combination of stances produces an interesting paradox in that the more we listen for lexical leakage, the less we are likely to find, whereas the more we disregard leakage, the more it is likely to happen! A second pair of conditions applies to the insistence of the background theme. If it is too insistent, it will probably disrupt sentence formation to the point where leakage stops and more obvious speech faults begin; on the other hand, if it is not intrusive, no leakage will develop. A third pair of conditions applies to the speaker's conflict over the background factors: with no conflict, the themes can be openly expressed (and no leakage will develop); with too much conflict (as with our defended patients in the cancer study), only extreme transformations will be allowed into the sentence frame and leakage becomes very difficult to detect.

It is partly as a consequence of the first paradox that lexical leakage has remained unnoticed and unstudied for so long. The ordinary listener, listening in a syntagmatic mode, is not aware of individual words; the interested listener, listening in a paradigmatic mode, conveys his interest in particular words and damps down their occurrence. Only the disinterested listener is exposed to a significant amount of leakage, but because of his disinterest, he is not aware of what was happening. Participant observers are clearly disqualified for studying this phenomenon; the answer lies in developing statistical procedures for the analysis of changes in word frequency over time, and linguistic procedures for the detection of subtle variations in usage. Lexical leakage lies all around us, waiting to be discovered; future studies will indicate the scope and significance of the phenomenon.

7.7. References

Baars, B. J., & Motley, M. T. Spoonerisms as sequencer conflicts: Evidence from artificially elicited errors. *American Journal of Psychology*, 1976, *89*, 467–484.

Bokert, E. G. *The effects of thirst and a related verbal stimulus on dream reports.* Unpublished doctoral dissertation, New York University, New York, 1967.

Bransford, J. D., & Franks, J. J. The abstraction of linguistic ideas. *Cognitive Psychology*, 1971, *2*, 331–350.

Brown, R., & McNeill, D. The "tip of the tongue" phenomenon. *Journal of Verbal Learning and Verbal Behavior*, 1966, *5*, 325–337.

Cuddon, J. A. *A dictionary of literary terms.* New York: Doubleday, 1977.

Culler, J. *Ferdinand de Saussure.* New York: Penguin, 1977.

Deutsch, F., & Murphy, W. F. *The clinical interview.* Vol. 1. New York: International Universities Press, 1955.

Freud, S. *The interpretation of dreams* (Vol. 5) (J. Strachey, Trans.). London: Hogarth, 1953. (Originally published, 1900).

Freud, S. *The psychopathology of everyday life* (Vol. 6) (J. Strachey, Trans.). London: Hogarth, 1960. (Originally published, 1901.)

Goldman Eisler, F. *Psycholinguistics.* New York: Academic, 1968.

Graves, R., & Hodge, A. *The reader over your shoulder.* New York: Random House, 1979.

Jaffe, J., & Feldstein, S. *Rhythms of dialogue.* New York: Academic, 1970.

Klein, G. S., & Wolitzky, D. L. Vocal isolation: The effects of occluding auditory feedback from one's own voice. *Journal of Abnormal Psychology*, 1970, *75*, 50–56.

Korsch, B. M., & Negrete, V. F. Doctor-patient communication. *Scientific American*, 1972, *277*, 66–74.

Kübler-Ross, E. *On death and dying*. New York: Macmillan, 1969.

Luborsky, L. Momentary forgetting during psychotherapy and psychoanalysis. In R. R. Holt (Ed.), *Motives and thought: Psychoanalytic essays in honor of David Rapaport. Psychological Issues*, 1967, *5*, Nos. 2–3, Monograph 18/19, 177–217.

Luborsky, L. Forgetting and remembering (momentary forgetting) during psychotherapy: A new sample. In M. Mayman (Ed.), *Psychoanalytic research: Three approaches to the experimental study of subliminal processes. Psychological Issues*, 1973, *8*, No. 2, Monograph 30, 29–55.

Meltzer, L., Morris, W., & Hayes, D. Interruption outcomes and vocal amplitude: Explorations in social psychophysics. *Journal of Personality and Social Psychology*, 1971, *18*, 392–402.

Motley, M. T., & Baars, B. J. Semantic bias effects on the outcomes of verbal slips. *Cognition*, 1976, *4*, 177–187.

Natale, M. Convergence of mean vocal intensity in dyadic communication as a function of social desirability. *Journal of Personality and Social Psychology*, 1975, *32*, 790–804.

Sachs, J. Recognition memory for syntactic and semantic aspects of connected discourse. *Perception and Psychophysics*, 1967, *2*, 437–442.

Schmale, A. H., & Iker, H. Hopelessness as a predictor of cervical cancer. *Social Science and Medicine*, 1971, *5*, 95–100.

Spence, D. P. Language in psychotherapy. In D. Aaronson & R. Reiber (Eds.), *Psycholinguistic research: Implications and applications*. New York: Erlbaum, 1979.

Spence, D. P., & Dahl, H. *The general analyzer: Computer programs for processing clinical text*. Unpublished manuscript, 1972.

Spence, D. P., Scarborough, H. S., & Ginsberg, E. Lexical correlates of cervical cancer. *Social Science and Medicine*, 1978, *12*, 141–145.

Tweney, R. D., Tkacz, S., & Zaruba, S. Slips of the tongue and lexical storage. *Language and Speech*, 1975, *18*, 388–396.

Welkowitz, J., & Feldstein, S. Dyadic interaction and induced differences in perceived similarity. Proceedings of the 77th Annual American Psychological Association, 1969, *4*, 343–344.

Marshall Edelson

LANGUAGE AND MEDICINE[1]

8.1. Introductory Remarks

Today's lecture will be somewhat longer and more formal than usual, for reasons I hope will become apparent to you. Some years ago, a senior faculty member, who occupied an important position and who was a person for whom and for whose ideas I had considerable respect, was discussing the curriculum of this medical school with some other faculty members, including myself. He was trying to find the example par excellence of a subject irrelevant for the education of physicians. He did not know I had any special interest in language. Quite unmaliciously he hit upon what he considered to be the ideal example of irrelevance— the subject of linguistics. You know what it's like, after such a conversation, to think of all the good things you might have said. In this lecture, I am among other things replying—belatedly—to my colleague. You shall be the judges whether or not it is likely even now that my reply would shake his conviction one whit.

What I wish I had said to him at the least is that those of us who use language, we physicians, do indeed need to know what those who study language, linguistics, have to say about it. Physicians use language

[1] This is a somewhat revised version of a lecture given to the first-year class of medical students, Yale University School of Medicine, October 17, 1977, as part of a year-long course in behavioral science: "Mind, Brain, and Society: The Psychological Basis of Medical Practice."

Marshall Edelson ● Department of Psychiatry, Yale University School of Medicine, New Haven, Connecticut 06519. The author was supported in part by NIMH Psychiatry Education Branch, Grant No. 5–T02–MH11953–08.

to influence patients. Language as a medium of influence is as important a part of the clinician's armamentarium as the drug or scalpel. "Talking" is as powerful an intervention as a "medical" or "surgical" intervention, and requires as much knowledge and skill. In addition to looking, touching, and laboratory investigation, physicians use language to elicit information—which is, in turn, conveyed in language—about patients. From such information, the physician draws clinical inferences about the patient and his illness.

It follows that physicians who use language should know something about what those who study language have to say about it. Paradoxically, physicians appear to have little interest in modern linguistics as an essential foundation in knowledge for the skillful use of "talk" in clinical practice. They are not convinced of the relevance of this knowledge for skills which seem to them intuitive and somehow "given." This conviction is not supported by the wide variations in skill with which physicians use "talk" in medical practice to elicit information about patients and to influence patients.

Insofar as physicians influence patients by means of language, knowledge of the patient as language-user, the target of such influence, is a foundation for clinical skill. (In the same sense, physiological processes or anatomical structures are targets of pharmacological or surgical interventions, and knowledge of these processes and structures is also a foundation for clinical skill.)

For the physician, it is an important fact that both the physician's thinking about disease and the patient's thinking about his illness depend nontrivially on the language used.[2] The etiology, manifestations, and course of any illness are affected by what illness *means* to the patient. The physician must not only understand those effects of medicines, surgical procedures, hospitalization, and other interventions that do have to do with their intrinsic properties or efficacy, but also what these things, acts, people, and institutions *mean* to the patient.

For the physician, it is an important fact that language is a major instrumentality used by the patient to regulate his own behavior (Luria,

[2] F. G. Crookshank (1923), using a history of conceptions of poliomyelitis, argues that language affects how the physician thinks about disease and disease entities. Balint (1973) demonstrates how important a name of what is wrong with him is to the patient and what decisive consequences the choice of such a name by the physician may have for the organization of the patient's hitherto vague, fleeting, or disparate symptomatology and for the patient's subsequent clinical course.

1959). Habitual patterns of language lead to errors of thinking and problem-solving (Whorf, 1964). Ways of seeing and thinking about reality and feeling have their origin in innate cognitive, perceptual, and affective modes investigated in the laboratory (Shapiro, 1965). A particular way of telling a medical history, for example, should be understood, in part at least, as reflecting the way the patient always has chosen and always does choose to organize his experience, and not necessarily as a motivated expression(e.g., a sign that the patient is cooperative or uncooperative). These facts have implications for the way in which a physician communicates with a patient and responds to a patient's communications—for the way in which a physician conveys instructions for taking medication, for example, and assesses the extent to which a patient is able to regulate his behavior through self-directed internal verbal instructions and the extent to which these must be reinforced by external verbal instructions.

For the physician, it is an important fact that particular uses of language are culturally prescribed or related to coherent value systems. The way a patient expresses pain should be understood in the light of his cultural background and values, rather than as a mere idiosyncratic expression of personality style or disorder or as a means of annoying or inconveniencing the physician (Zborowski, 1969).

For the physician, it is an important fact that particular uses of language (by members of minority groups, for example, or of particular socioeconomic classes) are rule-governed dialects and not signs of intellectual deficiency or cultural deprivation (Labov, 1969). Without knowledge of facts like these, the physician may make grave errors in assessing a patient and responding to his communications.

For the physician in these times, when "explaining to the patient what is going on," "informing the patient about the gravity of his condition and his prognosis," and "soliciting informed consent" are considered obligations of the physician, it is an especially important fact that symbols (especially linguistic symbols) have in themselves profound functional and dysfunctional effects and can be effective in themselves in altering a patient's physical state (Lévi-Strauss, 1967). This fact clearly has implications, at the least, for considering the "placebo" effect of medications or other interventions, including a change of regimen or a withdrawal of medication, in the light of what such interventions mean or symbolize to a particular patient. At the most, there are implications suggesting here what might be accomplished by the physician through words alone. If words alone are sufficient, they are the preferred intervention; the physician who understands language will not despise them or feel that he is being unscientific or failing to do enough when he uses them.

Finally, it is likely, however improbable on first thought, that the clinician's tacit or unwitting recognition of and response to linguistic phenomena (the semantic, syntactic, phonological, and rhetorical features of a patient's speech) account for a large part of what we call interpersonal skills, clinical art, or intuition about patient or illness. This hypothesis has practical implications for improving skills in the use of "talk" in the assessment and treatment of patients.

8.2. Language and Medicine: Two Questions and Four Assertions

What I talk about today will circle mainly around two fairly big questions:

1. To what extent and in what way does the physician's clinical skill depend upon having adequate empirical-scientific (as opposed to philosophical or commonsensical) knowledge of human language and how language is used in thought and speech?
2. What is language? What is a human being capable of, by virtue of his possession of language?[3] What is the difference between the natural language of the human species and other kinds of signs and sign systems? What ideas about human beings—about how they think, perceive, and act—are ruled out by what we know about language?

On the basis of a consideration of these questions, I shall conclude my lecture with four assertions to my colleague:

1. The study of language is the key to the study of man.
2. The study of language provides a model for thinking about other human capacities.
3. The physician's attention to and understanding of linguistic phe-

---

[3] I'll use the pronoun "his" throughout, and depend on you to provide "his or her" as wherever it is called for.

nomena lead to a deeper understanding of the patient and his illness.

4. At the least, the clinician's tacit or unwitting recognition of and response to linguistic phenomena account for a large part of what we call clinical skill, art, or intuition.

These are big claims.

Evidently I'm going to be covering a lot of ground in a brief period of time. On top of that, I shall be referring to material you have yet to read in this course—introducing you to it, so to speak—as well as material you have already read. You have already had the experience in other lectures and seminars in medical school and in this course of being deluged by unfamiliar ideas and vocabulary. There is no easy way out of this. There doesn't seem to be any place to start but in the middle. But, from our own experiences, I can assure you that things do come together, often quite happily, eventually. Meanwhile, it's probably best if you do not try too hard to follow and grasp every detail, but rather sit back and get an overall sense of where I'm going, what I'm interested in, and how some of us are thinking about this subject.

8.3. Talk in Medical Practice

I'm not sure how much needs to be said to convince you of the ubiquity and significance of talk in medical practice. Probably most of you are already convinced. After all, you've been patients, if not yet physicians. Patients talk about what they want to get rid of. They use words like "pain," "ache," "hurt," "sore." These words are a primary set; each one may appear in more than one syntactic form—noun, verb, adjective, or adverb. Patients also use other words, which tend to be verblike, such as cutting, rubbing, pulling, pressing, crushing, sharp, burning. Sometimes these are used instead of one of the members of the primary set. They designate features of pain, or create metaphors of the quality of pain, what kind of change of state, damage, or destruction the patient imagines. Still other words, used in many other contexts as well, convey facts about intensity, time, space, or the affective meaning of pain, such words as deep, intense, mild, steady, shifting, depressing, tingling (Fabrega & Tyma, 1976).

What must the physician know about language as well as disease to make warranted inferences about why the patient makes the choices he does among all these possibilities? (1) To what extent do such linguistic choices depend on the source of pain in the organism, on thresholds of pain determined by the organism? (2) Do such linguistic choices depend on the cultural background of the patient, his values, his conception of pain and the proper response to it which follows from these values? (3) Do such linguistic choices depend on the relationship of the patient to the physician, what the patient thinks the physician expects him to say, what the patient imagines the physician will respond to the various things he might say? (4) Do such linguistic choices depend on the psychological state of the patient, his conflicts, the idiosyncratic meanings pain has come to have for him, his fantasies about what is happening to him and why it is happening?

Then, you already know from your reading for the first seminar session of this course about what happens when a recording of a contentless flow of vowel tones is played—that is, a recording from which the acoustic frequencies of consonants, those noises determining the sense of speech, have been entirely omitted. Judges are able to agree, listening to such a recording, upon the emotion of the speaker (Freedman, Kaplan, & Sadock, 1976, p. 42). What must a physician know, wittingly or unwittingly, about language, about patterns of vowel tones (the music of speech), to make warranted inferences about his patient's feelings—without regard to the semantic content of what the patient says, without even listening to the words we have just mentioned (or by listening beyond these words), without even knowing *what* the patient is talking about (or by knowing more than *what* the patient is talking about)? Can we imagine that a physician might also make similarly important inferences from patterns of syntax alone?[4]

All physicians talk with patients. What physicians and patients say to each other affects the relationship between them. The degree and quality of the collaboration between patient and physician—their ability to join together to cope with the patient's illness—are built to some large extent on the risky foundations of "talk." The patient's conception of his illness and his response to it are shaped, in part, by the way in which his physician uses speech to question, inform, advise, and instruct. In some ways that we do not fully understand, what the physician says—

---

[4] Edelson (1975) discusses these questions and in particular extensively the "music of speech."

by altering how the patient thinks and feels—may directly affect (independently of other interventions) the state of illness itself.

The physician probably depends on language more than he knows. The speech of the patient, elicited by the speech of the physician, provides the latter with data from which he makes a stream of critical clinical inferences—even before he makes use of any more complex technologies or physical interventions. At the least, from speech the physician forms hunches about what to look for, where to look for it, and how best to go about looking for it. However tentatively, from speech he more or less quickly forms conclusions about what kind of person the patient is.

The physician tends to suppose that the patient's speech is only a vehicle for the transmission of information the patient intends to convey through its use. The physician pays no focal attention to the speech itself—only to what it "means." He hears through speech, as if it were transparent, to what it means. However, the patient's utterances are objects in themselves. Yes, words, sentences are objects in the world—just as tables, chairs, numbers, and electrons are. They have properties as other objects do. Many of the properties of these utterances (as we have noted at least some investigators report) are unknowingly built into them by the patient who makes them, and only tacitly observed by the physician. It is an important possibility that these data, which include the grammatical form of utterances, as well as sound patterns, rhythms, ambiguities, and various kinds of deviance, do not receive focal attention by either patient or physician but nevertheless influence clinical inference.

We do not know to what extent the physician's clinical inferences depend on his unwitting observation of properties of speech itself. For should that be the case, and whenever it is the case, the physician is likely to attribute his clinical skills to "intuition" or "art." He certainly does not usually regard knowledge of language as part of the foundation of his clinical skill or believe that the study of language is a necessary part of his medical education.

Yet, the many properties of speech and different kinds of language use—no less than pain or cardiac murmur—are symptoms or signs. Today, the term *semiotics* has been preempted by logic, philosophy, and literature to refer to a general theory of signs and symbolism, which has as its branches syntactics, semantics, and pragmatics. Long before it was so preempted, this term belonged to medicine (and perhaps should be reclaimed by it). In 1625, Hart wrote in his *Anatomy*, "The chiefe . . . part of Physicke diagnosticke or semioticke, which teacheth us to know the nature, causes, and substance of the disease by the signes and grounds of the same" (O.E.D.). Aspects of the patient's language are signs of the disease and of the patient's conceptions of, attitudes toward, and responses to the irreducible triad: himself (and, in particular, his body), his disease, and the physician.

Suppose we distinguished physical signs of disease from symptoms of disease. Physical signs are discoverable by the physician in the course of a physical or laboratory examination. Symptoms are complaints of the patient conveyed to the physician most usually through the use of speech. Then we want to know if there is any difference (and, if there is, what difference) between inference from physical signs and inference from symptoms or complaints.

We want to know in what respect linguistic signs are different from any other the physician uses in arriving at conclusions about a patient. In what ways does any so-called animal language, any index or physical "sign" of some immediate existent thing (under the skin, for example), any arbitrary signal such as you have studied in conditioning paradigms that may set your patient's heart racing or his gut twisting, any icon, any expressive or emotive symbol, any agreed-upon code, differ from a natural language (the class to which human verbal utterances belong)?

8.4. Language and Behavioral Science Foundations of Medicine

A major revolution in the so-called behavioral sciences has occurred since the 1950s, following developments in the science of linguistics initiated primarily by Noam Chomsky (1957). These developments, in turn, would not have been possible without less generally well-known work in symbolic logic or mathematical logic, which since the last half of the nineteenth century has advanced at a rate and magnitude argued by some to dwarf all the achievements in logic of the preceding two thousand years. This work has had widespread ramifications for many endeavors; for example, the development of the logical foundations of mathematics, and the consequent unification of its many branches; the invention of artificial languages and simulation models in the computer and communication sciences; the study of learning, cognition, and the brain and mind of man; and the investigation of the scientific enterprise itself, the construction of its explanatory theories, and the ground of deductive and inductive inference. Indeed, Whitehead and Russell's *Principia Mathematica* and Freud's *The Interpretation of Dreams*, published within a decade of each other, ushered in, according to Susanne Langer, a new intellectual epoch, a new world view, whose theme is "the power of symbolism" in all the works and the life of man (Edelson, 1972, 1978).

This revolution in the behavioral sciences, born of work in linguistics, is in many ways as significant as, and certainly congruent with, that wrought earlier by Freud. We may argue that the two revolutions to some extent, at least, are one, since for both the problem of signs—their significance, their interpretation, and their organization into sign systems—is central. One of Freud's great discoveries, if not indeed his greatest discovery, was of two different processes or sign systems—primary and secondary—according to which representations or presentations of meaning come to be constructed. For both primary and secondary process, language is crucial (Edelson, 1975, 1977). This aspect of Freud's work is necessary for conceptualizing how internal representations are used in the kind of computations we include under the rubrics of thinking, planning, and seeking. More than any other, this aspect of his work also has direct links with theories of brain, on the one hand, and, on the other, with theories of the works of man or culture—the matrix in which humanhood is acquired and manifested.

A major paradigm shift is occurring in the behavioral sciences. The central idea is *language*. Theories of mind, brain, and society are being drastically revised to take into account our knowledge of language. We speak of genetic codes and of neural transmission codes in the organism, of symbolic media in social systems, of the symbolic function in personality systems (Edelson, 1976). Within a few years perhaps, if not already, no physician will be able to evaluate the literature in many (perhaps not in any) of the behavioral sciences without an adequate background in linguistics—without at the least an adequate mastery of the technical vocabulary of linguistics.

Moreover, the physician will increasingly find that views of the human being who is his patient—whose humanity is perhaps nowhere more evident than in his acquisition and use of language—are determined by stands taken on the nature of language. The physician's own view of language will govern his conception of his patient as human being and thus, however subtly, nuances of his relationship with his patient.

Sociolinguistic studies are already clarifying difficulties in the interactions of patients and health professionals from different cultures, whose different value systems prescribe different ways of talking—different ways of expressing pain in language, for example. What for one person is sharing feelings to create solidarity with others is for another person hysterical hyperbole or betrayal of weakness. What for one is cooperation through a dispassionate transmission of helpful information is for another a soulless surrender of autonomy, a going against the conviction that after all a person is supposed to know better than anyone else what is wrong with him and what is best to do about it (Zborowski, 1969).

Patients and health professionals speak in different tongues. They see the world from the perspective of different terminologies. John Dewey referred to that condition in which a person's perspective on the world is constricted by one specialized terminology as an "occupational psychosis," so serious are its consequences. This confusion of tongues and the automatic unthinking use by health professionals of an arcane terminology, without awareness of its impact on the uninitiated, interfere with the care of some patients at least and contribute to the dysfunctional impact of hospitalization itself and to unwelcome side effects of many medical and surgical interventions (Baziak & Dentan, 1960).

Medical science will inevitably also be affected by developments in linguistics. The literature on speech disorders offers a convincing case study of how studies carried out by investigators with inadequate or different conceptions of language may miscarry. In one study after another attempting to correlate neuroanatomical or neurophysiological facts with language functioning, the data are inadequate in the light of what we now know we need to know. Data from one study, collected by means governed by one conception of language, are not comparable with data collected by means governed by another conception of language. Needless to say, advances in this area have been almost nonexistent, despite the plenitude of clinical case reports—with no work able to build on any other (Lenneberg, 1967).

One moral is clear from much of this work. One cannot draw conclusions about the brain and any of its functions without an adequate description and theory of the nature of the function itself—and of other functions as well. Psycholinguists study how a person comprehends and produces speech and what relation exists between language and thought. Their studies suggest to what an extent an adequate understanding of language must be joined to a comparable understanding of other functions—for example, memory, perception, and attention—if an adequate solution of these problems is to be found (Luria, 1973).

8.5. Capacity and Motivation

It is interesting that, to know something about human language, we must take a kind of interest in human beings that is more customary in medicine than in much of social science. Social scientists tend to be distinguished by interest in motivation, in purposive dispositions manifested in actual performances, rather than interest in structured capacities, which (if taken at all) tend to be taken as given. Until recently— that is, specifically, until the interests of cognitive psychologists, in general, and psycholinguists, in particular, received a powerful impetus from the work of the linguist Chomsky—many psychologists, for example, were more likely to ask why a person was doing something, in the sense of what motive he had for doing it, than to ask what about the person made it possible for him to do it at all (Miller, Galanter & Pribram, 1960). About a verbal utterance, then, a psychologist might ask what motivated a person to utter under particular circumstances a particular sentence rather than ask what made it possible for the person to form and utter this or any sentence at all, supposing that indeed the person wanted to utter it. (No physician who has ever faced a stroke victim who is aphasic, who is struggling to utter a sentence and suffering the full agonized awareness of his inability to do so, could ever again be unaware of the question, What capacity makes it possible to speak?— although physicians have not been remarkably successful in their attempts to answer it.)

To repeat, one question focuses on a capacity or kind of competence; the other question focuses on what determines the use made of that capacity or competence in some particular motivated or purposive act or performance. Both are, of course, legitimate inquiries—although there is reason to believe that the study of the nature of a capacity is logically prior to the much more difficult study of the determinants of its use in varying circumstances.

The physician, his attention directed to the organism, has traditionally been concerned with questions of capacity and incapacity, with what is necessary for something to be able to work—whether the "something" be digestion, circulation, or locomotion. Given intact capacity, the physician has not regarded it his province as physician to inquire why a person should use his intact capacities one way rather than another. Perhaps for this reason, many physicians find it difficult to become interested in motives or they feel that such an interest is irrelevant to their work—except when motives lead a patient to use his capacities in a way that is perversely inimical to cooperation with the physician (i.e., from the point of view of the physician, the patient does not make rational use of his capacities).

Many social scientists, on the other hand, find repellent or far-fetched formulations about language describing it as a structural component of a person like an arm, a leg, a brain, or a digestive or circulatory system. Psychologists have typically explained the actions of man as determined either entirely by environmental stimuli (actions are reactions to such stimuli) or entirely by drives or purposive dispositions to act in certain ways under certain circumstances ultimately grounded in physiological processes. Those correlating actions and environmental stimuli have attributed minimum internal structure to the actor (seen as reacting automatically to stimuli). Alterations in the actor, called "learning," have been presumed somewhat implausibly (given the complexity of these and analogous phenomena) to come about in accordance with the simplest sorts of principles.

Freud, to be sure, in his more complex sophisticated formulation, the complemental series, proposed that actions could only be understood as determined by both drives and external events, each category of determinants having a different degree of influence in different persons on different occasions or during different phases in the life cycle (Freud, 1953). However, for the most part, Freud tended to view drives as unorganized dispositions, in contrast to the structural components controlling or inhibiting their expression.

Freud made frequent allusions to constitutional ego characteristics, usually in the context of his rather bleak assessment of the possibilities of change (even given so radical and thorough a therapy as psychoanalysis). Ego psychologists, however, have only recently emphasized as part of psychoanalytic theory the existence of so-called inborn or innate autonomous ego apparatuses or capacities, such as memory and perception. These capacities owe their primary existence neither to drives and their vicissitudes nor to environmental input. Such inborn ego apparatuses or capacities (along with drives), in fact, guarantee that man is not enslaved by external stimuli, and also guarantee (along with external stimuli) that man is not enslaved by his drives (Hartmann, 1964; Rapaport, 1967). Language is now thought by linguists such as Chomsky to be one such inborn or innate capacity (Chomsky, 1975). It also guarantees man's freedom from domination by environment, on the one hand, and drives, on the other.

Despite these developments, many psychologists and psychoanalysts continue to be preoccupied with the role of motives or purposive dispositions—with what determines the use of a capacity rather than with the nature of the capacity itself. One cannot quarrel with this state of affairs, if it represents a division of labor in scientific work. But why is it so difficult for some to accept the legitimacy of regarding language as a capacity? Why must language be fixedly regarded by them as (of course, obviously) *nothing more than* motivated speech acts or verbal communications?

One might ask whether the rejection of a study of man in terms of the nature of his capacities may have its origin in a bias. For example, in our culture at least, the term *capacities* has the connotation "limitations." A belief in the influence of experience or drives goes with a perhaps utopian, certainly optimistic ideology asserting that the possibilities of bringing about change by controlling or manipulating the environment or physiological states are unlimited. A simplistic environmentalism returns in the guise of an emphasis on the importance of object relations and socialization in development that, valid as it is, is vitiated by an unwarranted assumption that human beings are tabulae rasae and almost infinitely plastic. A simplistic drive theory returns in the guise of analogies excessively ethologizing man's social and psychological life. In reaction to these assumptions, perhaps the best example of a simplistic emphasis on capacities would, I suppose, be the belief that man's fate, including his particular performances or uses of capacities, is primarily, if not entirely, determined by his genes.

Physicians, who by the nature of their work must struggle with the fact of incapacity and face the tragedy of irrevocable alteration in a capacity, may find it easier in the long run than most social scientists to accept a study of language as a kind of competence like being able to walk, breathe, or digest food. (The problem here rather, as I have suggested, is that many physicians may not see the point for their work in any study of language at all.)

An interest in language as a capacity or competence leads to a theory of language that attempts to answer the following questions: What is linguistic competence? What are some of its properties? What are the properties of the agent, the person, possessing this competence? If we can answer these questions, we can demarcate human speech from the other kinds of signs physicians use in making inferences about patients and their illnesses. Incidentally, if we can answer these questions, we can also demarcate human language from the so-called languages and language behavior of other animal species (which have been the subject of so much interest in the recent literature, not to mention television and the popular press).

8.6. Language and Language Users: Facts and Hypotheses

Speaking of linguistic competence, we may ask what does a user of a natural language know—"know" in both senses: he "knows that" and he "knows how to." We may ask what do we know that he knows and what do we infer that he knows. In the following discussion, I shall differentiate between facts and inferences—for example, between what knowledge we observe the language user possesses (i.e., knowledge apparent in his intuitions and judgments, and what we observe he knows how to do with language) and inferences we make about the underlying linguistic competence (formulated in a theory of language) for which such facts are evidence. In other words, in each case, facts mentioned follow from the properties assigned to language or to the user of language by inferences formulated as hypotheses or statements in a theory of language (see Figure 8.1.).[5]

8.6.1. Fact

Any user of a natural language, any speaker of such a language, knows that a particular sentence is grammatical or nongrammatical, well formed or not well formed. He can make this judgment whether or not he has ever encountered the sentence before. He can make this judgment without regard to the comprehensibility of the sentence. He knows that *this* particular sentence, which is easy to comprehend, is nevertheless not well formed; it is nongrammatical. He knows that *that* particular sentence, difficult to comprehend, is nevertheless well formed; it is grammatical.

Faced with a sentence he judges to be not well formed or non-

[5] The form of the following discussion owes something to the clarification of some of Chomsky's more controversial concepts by Moravcsik (1974).

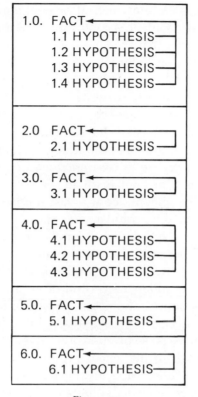

Figure 8.1.

grammatical, a person knows (he might say, intuitively) that some rule (or perhaps more than one) for generating sentences has (or have) been violated. ("Generate" is used here in the same sense an algebraic equation "generates" different numbers when its variables are assigned different values. How the sentence is actually constructed or produced, and in what way and when rules are involved in the production of sentences, are other questions, not being considered here.) Nevertheless, it is likely that he cannot say what rule (or rules) has (or have) been violated. He may not be able to give the rule a name or explicate it— even upon prolonged reflection, even if, in fact, he is a linguist.

In summary, the language user acts as if he had knowledge of an internalized set of rules, and as if this knowledge were tacit or unconscious—reflection and introspection being not sufficient to bring this knowledge to consciousness.

8.6.1.1. Hypothesis. From the language-user's ability to make judgments that sentences are grammatical or nongrammatical, and his intuition that the former sentences conform to and the latter violate rules, we may justifiably infer that the language-user's linguistic competence is best represented as an internalized set of rules he knows. (In the unusual cases where he is doubtful whether a sentence is grammatical or not, the set of rules which accounts better than any other theory for the demarcation between clear-cut cases of grammaticality and nongrammaticality decides the issue. If a sentence is generated by members of this set of rules, it is grammatical; if not, it is nongrammatical.)

It should be emphasized that *a priori* assumptions about how this knowledge is acquired are not justified. However, that the language user can make this judgment about a vast number of sentences never before encountered tends to count against simplistic ideas about the way in which language is acquired; for example, that language is made up of acquired habits, "learned" by practice and generalization based on the recognition of sentence-pattern similarities,[6] or by a time-consuming process of instruction under the control of externally granted rewards for approved performance (Chomsky, 1964; Hilgard & Bower, 1975).

It should also be emphasized that we do not know how or when the language user makes use of this knowledge, this internalized set of rules, in performance, in the actual production or comprehension of sentences. (Obviously other capacities such as perception, memory, and heuristic problem-solving devices or strategies enter also into the actual production and comprehension of sentences.) We are not justified in assuming *a priori* that production or comprehension in performance always involves using knowledge of this set of rules, or that in some way a theoretical description attempting to account for production or comprehension will conform (with regard to a sequence of steps, for example) to a theoretical description of what this set of rules should be like to account for the ability to judge sentences as grammatical or nongrammatical. Such assumptions are rather matters for empirical investigation.[7]

8.6.1.2. Hypothesis. From the inability of the language user to arrive at rules for generating sentences by introspection, we infer that his knowledge of these rules is unconscious. The attribution of unconscious

---

[6] The idea "similar" is problematic. How do we know when two entities are "similar"?
[7] Many apparently critical tests of Chomsky's theory of language fall wide of the mark, because they assume his theory is a theory of the actual production or comprehension of sentences, which it is not.

knowledge to a human agent need not surprise us. It accords with our everyday acquaintance with skills such as swimming. Swimming involves knowledge the swimmer is unable to explicate; furthermore, we often do not know how knowledge is used in a skillful performance. It also accords with the by now indisputable empirical findings of psychoanalysis that a person may have knowledge of a great deal that profoundly affects his actions, and that yet is ordinarily not accessible to introspection. It is unconscious. Only under exceptional circumstances, if ever, can it become conscious.

8.6.1.3. Hypothesis. From the independence of the language user's judgments about the form of sentences and judgments about their communicative efficacy or comprehensibility, we may infer that the syntax or form of sentences is in some way independent of semantics or the meaning of sentences.

Furthermore, we may infer that language as a tool and the function of communication do not coincide—are not indissolubly one. Although obviously language may serve the function, among others, of communicating information, its rules are not determined solely by requirements of communication. In fact, rules governing the form of sentences are quite different from rules, supposing there are such, governing the use of sentences in various kinds of communicative discourse. (This distinction is neglected by those who focus on "speech acts" and their situational contexts.) The ability to abstract the form of a sentence from its content and the circumstances and aims of its use is clearly part of linguistic competence.

That language is not governed by communication and its requirements, that it is abstractable from situational and communicative contents, and that it is available for thought and poetry and other uses as well, make it a different kind of sign system from most others—in particular, so-called animal languages.

8.6.1.4. Hypothesis. From all this follows a conception of natural language as the set of all and only the sentences generated by a finite set of rules. It turns out that this set of sentences, for reasons we shall see, is infinite. The language user possesses a finite device that enables him to create an infinite set of sentences.

8.6.2. Fact

A language user knows how to produce an infinite set of sentences.

Of course, the length of any actual sentence may have practical limits in a particular context of use, given the limits imposed by such nonlinguistic factors as memory.

However, all sentences are theoretically unbounded. Any sentence, no matter how long, may be made yet longer by adding another adjective, phrase, or clause. In other words, there are a variety of operations for combining sentences. Any sentence at all may be made longer by using such an operation, which adding a word, phrase, or clause yields yet a different sentence, which itself may be so operated upon.

8.6.2.1. Hypothesis. We infer from this fact that the user of a language is creative in one sense we shall use the term "creative." Possessing finite resources, he is able to produce an infinite set of sentences.

There is nothing about language itself as a sign system that limits what thoughts it can be used to express. If the sentences a language user were able to produce depended on no other factor than his knowledge of all the rules (phonological, syntactic, and semantic) for forming simple grammatical sentences and the operations for combining these sentences to form more complex grammatical sentences—not on his knowledge of the world, or his store of concepts, or the size of his vocabulary, or his rationality, or his stock of memories, or his ability to think clearly, or the integrity of his physiological apparatus—then there would be no limit to the content of the messages he could produce. He could say anything at all.

We may infer also that the rules of language must possess recursive devices. That is, these rules must include operations such that whatever entity is yielded by such an operation can be operated on once again to yield still another such entity. For example, "The dog chased the cat" may be combined by a rule of language with "The cat chased the rat" to yield "The dog chased the cat that chased the rat," which may be combined by the same rule with "The rat sought the cheese" to yield "The dog chased the cat that chased the rat that sought the cheese," and so on, without end.

Language as a sign system is different from any signals or codes—whether these involve animal grunts (or other ejaculatory vocalizations) or flag signals—that are capable of representing only a finite set of messages.

Human language as a sign system is also different from the so-called languages of certain animal species (for example, the dance of the bees) that are capable of representing an infinite set of messages. Unlike human language, however, such a sign system is organized by the location of a message on a limited number of continuous dimensions; for example, movement that is vertical or horizontal in space, or of a certain degree of intensity. Since these continua possess infinite degrees, it follows that the set of messages such a "language" can transmit is also infinite. However, there are a very limited number of such continuous dimensions. Location upon such continua, again quite unlike the organization of human language, is strictly correlated in a one-to-one relation with specific features of the world—for example, the distance from the dancer to source of honey and the location of source of honey in physical space. These limitations in turn limit markedly what the messages generated by such a "language" can be about.

8.6.3. Fact

The language user does not produce or understand a sequential chain of arbitrarily associated links, connected by "habit" (whatever that is), for he knows far ahead in a sentence what word must be chosen to agree syntactically with a word or phrase that will not occur until much farther along in the sentence. An example is the tense of a verb which agrees syntactically with the singular or plural noun widely separated from it.[8]

8.6.3.1. *Hypothesis.* The language user cannot be a finite-state automaton. If he can be modelled by a computer, it must be a much more complicated one than a finite-state device, in which each successive state in a chain of such states depends only on the state immediately preceding it.[9]

8.6.4. Fact

The language user knows more about a sentence than is given by the sentence as a physical signal. He hears and treats what is a continuous flow of sounds as discontinuous segments. He knows, and he can be brought relatively easily to an awareness, that a given sentence is a number-of-ways ambiguous. He knows that a sentence may have more

---

[8] Some examples given by Lyons (1970) are: <u>Anyone</u> who says that <u>is</u> lying. <u>Anyone</u> who says that <u>people</u> who deny that <u>are</u> wrong <u>is</u> lying.

[9] It is rare for a social scientist to prove that a certain hypothesis about man—in this case one widely held in the 1950s by those enthusiastic about the possibilities of computer simulation and information theory—is in fact impossible. Chomsky's rigorous proof that given the facts about natural language, man cannot be a finite-state device is one such rare achievement.

than one sense, and that he can use the same sentence in different contexts since its sense in any utterance of it can change depending on the context in which it is used. Ambiguity is not necessarily semantic, that is, dependent on a particular word having different senses. The ambiguity may be phonological as in "I said 'through the glass'" and "I said 'threw the glass'" (see Figure 8.2.). It may also be syntactic as in "Obliging physicians can be dangerous" (see Figure 8.3.). This sentence receives two different syntactic readings. It is two-ways ambiguous. It may be used to assert that if a patient is too obliging he may incautiously subject himself to a risky treatment recommended by a physician; or it may be used to assert that, if a physician is too obliging, he may endanger the patient's life by not carrying out a necessary treatment to which a patient objects. The following sentence may be analyzed syntactically in two different ways. "The doctor prefers to have old men and women as patients," may be used to assert that the physician is devoted solely to geriatrics or to imply that he is devoted to lecherous pursuits as well (see Figure 8.4.).

The language user also knows that sentences include presuppositions as well as assertions: "The present head of Yale–New Haven Hospital is bald" presupposes that there is at least one and at most one head of Yale–New Haven Hospital and asserts that he is bald. "The overconscientious physician decided to treat more rather than less patients," presupposes but does not assert that the physician to whom reference is made is overconscientious and thus implies but does not assert the reason for his decision.

The language user knows further that two sentences may have the same syntactic form, and yet words which are assigned to the same syntactic category in the sentence actually possess a different syntactic

Figure 8.2.

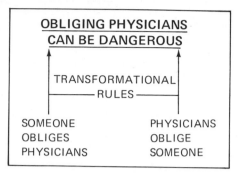

Figure 8.3.

function. "The patient was easy to please" and "The patient was eager to please" both receive the same syntactic analysis, although in one case it is clear that someone, perhaps the physician, pleases the patient and that in the other it is the patient who pleases—perhaps the physician (see Figure 8.5.).

The language user similarly knows that, in two sentences that receive quite different syntactic analyses, the same words assigned to different syntactic categories actually possess the same syntactic function. A patient with a fracture may say, in answer to one question, "My *brother* tripped me," and in answer to another, "I was *tripped* by my brother." "My brother" and "I" are, respectively, subjects of the two sentences but in fact the cognitive sense of the sentences, that proposition which is either true or false, is in both cases the same, and the subject of that proposition—the agent rather than the object of action— is "my brother."

8.6.4.1. Hypothesis. The language user's knowledge of language is not limited to the physical characteristics of the acoustic signal he re-

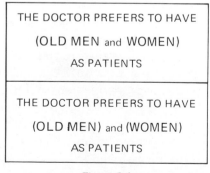

Figure 8.4.

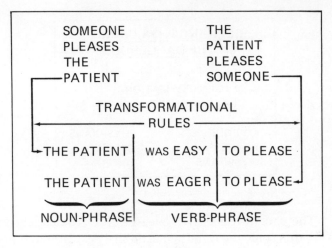

Figure 8.5.

ceives or even to the abstract syntactic segmentation of surface sentences produced or comprehended. He is not stimulus-bound; neither his production nor his comprehension is stimulus-governed.

The behavior of the language user cannot be understood by correlating behavior and stimulus-input. Understanding the behavior requires postulating the categories and rules the language user knows and uses in producing and comprehending not only language but any kind of action at all.

To account for the facts, we infer that he possesses a theory of language. This theory includes three independent levels of analysis, three ways any sentence can be analyzed. Each level, phonological, syntactic, and semantic, has an independent set of categories and rules.

The language-user's theory of language clearly must be underdetermined by the data to which he is exposed, since he might just as well have formulated some alternate theory to account for the data.

8.6.4.2. Hypothesis. Phrase structure rules, simply segmenting sentences as given, do not provide a sufficient theory of language. One theory of language that is more adequate follows. A surface syntactic structure gives what syntactic information is necessary to interpret the sentence in an appropriate sound and intonation pattern. Or more technically, a phonological representation, which is an analysis using phonological categories, can be assigned to a surface syntactic structure. An inferred deep or underlying syntactic structure gives what syntactic information is necessary to interpret the meaning or propositional content of the sentence. Or more technically, a semantic representation, that is, an analysis using semantic categories, can be assigned to the deep or underlying syntactic structure. As we have seen, a sentence with a given surface structure can be associated with more than one deep structure. Also, one deep structure can underly sentences with different surface structures.

The relation between sound and sense in natural human language is not arbitrary, although it is often characterized as such. It is not conventional in the sense that it comes about by a process of social agreement, as in the use of a code. The relation between sound and sense is mediated by syntax or form. In particular, rules of formation or phrase structure rules of syntax, together with a dictionary-like lexicon, generate deep syntactic structures, which receive semantic interpretation. These deep structures are operated on in their entirety by transformational rules of syntax. These rules generate surface syntactic structures, while holding important aspects of cognitive sense invariant. These surface structures receive phonological interpretation.

When the relation between a phenomenal representation or vehicle and what it represents is some kind of resemblance or similarity between the two, then we have an iconic symbol. Piaget has considered the symbolic play of children as involving iconic symbols (Piaget, 1962). The symbols in dreams and folktales, considered by Freud, are also iconic symbols. A diagram of the nervous system is an iconic representation of it, and if you came across such a diagram, even if it were unlabeled, it might indeed bring to mind the nervous system you have been studying.

Such icons contrast, as ways of signifying meaning, with natural language, in which there is no necessary similarity between sound and cognitive sense, although such similarities may be exploited—as in poetic or rhetorical utterances—to convey emotional states or attitudes. In language, the relation between sound and sense is mediated instead by the transformation of syntactic forms of one kind into those of another.

8.6.4.3. Hypothesis. Transformational rules of syntax appear to be structure-dependent operations. That is, such rules operate on entire structures as defined by abstract categories—rather than any item in a particular position—and operate on such structures cyclically (rather than on any item in a given category). For example, a transformational rule moves an entire noun phrase to a new position, but does not operate on a noun embedded within that noun phrase. There is no *a priori* reason to suppose that such rules should be structure-dependent. That they are, suggests that there are species-specific linguistic universals. It also suggests that these universals are not simply substantive. Substantive universals include the finite set of distinctive phonetic features from which every language draws to form its own sounds or phonemes. Each phoneme is a bundle of such features. Another substantive universal is the syntactic rule that rewrites every sentence in the deep structure as a noun phrase followed by a verb phrase. Linguistic universals are formal as well. That transformational rules are structure-dependent is such a formal linguistic universal. Formal universals constrain what kinds of rules may be part of a theory of natural language.

I suggest to you that when you consider the Sapir-Whorf hypothesis (Sapir, 1966; Whorf, 1964) and various writings emphasizing differences between languages, and how such differences limit what is possible for those who speak different languages to think, you should keep in mind (1) the distinction between vocabulary, which does, of course, reflect the interests of a culture, and the grammar or rules of language; (2) the distinction between rules generating surface structures (which, of course, may differ widely from language to language) and rules generating deep structures; (3) the evidence for linguistic universals; and (4) the fact that no human language has ever been discovered that can be considered intrinsically more primitive (or animallike) than any other human language.

8.6.5. Fact

The language user knows how to comprehend a sentence never before encountered and how to produce a sentence never before encountered appropriate to the circumstances in which it is uttered. Whatever we mean by appropriate, we do not mean that the production of a sentence is governed by, or can be predicted from knowledge of, external stimuli or drive states. As Chomsky has ably argued, it would be difficult indeed, before the fact, to identify the stimulus "causing" a particular verbal behavior of the language user. Except in rather bizarre circumstances involving a large degree of coercion, much as in the classical conditioning paradigm, the set of possible appropriate utterances in any particular situation are apparently infinite. The probability of the occurrence of any one utterance in a particular situation is close to zero. Utterances are not only appropriate, but also novel.

In addition, we note that the language user is able to use language to talk about language and to invent languages.

8.6.5.1. Hypothesis. The human language user in this sense is creative in a way no other species is, although the nature of this creativity is still largely a mystery. Natural language is by this criterion held to be species-specific.

Speech as a sign is not "caused" by a somatic state or the environment or whatever it signifies or is about. It may be distinguished, therefore, from indices, which are also used as signs and, in fact, are often so used by physicians.

In Piaget's work on symbolic functioning, an index functions as a sign by virtue of its intrinsic physical relation to that which it signifies. It is a part of, or related as cause to effect to, what it signifies (Piaget & Inhelder, 1969). A palpable protuberance is a sign of a tumor; a fever or inflammation, a sign of foreign invasion; a scream, a sign of pain.

Because the physician is so alert to indices, he may carry over the same set in interviewing a patient. He may mistakenly regard the patient's responses to his questions or instructions as necessary effects of them, and, indeed, conduct the interview in such a way that he coerces responses rather than creates the conditions in which the patient's creativity may manifest itself. For similar reasons, perhaps, a physician may be prone to accept without question extrapolations from studies of language using an animal population to the human species despite the marked relevant differences between the two populations.

8.6.6. Fact

Children acquire rules of language (their mistakes are systematic), without formal instruction, from experience with a set of debased and imperfect utterances in an extraordinary short time and are able to comprehend and produce sentences never before encountered. This acquisition is not correlated over a large range with intelligence. Children arrive at the correct grammar among all the many possible grammars of the language that would have fit the data to which they are exposed. Any child is capable of learning any language whatsoever.

8.6.6.1. Hypothesis. There are substantive and formal linguistic universals. These are part of the innate equipment of the human child.

If we postulate a linguistic universal from the intensive study of any particular single language, we formulate a strong empirical hypothesis subject to disconfirmation by the intensive study of another language.[10]

All these facts and inferences about language tell us something about the nature of human beings and have implications, as a number of readings in this course point out, for our understanding and theories of, for example, memory, perception, and action (Pribram, 1971). In each case we must postulate internalized capacities, which make possible the ability to recognize or comprehend the significance of some representation, as well as the ability to produce a representation according to some plan, set of instructions, or rules (Fodor, Bever, & Garrett, 1974).

8.7. Conclusion

For the physician, then, the primary payoff from a study of language is a better understanding of man and an increased ability to evaluate the various suggestions in the literature concerning his fundamental nature and what theory is most likely to be fruitful in capturing it.

In addition, however, the physician may be led to more awareness of his patient's speech, to its distinctive characteristics, and to individual differences in it from patient to patient and in the same patient from time to time. Since the physician knows the rules of language, as every human does, he can recognize departures from such rules, and features of utterances that are not constrained by rules and are therefore freed for expressing emotions and attitudes. An example would be alterations in the rate or volume of speech which do not affect sense but do convey feelings. A patient may show a preference for an unusually frequent use of one kind of vocabulary or, more interesting, one kind of syntactic transformation or one set of sounds over any other. Some patients use pronouns in a way that makes reference hard to follow. Some patients prefer to use transformations that result in surface sentences in which the subject is an *individual* such as "John"; or a *state*, such as "Being ill"; or an *event*, such as "Being hit on the head"; or a *fact*, such as "That my husband doesn't come around much." A patient may use transformations-that-delete, more than other patients or on some particular occa-

---

[10] Therefore, rejection of Chomsky's theoretical work as nonempirical or philosophical is not justified. Neither can the theory be rejected as incapable of making statements about linguistic universals even if the data so far were, as they are not, limited to the study of one language.

sion or suddenly within a particular interview more than is usual for himself. Given the unbounded nature of language and the creativity of language users, the set of a particular patient's utterances may seem unusually constricted, not just in vocabulary but even in type of sentence. Some patients' productions are full of all kinds of ambiguity that may be noted with profit by the physician if not by the patient as well.

In conclusion, as I promised to do, I shall state four beliefs:

1. The study of language is the key to the study of man.
2. The study of language provides a model for thinking about other human capacities.
3. The physician's attention to and understanding of linguistic phenomena lead to a deeper understanding of the patient and his illness.
4. At the least, the clinician's tacit or unwitting recognition of and response to linguistic phenomena account for a large part of what we call *clinical skill, art,* or *intuition.*

8.8. References

Balint, M. *The doctor, his patient, and the illness.* New York: International Universities Press, 1973.

Baziak, A., & Dentan, R. The language of the hospital and its effects on the patient. *ETC.: A Review of General Semantics,* 1960, *17,* 261–268.

Chomsky, N. *Syntactic structures.* The Hague: Mouton, 1957.

Chomsky, N. Review of B. F. Skinner's *Verbal behavior.* In J. Fodor & J. Katz (Eds.), *The structure of language.* Englewood Cliffs, N.J.: Prentice-Hall, 1964.

Chomsky, N. *Reflections on language.* New York: Pantheon, 1975.

Crookshank, F. G. The importance of a theory of signs and a critique of language in the study of medicine. In C. K. Ogden & I. A. Richards, *The meaning of meaning.* New York: Harcourt, Brace, and World, 1923.

Edelson, M. Language and dreams: *The interpretation of dreams* revisited. *The Psychoanalytic Study of the Child,* 1972, *27,* 203–282.

Edelson, M. *Language and interpretation in psychoanalysis.* New Haven: Yale University Press, 1975.

Edelson, M. Toward a study of interpretation in psychoanalysis. In J. Loubser, R. Baum, A Effrat, & V. Lidz (Eds.), *Explorations in general theory in social science* (2 vols.). New York: The Free Press, 1976, pp. 151–181.

Edelson, M. Psychoanalysis as science. *The Journal of Nervous and Mental Disease,* 1977, *165,* 1–28.

Edelson, M. What is the psychoanalyst talking about? In J. H. Smith (Ed.), *Psychiatry and the humanities: Psychoanalysis and language* (Vol. 3). New Haven: Yale University Press, 1978, pp. 99–170.

204   MARSHALL EDELSON

Fabrega, H., Jr., & Tyma, S. Language and cultural influences in the description of pain. *British Journal of Medical Psychology,* 1976, *49,* 349–371.

Fodor, J. A., Bever, T. G., & Garrett, M. F. *The psychology of language.* New York: McGraw-Hill, 1974.

Freedman, A., Kaplan, H., & Sadock, B. *Modern synopsis of psychiatry/II.* Baltimore: Williams and Wilkins, 1976.

Freud, S. *Introductory lectures on psychoanalysis.* Standard Edition of the Complete Psychological Works (Vols 15 & 16). London: Hogarth Press, 1953.

Hartmann, H. *Essays on ego psychology.* New York: International Universities Press, 1964.

Hilgard, E., & Bower, G. *Theories of learning* (4th ed.). Englewood Cliffs, N.J.: Prentice-Hall, 1975.

Labov, W., The logic of nonstandard English. In W. Labov (Ed.), *Language in the inner city.* Philadelphia: University of Pennsylvania Press, 1972, pp. 201–240.

Lenneberg, E. *Biological foundations of language.* New York: Wiley, 1967.

Lévi-Strauss, C. The effectiveness of symbols. In *Structural anthropology.* New York: Basic Books, 1967.

Luria, A. R. The directive function of speech in development and dissolution. *Word,* 1959, *15,* 341–352.

Luria, A. R. *The working brain.* New York: Basic Books, 1973.

Lyons, J. *Noam Chomsky.* New York: Viking, 1970.

Miller, G. A., Galanter, E., & Pribram, K. *Plans and the structure of behavior.* New York: Holt, Rinehart, and Winston, 1960.

Moravcsik, J. M. E., Competence, creativity, and innateness. In J. M. E. Moravcsik (Ed.), *Logic and philosophy for linguists.* The Hague: Mouton, 1974.

Piaget, J. *Play, dreams and imitation in childhood.* New York: Norton, 1962.

Piaget, J., & Inhelder, B. *The psychology of the child.* New York: Basic Books, 1969.

Pribram, K. *Languages of the brain.* Englewood Cliffs, N.J.: Prentice-Hall, 1971.

Rapaport, D. *Collected papers of David Rapaport* (M. Gill, Ed.). New York: Basic Books, 1967.

Sapir, E. *Culture, language, and personality.* Berkeley: University of California Press, 1966.

Shapiro, D. *Neurotic styles.* New York: Basic Books, 1965.

Whorf, B. L. *Language, thought, and reality.* Cambridge: The M.I.T. Press, 1964.

Zborowski, M. *People in pain.* San Francisco: Jossey-Bass, 1969.

Theodore Shapiro

TALKING TO CHILDREN AND ADOLESCENTS

One can see how many times patients have failed to convey a sense of self because a therapist has interpreted a snake as a penis symbol. (D. W. Winnicott, *Therapeutic Consultations in Child Psychiatry*, 1971, p. 10.)

Child therapists frequently admonish their supervisees to speak at the level of the child. Surely, this does not signify that one speak with the speech of the child, but rather at the level of the child's linguistic competence and ability to grasp what is being said. Thus, the words and grammatical structures that we use ought to coincide as closely as possible with the child's general cognitive abilities and the actual lexicon that he or she uses. Indeed, this might well be considered a general dictum in adult therapy. Significantly, the impact of using a patient's own words as opposed to using an alien vocabulary is manifestly effective. We certainly should avoid speaking to patients in metapsychological terms or in the argot of our particular theoretical framework. So why should we use one of the many pretentious codes unless our aim is to further distance us. Instead, we should substitute for classic Latinisms the lingua franca that dominates the therapeutic milieu. Furthermore, since the patient should be doing most of the talking, it ought to be his brand of lingua franca. This task becomes even more controversial when we deal with age-stage related abilities of children and

---

Theodore Shapiro ● Cornell University Medical College, New York, New York 10021. This chapter, with slight modification, originally appeared as Chapter 11 in *Clinical Psycholinguistics* by Theodore Shapiro, 1979, Plenum Press, New York, N.Y.

especially those of adolescents wherein the particular variations in linguistic performance characterizing that stage confound our comprehension still more.

Talking to preschool children in which the dominant activity in the
therapeutic session involves play requires the largest modification in
technique. The therapist does well to begin with designating the activities carried out by the youngster in his play behavior. The child is con-
fronted naturally with the naming-describing function with which he
is familiar. He also gets the idea that doing is complemented by saying
and that saying is an aim of the interaction. We will examine a series
of descriptions concerning the play and the action that is called forth
in the play.

The tendency for nursery teachers and therapists to use the present
progressive tense is well worth noting insofar as the /-ing/ ending of
that tense dominates the linguistic activities heard during such interactions: "Jimmy is *playing* with a block" or "Jimmy is *building* a castle"
or "He's *putting* mommy in the castle and now *knocking* the castle over."
The next step after such descriptions in the present progressive tense
usually involves a semi-interpretative remark that recognizes a wish, a
motivation, or, in young children the beginnings of designating affects
as opposed to acting upon them: "Jimmy is angry at his mommy." If
this response is to the negative, then one might begin to point again to
the play: "The blocks and the castle did tumble down about her?"

The latter confrontational exchange is stated without using a /wh/
phrase—what, when, who, where—which tend to be rather confusing
and poorly understood by young children. Since they learn these pro-
forms (substitutes for nouns or pronouns) somewhat later, the earlier
period of confrontation ought to exclude /wh/ forms. Moreover, the
promiscuous use of /wh/ form is taken by young children as an accu-
sation, especially in the word *why*. This is because the young child has
so often heard the word *why* following a minor misdemeanor in which
a parent has said "Why did you do that?" or "What did you do?" The
intention of the therapeutic intervention is to bring a behavior under
the ego's control and not to serve as an anlage for superego chastise-
ment.

As we consider the possibilities of being able to make more than
confrontations to children and which terms in what language to use,
we must try to find a way to convey intrapsychic conflict without confusion. To do this, we have to state the conflict in terms that the child

can deal with himself. In the simplest language of the child, it might be best to state two opposing wishes back to back, rather than saying "You are conflicted by," or to state an apposition. For example, the therapist might say "You want to go, but you also want to stay"—or if the *but* seems too advanced—"You want to go, and you want to stay" and adding the general clarifier "both at the same time," if he can take a sentence of that length. Children with attentional deficits might not. Moreover, children with nagging parents turn off after two words. Laconism wins that session not loquatiousness. One can easily move toward an affect following such a statement by saying "and that makes you feel fidgety in your hands" or "restless so you run around" or "worried inside." Each of these statements places the feeling state closer to a cognitive concept moving first from an observable body state that can be called by name.

As we discuss the matter of talking to children, it becomes clear that one of the tasks in the therapy of youngsters concerns the linking of behavior, qua activity, with their verbalizations to state what we generally call *affects* or *feeling states*. For the most part, preschool children have not learned to designate the nuances of feeling and less frequently to equate them with situational circumstances in which anticipation and control become possible if the linkage is appreciated. One of the earliest tasks in therapy with young children and even older children who have not been exposed to the nuances of language is to teach the words that match their feelings and how they relate to the situation that gives rise to such varied body and mind states. For example, "You do this when you feel Y or Z." "You knock over blocks when you feel worried that I am going to say 'no' to you." "You always become quiet and silent and stop playing when you feel angry." "You are afraid that I will punish you for doing an angry thing." "Oh, your daddy went away! That feeling you have which makes you want to cry while you're holding back the tears is called sadness." You may wish to offer the possibility and sense of the universality of feeling sad by saying "and everybody feels that way when somebody who is loved has gone off." This may seem didactic rather than analytic but it represents a significant step in making what seems private, public or what seems magical and isolated, social.

Teaching the names of affects is only part of the story, because these affects must be linked to ideational and situational content or else the names remain dangling as designations of mental states devoid of content and devoid of anticipatory power, to be called forth when certain circumstances recur in the life of the child. The aim of therapeutic communication with children as with adults concerns the possibility of offering a verbal lexical vehicle by which he or she can designate what used to be an unknown mysterious thing and change it to a current familiar thing that can be rendered less overwhelming.

There are two difficult problems in interpreting the unconscious to a child: the first concerns the tendency to turn the unconscious into an out-of-awareness, out-of-control animus that permits lack of responsibility; the second concerns his or her cognitive and linguistic capacity to comprehend that current behaviors may be dictated by prior patterns and prior experiences. The therapist has to be sure that the child understands such phrases as "when you remember" or "the difference between before and after" which are linguistic forms that are arrived at somewhat late, compared to the early lexical ability to designate the here and now (Harner, 1976; Miller, 1977). For this reason, we often stick to the description of the play activity on displaced objects and discuss affects, feelings, and inner conflict states in terms of play material, prior to bringing it home in relation to the past and current life situation or in the transference. If language is to serve as a scaffolding for ideation, it is the scaffolding which links the past with the present and the present with the behavior of the child in the therapeutic situation, either as a current reality or as a transferential phenomenon.

As the therapist advances towards the period of latency and the stage of concrete operations, the child also has a better grasp of nuances of grammar and lexical possibilities exemplified by his understanding the passive voice phrases or the flow of elements from the past into the present. Even the mastery of sequences such as days of the week bodes well for linguistic grasp. One might even suggest that latency signifies a significant cognitive event as well as a dynamic event (Shapiro & Perry, 1977) in which one clearly has to work with the unconscious as well as the conscious activities. Repression is more clearly evident and obsessive rigor has covered over the linguistic charm of earlier phrases and phases. However, although children of this stage have achieved a good deal of comprehensional ability, they are still not in the stage of abstract operational thought. As such, the therapist not only has to continue to speak in their language, choosing vocabulary carefully, but also has to speak at the complexity level that they are used to handling.

The child is much more likely to be engaged in some direct play activities or direct verbal interplay with the therapist and may even be able to bring in his or her feelings as something to talk about as well as be able to designate nuances of sadness, elation, disappointment or rage. The tendency toward acting out in some children at this stage has to be stated very carefully in terms of fantasy activity influencing behavior—a matter which is not apparent to many adults or children. One of the most useful therapeutic activities in this period of life is to make the distinction between *thinking* and *doing* while at the same time helping the patient to see that doing is used sometimes instead of thinking about things. These dicta are already a part of the general activities of therapists who deal with adults, but must be highlighted for routine use with children. There is a tendency to undercut the importance of such distinctions by their apparent banality and to surmise that they are generally known.

Encouragement of the child that the task of the meetings is to talk about feelings and problems must be at the forefront of a therapist's activity. However, many new therapists sometimes tend to fall into what seems to them like "nagging" rather than "interpreting" behaviors. Making sure that the child understands what he is doing may also be contrary to the aims of the meeting which, in the initial phases, are to establish a basis for unpressured communication in which the usual demands of the day-to-day world are suspended. In the words of Anthony (1974), therapeutic space is a land "between yes and no."

While we attempt to understand, the child is at a stage of development in which his wishes may become manifest during the therapy by a series of attempted exploitations: "Will you take me for a soda?" "Let me call my mother." "Oh, can I take home this toy?" "Oh, I would love to have the magazine in your waiting room." All these wishes can be satisfied easily enough, and, indeed, at times, when one is doing ego supportive activity or work that requires some compensation for parents' neglect, one may acquiesce. Even in child analysis many analysts offer the child some nutriment, especially after a long school day, with the knowledge that a little hypoglycemia impairs the attention to the therapy. More important, there is the natural expectation that the interaction between an adult and child is such that the adult is nurturing, giving, as well as understanding. That difficult step between "what do you give" and "how much do you avoid the giving" so that the *wishing* becomes apparent as a thought is one which only the sensitivity of practice and adequate supervision can teach the therapist. In unconscious terms, what you say to the child is also nutriment and must therefore be couched in digestible terms, both sweetened and strong enough to be effective. But if we need a way to the digestive center, a pinch of originality pays off. The child all too readily falls into your locution and begins to ignore what you say and even tells you how boring you are in your repetitiousness if you lack spice in your delivery. The child patient may fail to see repetitiousness in his own play behavior as the source of why you, the therapist, are repetitious. But it is possible that the lack of color in what is said does poison the content so that the child cannot tolerate it. This brings us to the possibility of peppering one's confrontations and interpretations from early childhood on well into adolescence with a lot more of the paralinguistic and prosodic music than we may be accustomed to in adult therapy.

It is truly condescending, however, to speak to a child in the high-pitched falsetto that signifies his or her inequality with you. Most children find this offensive. On the other hand, it *is* possible to use a grammatical form which is closer to their own, while at the same time appropriately raising and lowering the pitch of your voice, show appreciation and excitement or offer encouragement in the way in which you say something. If we remember that the affective envelope of what we say is probably learned prior to the content of what we say (Stern, 1979), in being closer then to that period when words were not available to a child, we do well to maintain the affective envelope if we are to keep the therapeutic alliance and make communicational sense. Besides, there is nothing so monotonous as the "hm" or mumbling of pat analytic phrasing. Since the task of therapy with children is to bring them back into life, a little liveliness in the way in which things are said is very helpful to the child and increases his or her willingness to receive what is said.

Chronological age alone would not dictate the syntactic and lexical forms that are used. We must also know something about the intellectual capacity of those ages or the degree of psychosis which may have its secondary effect on understanding. Watch how simply the child himself speaks; there may be minor retardation. The quality of the interpretation has to follow the degree of social sophistication, too. In a similar fashion there are a group of children, some of whom are psychotic, some of whom are simply obsessional, who use a broad-range vocabulary and rather pretentious Latinisms. Although we might not want to speak in the language of an unskilled laborer to this type of child, we might make such a child understand that we grasp what he is saying by not confronting him with his pretensions but answering him in kind, without mocking. Because he becomes so accustomed to alienating himself from others by his mannerisms, it may be comforting that our speech is non-judgmental. The look of appreciation that the therapist receives when the obsessional child is given something back in kind, this time with a gestural or mimetic twinkle (as well as a prosodic lilt), might be very useful in establishing contact especially in initial interviews.

Some psychotic children go so far as to create entire new languages made up of complex phonemes and morphemes and new lexicons. Strictly speaking, these are not likely to be new languages in a grammatical sense, for the syntax is rarely changed, but the new vocabulary is the focus. One suspects the referential change is in the service of shunning the things of this world. Such children are usually all too willing to share with you the nature of their supposed genius. Indeed, this is their very specialized message which says in essence "I am cut off from my peers and everyone else, but what I am looking for is a special group of people who will be able to not only admire me, but also will wish to communicate with me in kind." They also offer the challenge of meeting them more than halfway by learning a new tongue. I am suggesting that the message-carrying unit on the child's part may be simple verbalization, but, if we paid greater attention to the form as well as the content, we might be able to decipher and dissect some of the origins and intentions of the production so that the perlocutionary force of these speech acts may be interpreted in the appropriate framework, and all is not lost on the narrow focus of the words, grammar, or prosody.

Although children may not consciously speak in metaphors, it is interesting how metaphoric their speech can be. Indeed, the child's capacity for imaginary companions or the tendency to humanize a pet dog provides useful vehicle from which one can begin to understand the nature of the individual and idiosyncratic human relations and wishes. A. A. Milne (1961) in his poem, "Binker," describes a relationship with an imaginary companion. The child in the poem suggests that Binker liked sweets and that is why "he always asks for two." One comes to a full understanding of the existence of Binker as a "talking companion" by the end of the poem, and the realization that all the adults in this child's life seem available too infrequently for this child's needs. However, his wishes are revealed via displacement to the needy companion.

Some of the sociolinguistic models are instructive with respect to

how children respond to what the therapist says. We have already mentioned the tendency of children to take /wh/ questions as accusations.
They also have tendencies to take other comments in an accusing, pun-
ishing way. For example, if you walked into the room and said "The
window is open," it might sound like a simple description of the state
of the window sash. However, if you are sitting in a room and the two
of you are shivering and one of you is closest to the window, and you
utter the phrase "The window is open," surely it will have the illocu-
tionary force "Close the window!" You can imagine that the impact of
such a comment would be even greater on a late latency child in the
room with an adult, because it is so often the tendency in many households that the younger child as opposed to the adult is expected to do
the bit of work that is required to drop the sash. Of course, the reverse
might be equally possible in households where affluence is the case and
"thank God the child doesn't have to move." We can see how descriptions are sometimes turned into prescriptions by certain children.

In confronting the child, the therapist must take care and be certain
it is clear in describing a state of affairs that it does not mean that the
therapist necessarily wishes him or her to change, that the intention to
change has to come from within, and that the choice to change is free
if the wish is that certain circumstances are to be brought about. It is
therefore possible with children over eight that "if . . . then" hypo-
thetical phrases might be used as a way of conveying the possibility for
change. In fact, phrases such as "Suppose you," or "Let's pretend that,"
or "Do you think if" might be used to introduce contrary-to-fact conditional ideas that the child might be interested in enacting. The consequences of those actions might be considered in the phrasing as described. During play sessions, one could make the easy displacement
of representation from the concrete to the inner life by analogy, once
one is assured that the child has preconscious grasp that the tasks em-
barked on concern the establishment of greater contact with his or her
feelings.

Let us consider a seven-year-old child who has begun to elaborate
a sequence of play with a small car. During a session, a ramp was constructed which is essentially an inclined plane that enabled the car to
move from a great height on the table to the rim of the table, accelerating
in speed as it fell. As the car went tumbling over the edge, the child
seemed greatly excited. A simple description of the behavior might be
put in terms of how fast the car goes and how excited the child feels

when he sees is going so fast. Thus far, we have not breached even the austerity of a behaviorist's principles. During the next step, the child might comment, "Yes, it goes fast, but look it crashed on the bottom." It might be possible to state that "Going fast is exciting, but the danger of getting broken is a real problem." If the child then suggested that the car should have wings like "Chitty Chitty Bang Bang" so that it could convert itself into an airplane to avoid danger, one might exclaim "What a wonderful car!" Were the therapy further along, "What a wonderful car; it not only goes fast, but it can fly and doesn't have to worry about the dangers below." If we wanted to emphasize the denial implied in the wings which prevent the crash, the therapist might say "Wouldn't it be wonderful if cars had wings?" That would then put the emphasis on the fact that both therapist and child understand that this is not so, and that it is merely a wish to protect against the overwhelming aspect of the excitement leading to danger.

During the same play, the child might construct a series of barriers at the bottom of the ramp or comment, as the car came to an abrupt halt, that it had marvelous brakes. The therapist might comment "What a wonderful car to be able to go fast, and be able to stop just at the point that the danger became very great." This would emphasize both wish and defense, excitement and inhibition, and offer the child the concrete medium in which to play out and begin to work through some of the ramifications of his wishes and their dangers if executed.

The ultimate transfer of such statements about the play to the child's own emotions would have to come at an appropriate point as a description of the sense of excitement and restraint within himself, either by analogy or by demonstration in the play situation. Or, if we had gone through this sequence over and over again and knew of similar circumstances in our young patient's life, a question might broach the gap between play and life: "Wasn't that similar to this and that?" or "When you wanted to go on a roller coaster you felt so excited, and then you had to stay home with a tummyache because you were afraid that the excitement would be too much—it was like this." These verbalizations would be ways of making the linkages that are necessary in treatment so that the child's grasp of his circumstances both in play, with the therapist, and with the world he lives in could be integrated, brought together, and become a usable structure around which he could anticipate future excitement and dangers.

Genetic links to the past are a problem in child therapy because they involve a certain amount of "as if" thinking. "You act now *as if* your mother had deprived you then" represents the general form in which we find that therapists make genetic reconstructions. For the child, it must be put much more in terms of his feelings and *what* he actually remembers. Phrases such as "You remember what you told me about you and mommy when you went to the movies when you were two" or "You didn't remember what you felt, but from what you said just now, we could guess that you felt alone and sad but couldn't say it then." Thus, language even in the quite young child permits a possibility for stating how the facts of your observations cohere with the facts that you are aware of in his or her life. Winnicott's book, *The Piggle* (1977), provides a number of examples of genetic interpretation to a very young patient and the degree of imagination necessary to grasp the meaning of play data. The linkages to knowledge of current life and concerns are essential.

Talking to adolescents provides another set of problems and also some of the same problems we have when talking to young children. We might begin by classifying the problems of talking to adolescents not in terms of the biology of their developmental stage, but, more importantly, in terms of their sociology. If we were to draw a systems diagram of adolescence, it would be best represented by that overlapping space in which childhood and adulthood intersect. Whatever rite of passage each culture offers adolescents to mark his or her march into this period, there are no formal rites of passage which involve the introduction of a secret language that arises naturally. And yet, adolescence, with its sociology of gang formation, chumship, and new group arrangements, creates a situation in which linguistic drift and usage take on a unique form. This has occurred during every stage of history. There is no period in development in which language variance from the general standard tongue spoken in the surround undergoes such rapid idiosyncratic changes. The Opies (1959) have described the language and lore of childhood in terms of the uniformity of game structure, rhyme, and jargon for latency by oral transmission. Similarly, adolescents have a network of linguistic movement which is carried by their music, their songs, and their propensity to play with language in small and secret group interchanges. The lingo of the bobby-soxer in the 1940s contrasted with the language of the "greaser" attests to the rapid shifts that take place in a brief span of 20 to 30 years.

If we begin by reiterating the notion that psychotherapy is a mutual enterprise between therapist and patient, both of whom are engaged in a quest for meaning, it is not a simple matter to discover what someone is thinking by what he says if we are not acquainted with his personal argot. This is especially so if we seek to discover the nuances of meaning that are so important to our adolescent patients who are all too prone to feel that they are misunderstood. When engaging an adolescent, we have to follow an example parallel to that of other patients. The formal code used must obey similar rules of surface structure formation and deep structural organization, for both parties to be understood. It is even more important to therapeutic encounters that the code be comprehensible, because, when we focus on the unconscious, the manifest language is a vital link to the language of that unconscious. While we reach for that language, the rules of discourse of each individual must guarantee at least potential agreement so that other levels may be reached. Indeed, as has been indicated earlier, the other levels may not be reached solely by the discourse itself, but in messages hidden in the form of the discourse and how it varies from person to person or group to group. When viewed from this vantage, a number of characteristic problems arise when talking to adolescents that may be treated linguistically. They can be subsumed under problems of interpreting the speech act and its significance, and more significantly to the quandary of reference. A set of principles about talking to adolescents should grow out of our respect for this problem. The three areas of reference that concern us during the adolescent period are linguistic drift, imprecision of usage, and adolescent argot.

Linguistic drift has been approached as a diachromic science; that is, words change in meaning and change in reference over time and geography. New words (neologisms) may even be created by cultural need as well as by individuals. When dealing with adolescents, we see a microcosmic short-term shift in meaning and lexicon at a synchronic level. Such shifts may be even more radical and sudden than longer term diachronic shifts.

Three types of drift may be noticed. The first concerns the changing meaning of the same word. A common word among adolescents during the 1970s is *fag*. By general agreement, most adolescents use the word fag to describe somebody who does not fit, who is a bit persnickety, who cannot take the rough and tumble; in short, somebody who may not be "one of the guys" or maybe a little bit outside of the group, more likely to be prim or bookish and nonsocial. In later adolescence, the homosexual significance is clearer. It was not so long ago during the 1950s early 1960s when a *fag* uniformly referred to a homosexual, so that to be called a fag by someone in one's group not only referred to the outsider's role but also to the outsider with a specific sexual orientation. If one goes back further in history to Tom Brown's school days, it is clear that a *fag* was somebody who did menial tasks for an upperclassman at school and became fatigued or fagged out. He was in no way looked upon as a homosexual except insofar as there was a sadomachochistic aspect to the same-sex relationship that might be attributable to features of both designata. There is also an additional common use of *fag* which may be detected from context. For example, in passing a cigarette an adolescent might say "Pass the fag." Tracing etymological history further takes us to the word *fagot* as *faggot*; *fag* derives from the word *fagot*, which refers to the bundle of twigs that was carried in the original *fasces* during the time of the Latin beginnings of our language. There is also a Greek equivalent *phakelos*. The word *fag* has had important designative significance then, but a meaning quite far from current adolescent usage. It is curious that currently to call somebody a faggot rather than a fag again refers back to the homosexual aspect of its various meanings when used by an adolescent.

Linguistic drift is also evident in phrases as well as words. Phrases such as "going out" in the terminology of the 1940s and 1950s referred to the fact that an adolescent was seeing someone on a single date, or possibly more than one date, but not with serious intentions. Currently, it is the rough equivalent of what adolescents of the 1940s called "going steady" and adolescents in the 1920s referred to as "keeping company." Similarly, "making out" might refer to kissing and petting, but certainly not to coitus these days; in former years, it might have referred to all three. The newly invented phrase "getting on over somebody" involves the ultimate aim of the foreplay referred to. "First, second, third, and home base" are not only used to designate the male adolescents's preoccupation with baseball but also his anatomical interest in a female conquest when he describes the progress of his sexual victory.

There is a phrase drift, too, that occurs in the opposite direction, that is, from the figurative to the literal. "We slept together" is one such example. It might currently mean nothing more than that; specifically, the act of being in a somnolent state in the same bed with somebody. In former years, it was a euphemism for coital interaction. Recent adolescent terminology also borrows heavily from psychiatric discipline.

Somebody might say "I got crazy" and mean "I became excited" or say "He's paranoid" and not be referring to a fullblown psychiatric state but rather the idea of becoming suspicious, especially when under the influence of marijuana. Thus, we have to adjust our receptive understanding so that we do not confuse the same reference as having a constant referent when talking to an adolescent. That which is usually signified may be quite different in the language of the adolescent. Moreover, he or she may be carrying it to you in just that way in order to confuse rather than to inform, or to test your understanding of adolescents as a group. This brings us to Freud's important discovery in the interpretation of dreams; that we dare not use standard symbol translation to interpret dreams. The individual associations and the context of the dream are more important to on-target understanding. The caution is similarly important in understanding the language of the adolescent.

The second feature of adolescent usage is its imprecision. One example of a problem that arises comes directly from the popularity of psychological thinking in our time, especially that focused on Erik Erikson's view of identity. The anomie of the twentieth century is translated by the intellectual adolescent into "I don't know who I am." Therapists dare not look at statements such as that, as comments that do not need translation into the language of the unconscious. The simple answer to "I don't know who I am" is "You are what you do." This may sound too pragmatic and operational to satisfy the troubled youngster, but it clearly shifts focus from the abstract to the action–self. The philosophical implication of "I don't know who I am" seems to stem from the romantic interest of young adolescents in the books of Hermann Hesse, or of Buddhism, transcendental meditation, and mysticism. Psychologically, such problems may be better described in the language of Mahler concerning merging, as-if personality, and identity formation. They may correspond to trendy conversations and be reflections or residues of conversations that adolescents have with other adolescents rather than true pictures of what is in reality the inner state. This wish for immediacy also corresponds to the protest implied in "I gotta use words when I talk to you," when the adolescent in the psychotherapeutic process finds that he has to move toward the therapist by using his language, instead of the therapist moving toward the adolescent with his language.

A second area of imprecision comes from the problem of defining feelings. General statements such as "I feel upset" or the popular use of "being uptight" reflect a vagueness which serves a defensive purpose for the adolescent by claiming ignorance of the nuances of feelings in relation to ideas. The therapist in that instance must break through the vagueness and introduce the possibility of greater precision as a means of "teaching" control and anticipation and those aspects of ego mastery with which the adolescent would feel better were he not so much victimized by his own feelings. Indeed, the vagueness may hide a myriad of fantasies which he believes might make him feel even more upset or uptight were he to confront them. Imprecision is further ensconced within our language in such locutions as "you know" or "like man" which become continuing verbal confessions of the uncertainty of the adolescent's verbal skill in conveying his feelings and/or ideas. They reveal a technique in code which is continuous with the secret codes of latency and are reflected in an identification with subgroups that ensures a lack of hope for contact with the larger group—especially with those individuals who are over 30.

The latter issue brings us into the homeground of adolescent language—his argot. "I dig my head better when I'm on grass." "After all the shit has gone down, I've gotta cover my ass, because I was sure he was gonna lay it on me." What could possilby be the meaning of these phrases? They certainly correspond closely to the syntax of English, but the lexical items are used in an unusual manner. The references are different than those that usually come to mind. They sound very much like Chomsky's "colorless green ideas sleep furiously." Perhaps there are two languages: yours–mine, and the language of my people. These languages are continuous with the code of the 7- to 10-year-old children and the secret social clubs of that age period. The codes are colorful, too, and function to keep these children separate from adults, almost like a new ethnic group. The newer trends reveal an identification of adolescents with subcultures that usually have been considered to be outside upper- and middle-class white communities. The modern adolescent dresses in inexpensive blue jeans designed for work, and sport patches over their holely trousers to identify with the idea of what poor people and blacks must tolerate. In their language, too, they have tried out the phraseology which belongs to the language of these varied groups. The adolescent style also treads a rather narrow line between condescencion and arrogance. He tests the therapist for his bilingualism. He asks in innumerable ways to see whether he will be understood if he uses his own language, and he always tempts the therapist to inquire if he is understood. The fact is that the therapist does have to make an adaptation to the new language, and these adaptations require a certain amount of technical skill and extra understanding if communication is to be established. Some of this technical skill and understanding may come from prior knowledge of the linguistic form that the adolescent uses.

The first general rule therapists must cherish in talking to the adolescent concerns keeping the quest for meaning at the forefront. Discussion about "speaking the same language" may then be looked at in terms of how to approach a translation rather than adopting the adolescent's style. The therapist must beware of frightening the adolescent by what he says. Because of the average clinician's imprecise knowledge of his patient's language, he may make wrong interpretations because he uses his patient's language incorrectly. He then seems like another "somebody" who doesn't understand. The excessive zeal of new therapists sometimes makes them talk too much or talk in a way that parallels the adolescent's patter. Homosexual fantasies of intrusiveness, of being too much at the patient's level may confound communication. Instead of meaning Y, the adolescent means X. In fact, one of the important things to be established is that our jargon is not his, and his jargon is not ours: we are in somewhat separate worlds, but they can be bridged via a slow process of talking together. An old saw in clinical work is worth mentioning at this juncture. When a patient asks whether the therapist saw a movie or read a particular book, the response should be the same. "Even if I did see (or read) it, I'd like to know what you thought of it and how you thought of it and how you saw the story from a personal vantage." Communication should and need not imply merging and loss of separateness. Pluralism is tolerable. Translation assumes work to bind people. While acknowledging that his thoughts are personal and only yielded up on an act of volition, the therapist provides a space in which such voluntary discussions are possible.

Another technical rule concerns the information-seeking mode "Why did you say that?" or "How come you said it in that way, when you talk another way usually?" Generally, a shift in mode of expression might indicate a shift in significance, and the formal change addresses the particular content at that moment. It might be best to hold one's fire—listen—and see if the content fits the form. The lisping baby talk may be regressive, but it might also be flirtatious. The high-flown language may be defensive when threatened and not simply arrogant. Similarly, one must take extra care when making a confrontation to adolescents. For example, comments such as "While you're talking, you're sitting in such a way that shows me you intend to be seductive" can lead to extreme guilt and the feeling of being accused. Such a sequence frequently leads to a variety of action which carries the message "If I'm going to be hung for a lamb, I might as well be hung for a fox." "I might as well do that of which I am accused." It is important that the language of the therapist be not only appropriately timed but issued with the tact required of somebody both in the role of the compatriot as well as the potential object of a strong transference. Frequently, patients in this age group will deal not only with confrontations but also with descriptions of their behavior as permission for activity—the description that becomes the prescription mentioned so often represents the favorite distortion of adolescents in therapy.

Another factor to be considered in our adaptation of the adolescent's language is that our street language may not be seen as comraderie, but as a lie. We have to be careful that this lie does not alienate the adolescent completely from activity of exploring his unconscious or even his conscious behavior. There is a way to talk to adolescents at their level in our own words even though not in their argot. If we take up his argot, it demonstrates his power control over us. We become passive and unable to help and also open to the same ridicule and self-accusations that the adolescent may feel about himself. They may even meet us with the same condescension that is projected onto their own group. If we wish to be "let in" on the adolescent's world, we must use the same general rule of respect as used with other patients.

Although attempts at understanding and translation and striving for specificity are used universally with adolescents as with adults and younger children, nothing has been said, as yet, about the nonverbal or empathic aspects of discourse with adolescents. Empathy should be apparent in our mode of listening, our facial expression, our gestural and mimetic sympathies, and our paralinguistic tones. There is, to be sure, a complementary set of activities that occur in therapy which may be grasped while we listen, but each particular performance requires a general linguistic competence that we assume both therapist and adolescent carry.

In general, I would doubt that the formalisms of adolescent language differ very much in their structure and organization from that of the species-specific community of languages. If we were to subject adolescent language to the Whorf–Sapir hypothesis of linguistic relativity, we would examine the sociolinguistic structure of adolescence in terms of how noun, verb, object were arranged and the variety of choices that were made around the specific word options or the idiosyncracy of linguistic form. Although each of these sectors may be translated point-by-point into any other language, there are special nuances created by adolescent idiolects which make of their words more than simple labels. They are labels which carry affectful, secret things that point to important inner concerns, as for example, the proliferation of names for the genitals. The speech act and pragmatic frame of reference apply to adolescent language as they do to any other delivery or communication system. The problem ought to be studied as one would study a subculture with its idiosyncratic social control rules. To be an adolescent psychiatrist and listen to adolescent language is to be more expert than others in a variety of communicational modes which are subject to rapid change and continually created new forms. Vigilance to such change keeps us in a rapidly changing inner circle of great variety from social class to social class but also from day to day, from one school to another.

9.1. References

Anthony, E. J. Between yes and no. *Journal of Psychosocial Process: Issues in Child Mental Health*, 1974, 3, 23–46.

Harner, L. Children's understanding of linguistic reference to past and future. *Journal of Psycholinguistic Research*, 1976, 5, 65–84.

Miller, G. A. *Spontaneous apprentices: Children and language.* New York: Seabury Press, 1977.

Milne, A. A. *When we were very young.* New York: E. P. Dutton, 1961. (a)

Milne, A. A. *Now we are six.* New York: E. P. Dutton, 1961. (b)

Opie, I., & Opie, P. *The lore and language of school children.* London: Oxford University Press, 1959.

Shapiro, T., & Perry, R. Latency revisited: The age 7 + − 1. *The Psychoanalytic Study of the Child*, 1976, 31, 79–105.

Stern, D., & Wasserman, G. *The language environment of preverbal infants: Evidence for the central development role of prosodic features.* Unpublished manuscript, 1979.

Winnicott, D. W. *The piggle.* New York: International Universities Press, 1977.

INDEX